BACK IN TOUCH

Stanley & Mila Matthews
BACK IN TOUCH
with a helping hand from Don Taylor

Arthur Barker Limited London
A subsidiary of Weidenfeld (Publishers) Limited

Published in Great Britain by
Arthur Barker Ltd
91 Clapham High Street
London SW4 7TA

ISBN 0 213 16806 5

Printed in Great Britain by
Butler & Tanner Ltd
Frome and London

Illustrations

Introduction

This book is more explanation than autobiography. 'Whatever happened to Stanley Matthews?' ask some people in England. Well, now I can tell them. Perhaps I could have told them before. Perhaps I *should* have told them – but the fact is I didn't, even though I wanted to often enough.

The truth is I fled England in 1968 for fear of public opinion. I left my home, football, friends – everything I considered important. My whole life had been turned inside out and upside down, so I just boarded an aeroplane and flew away, not knowing when, or even *if*, I would ever return. I justified it to myself in a way, saying it was a private matter which was of no concern to the general public. Yet even that was a half truth. The public had been good to me. For more than thirty years they had cheered me from the terraces in all sorts of weather. The Press had been kind to me – often writing such flattering things about me that I cringed with embarrassment. The Establishment had been generous to me – awarding me a CBE in one Honours List and a Knighthood in another. I had even lunched at Buckingham Palace and been invited for drinks to Number Ten. *Too many* people had been *too kind* for me to doubt that they deserved an explanation. Yet I couldn't give them one, not then, because I felt sure they would never understand. So I fled the country.

So what makes the telling of it easier now? Time, I suppose. Attitudes change with the years, and people look at life in a different way as each generation adds its own set of values. Take divorce, for example. Nobody gives it a thought today. If a marriage is unhappy, then end it. I don't mean the odd row, or even a major difference of opinion, but if a marriage has broken down beyond repair then most people think it right to call it a day. But divorce was disgraceful not only when I grew up, but for many years after. Even in the sixties the divorce laws of

England were very different from what they are now. Times have changed – more than we sometimes realize.

But of course the other reason why an explanation is easier is that I can laugh at it now – and some things are very funny in retrospect – although I was too tensed up at the time to even think straight, let alone talk about it.

So here it is – warts and all. My wife Mila helped me write it – not that I could have stopped her butting in anyway! Unfortunately neither of us kept a diary, so a date may be wrong here and there, but overall I think we have it about right – how it *actually* happened. Whether I was right or wrong to act as I did in 1968 I leave you to judge, but at least I am now able to say thank you for the many kindnesses bestowed upon me by so many people. They were never forgotten or taken for granted. I always hoped that I might be able to explain – *one day* – and now that day is here and I am back in touch.

Sir Stanley Matthews CBE

Stan

It must have been 1965 when I met Irving Toorchen. Early that year, and certainly before my 'Farewell Match', because although I forget exactly when I met Irving, I shall never forget the date of that match. It was 28 April 1965, and you couldn't move in Stoke for footballers. Everyone in the game was there that day, or so it seemed. Players from all over the world: Yashin from Russia, Johansen from Denmark, Van den Boer from the Netherlands, Puskas from Hungary, Di Stefano from Spain – and so many more. In fact so many that the organizers picked four teams and we played two matches. Nobody really cared who they played for, as long as they got a game. I remember Jimmy Hagan, Nat Lofthouse, Stan Mortensen and Tommy Finney, lining up for the team skippered by Harry Johnson – and Jackie Mudie, Jim Dickinson and Jackie Milburn being among those who turned out for the Wally Barnes side. That was the curtain raiser and Harry Johnson's Eleven won 5-1. My team played the international eleven – although *eleven* is misleading because there were players to spare, so team changes took place at half time to make sure everyone got a kick of the ball. Ron Flowers, Johnny Haynes, Cliff Jones and Jimmy Greaves were among many old pals on my side and we lost 6-4, after being a goal down within the first minute of a scorching game in which Puskas scored two tremendous goals.

Goals are what the game is all about, and the fans saw sixteen of them on the same bill. And what an event it was – it was like a *carnival*! Dennis Howell, the Minister of Sport, refereed one game, and Arthur Ellis, the world cup referee, took charge of the other. A regimental brass band played the popular tunes of the day before the first match, then the Dagenham Girl Pipers piped the teams on to the field, and – in case that wasn't enough – Charlie Chester teamed up with dozens of other entertainers to amuse the crowd during the intervals. The Americans would have called it a 'soccer extravaganza' and even the more restrained British Press was full of words like 'unique' and 'unprecedented'.

Then Arthur Ellis blew the final whistle, and it was all over. Thirty-three years of playing in first-class football had come to an end. Charlie Chester said afterwards there wasn't a dry eye in the house. The entire stadium of 35,000 rose as one man and applauded me all the way to the dressing room. That's what they tell me at least – it's difficult to see what other people are doing when your own eyes are full of tears. Not that anyone saw how upset I was – I wouldn't have liked that. 'No fuss' was what my father had taught me, and although he was dead by then his lessons have served me all my life.

Of course, there was a huge party that night. A Farewell Ball and Cabaret at the King's Hall. My old pal Ted Heath brought his orchestra over to provide the music, and the cabaret was as crowded as the football matches, with more performers than time available to do them all justice – even though we went on well into the early hours.

I saw them all off the following day, at the station, or the airport, or in their cars. It was like the circus leaving town, and saying goodbye to so many old friends saddened me as much as the final whistle the day before. Of course I would see them around, because I was joining Port Vale as manager at the beginning of the next season and my links with them, and with football, would therefore continue. But I would never *play* again, not in truly competitive football. After thirty-three years it would take some getting used to and right at that moment the realization was still sinking in. Still, the game had been good to me. I was fifty years old then, so I'd had a good run, considering that most players retired in their thirties, and I had much to be thankful for.

But Irving Toorchen and I must have met *before then*, because he was invited to my Farewell Match – and the party afterwards. It was the very next day that we decided to form an advertising agency geared to sports products, which Ken Wolstenholme later joined as co-director. Then I went back to the Victoria Ground to help tie up the loose ends.

Of course things are a lot different today, but the rules about 'benefit' matches were very strict then. The club itself was not allowed to be directly involved, and a player's benefit match had to be organized by an outside committee – generally people 'co-opted' from the Supporters Club. My committee was twelve strong, which sounds a lot until you consider the amount of work involved. Charlie Chester was chairman (how Charlie ever found the time I shall never know), and the Lord Mayor of Stoke was another member. Between them they did a fantastic job. Altogether the big day netted a gross profit of some thirty thousand pounds – that's before expenses of course, it was a lot less afterwards. But even so there was enough for me to give gifts to all concerned, and to make a donation to the National Playing Fields Association, *and* to be left with a nice sum for myself. My share had to be banked for three years before I could touch a penny, otherwise most of it would go in tax. I wasn't even allowed to earn interest on the money. And another rule was that I could never play *professional* football again, or the 'benefit' would be deemed 'salary' and taxed accordingly. These days players get maybe three or four benefits in their careers, and even managers get them, but a benefit match then was very much a retirement thing, like a gold watch or, if you were as lucky as me, a golden handshake.

Mind you, my Farewell Match was nearly cancelled at the last minute. There was a terrible panic that FIFA would outlaw me and pass a judgement that our event was contrary to their rules. This was because Charlie and the rest of the committee had been so successful in persuading so many international stars to take part. It had never been done before. I remember a meeting at the North Stafford Hotel, two weeks before the big day, when George Birks, the secretary of our committee, announced that FIFA would not allow the event to take place. Pandemonium broke out. Well you can imagine – we had already sold the tickets and booked the players, and now we were faced with a cancellation. We spent hours trying to get Sir Stanley Rous, who was then President of FIFA, on the telephone. Finally we traced him to Zurich and dragged him out of a meeting. I explained the situation and then, along with the rest of the committee, held my breath until he replied. 'Stanley,' he said after a long pause, 'carry on, you have my blessing.' What a relief! Charlie ordered a bottle of champagne to celebrate and the work continued at a rattling pace. But I think my Farewell Match broke new ground and the rules were altered after that.

So there I was, at the age of fifty. By most people's standards I had nothing to complain about. I had paid for my house in Blackpool, I had two cars in the garage, money in the bank, good health, a new career as manager of Port Vale ahead of me – and I even had *something else*. I had Irving Toorchen.

Irving was an American advertising man who worked in London for a big agency. He had phoned me one day to ask about carrot juice. I used to drink it by the gallon in those days, and a client of his had seen me extolling its virtues on TV. Just how good is this stuff, he asked.

Well, we had a long talk and by the end of it he must have thought carrot juice did for me what spinach did for Popeye, because a few weeks later he phoned again. His client, Express Dairy, were thinking of putting carrot juice on to the market in a big way, and would I go down to London for a meeting? They wanted me to help promote it.

So I went, and we all had lunch together at the Savoy Grill. Present were a director of Express Dairy called Harry Mendoza, a representative of the firm whose carrot juice they were thinking of marketing, and of course the ubiquitous Irving. As the lunch progressed he became more and more expansive, so that by the end of the meal I had visions of carrot juice replacing tea as the national drink. Irving was genuinely enthusiastic. He had all the facts and figures of the drinks and beverages market at his finger tips, and by the time he finished it sounded as if even Coca-Cola might be swept away on a tide of carrot juice. 'Carrot juice,' Irving said, 'could be the biggest thing since sliced bread.' Then he quizzed me on the benefits of the drink and wrote my answers down in his little black book. I gave him everything I could think of but he was a difficult man to satisfy. 'Are you sure, Stan, that you cannot think of any other benefit?'

I racked my brains. It was obviously vital to help as much as I could. Even a *small* benefit might be of some use to him. So I said, 'Well, my daughter drinks it. She says it makes her all pale and interesting.'

Irving shot a look at our host, and shortly after that 'benefit' the lunch came to an end. I went back to Blackpool a happy man. My name was to appear on every tin of carrot juice produced, and I would receive a royalty on all sales. Naturally it would take a while to get under way – Irving and Harry had plenty to do, setting up production lines, growing carrots and working on the promotion plans – but they promised to keep me informed. All I had to do was sit back and wait for the royalty cheques to roll in. It was a comforting feeling – like knowing you're going to win the pools in a few months' time.

After my Farewell Match, I went to Canada on a two-month tour. It was a solo trip and I had made many by then, playing as a guest player for this club, and playing in an exhibition match for that one. Football was gaining popularity in Canada, and one of the leading lights was a man called Steve Stavro. Steve was of Macedonian origin and had built up a big business in Ontario. He was a real dynamo of a man – up at five every morning to work a fifteen hour day. In his *spare time* Steve diverted some of his phenomenal energy into football. I doubt that his business suffered, because Steve had more go in him than some whole football teams I've known. Within a short time he was persuading clubs like Juventus and Manchester United, and his own favourites Olympiad of Greece, to make summer tours of Canada. And he sponsored individual players like me. Steve and I struck up an immediate friendship which I'm glad to say is stronger than ever today. Now I wouldn't dream of going to Canada without seeing Steve and his wife Sally.

In 1965 Steve got together with George Gross (now sports editor of the *Toronto Sun*) and arranged for me to play a few games for Toronto City. It was all very light-hearted stuff and I treated the trip as a holiday. I knew I would need one, with the prospect of the Port Vale job to face when I returned home. But I would have help at Port Vale because I would be joined by Jackie Mudie and Len Graham. Jack had been with me at Blackpool and Stoke, and had signed up as my assistant manager, while Len Graham, the former Stoke trainer, had joined Port Vale six months before. We were like a little squad – all men from a big time club going to try our hands at running a little one. It would be hard work, we all knew that, but the Port Vale directors had promised plenty of support and we were excited by the challenge.

So within three weeks of my return from Canada, we all assembled at Vale Park, the Port Vale ground, and the players reported for the beginning of the new season. Len Graham started to whip the boys into shape after their summer lay-off, while Jackie and I cast nervous eyes over the squad we had inherited – and a fortnight later we went to the board with our proposals for team changes.

That was the first set back – no money was available for new players! The club was £120,000 in the red! 'But what about the support we were promised?' Jackie and I chorused. The directors gave a collective shrug of the shoulders and I went back to the drawing-board. Perhaps we should have resigned there and then? After all, the directors had broken their word. But we were new to management and neither of us could resist a challenge. We rationalized it by telling ourselves that even if *some* money had been available it was unlikely to be enough for us to compete in the transfer market against the big First Division clubs. So we adopted a youth policy. It would take time to achieve success – it might take three, four, or even *five* seasons to build a team good enough to climb up through the divisions. But we were in the Fourth Division then, so the only way to go was up. When we told the directors they listened, nodded – and finally agreed with our proposals. Looking back I think they were secretly relieved to see us take on the job of running the club on a shoe-string.

So the season kicked off and Jackie, Len and I really rolled up our sleeves. I continued to live in Blackpool, so I left home at about five o'clock most mornings in order to be at the ground by seven. And when I wasn't driving to Vale Park I was travelling the country, scouring everywhere – schools, youth clubs, recreation grounds – searching for talented youngsters. Big clubs have scouts all over the place, but at a little club you learn to do things for yourself.

How the game has changed! When I was fifteen I joined the Stoke City office staff at one pound a week and was thrilled – just to have a chance to play football. But by 1965 there was money in the game, and things were different. For instance I would maybe travel to Durham, or Newcastle, or almost anywhere in the country to watch a fourteen-year-old play. Not once or twice, but three or four times. Then, if I thought his game had potential, I would go home to meet his family. Dad would sit at the kitchen table, over a cup of tea, and say: 'See this bungalow? It cost ten thousand pounds.' And *that* was the fee Dad was looking for. If I pointed out that signing-on fees for youngsters were illegal, Dad would grin and say: 'Daresay you're right, Sir Stan' – and that would be an end to the matter. But a month or so later Jackie Mudie or I would read that the youngster had joined this or that big club, and we would know – Dad had got his bungalow paid for.

It's the way of the world. I've no wish to enter into the argument about the rights and wrongs of it, but it's hypocrisy for the FA and others to say it doesn't happen. Of course it happens, *every week of the year*! The game is starving for talented youngsters and football managers work under such pressure that some would *sell their soul* for a young Johan Cruyff or another Kevin Keegan. I never did, because – fortunately perhaps – the temptation was never there. Port Vale hadn't even the money to pay my salary, let alone buy bungalows for avaricious fathers.

But Jackie and I persevered. Many of the boys we wanted were whisked out from under our noses in 'bungalow deals' or, more honourably, simply because Dad felt his son would have a better future at a big club. I could understand that, without necessarily agreeing with it. A boy in football is no different from any young lad starting out in a profession – and the best newspapermen don't all start in Fleet Street, any more than the best actors start on Broadway. A spell in the provinces learning his craft isn't such a bad thing for a boy. The important thing is to *learn*, and that often depends on the teacher as much as the pupil.

So Jackie and I selected from the second layer of talent, and by the start of the season, things were looking up. We had assembled a squad of about sixteen young lads and we played wherever we could – generally against non-league clubs in friendly matches, with Jackie and I playing alongside the boys to give them experience. All in all I think we were about on target: another season and the bigger boys could be *blooded* into the first team and then, as far as we were concerned, the sky was the limit.

Meanwhile the first team was still very much as we inherited it. I transferred some players and the club received about sixty thousand pounds in transfer fees, but somehow the money got swallowed up in the general expenses, so there was never a penny spare to invest in a new player. But we struggled on. Match days were an exquisite kind of torture as far as I was concerned. I sweated buckets. If only *I could play!* I pleaded with my accountant, who in turn pleaded with the tax people, but they were adamant – if I played for Port Vale most of the nest-egg generated by my Farewell Match would disappear in tax! So I sweated it out in the dug-out every Saturday, and cursed every tax official from Land's End to John O'Groats.

Then I heard from Irving Toorchen. The carrot juice venture was about to become a reality. A prototype would soon be ready for us to sample. *Great!* I was so excited. Perhaps I could use some of those fat royalty cheques to satisfy the Inland Revenue . . . if I did that I could *play again!* And if that happened Jackie and I calculated I could buttress the team up until our young hopefuls were old enough for the first eleven.

Two weeks later, Irving telephoned again. The prototype was ready! Cases of sample tins were being delivered today, and one of them was on its way to my home in Blackpool. I dashed home and sure enough, a carton of twelve tins awaited me. My face and name were on the wrappers, and I could hardly wait to get the carton into the kitchen. Not just because I liked carrot juice, not even at the prospect of those royalty cheques, but for what they represented – *a chance to play football again!* I punctured a tin and poured some into a glass, ready to toast future success. Then I froze in horror. Something terrible had gone wrong! *It was dark brown!* The contents of the glass were brown – as brown as a cup of coffee – with a rim of scum forming a 'head'. I panicked. I opened another tin, then another. They were the same – brown, oily somehow, with a revolting smell. And I was reaching for a fourth can when the telephone rang.

It was Irving. He sounded very upset. 'Stanley,' he said, 'something is drastically wrong. I didn't know it changed colour.'

'It doesn't! I mean – *mine* doesn't!'

'Put it in a can and it will. I'll have to get on to Express. Forgive me, Stan, for wasting your time.'

He really sounded quite aggrieved. Later on, after contacting Express Dairy, he rang again, more calmly. They were worried, of course, but he told me they were trying to find a way of preserving the colour of carrot juice – and he would call me back in a day or two. But it was months before I heard from him again.

Meanwhile problems developed at Port Vale. The FA introduced a new rule which compelled clubs to pay players a signing-on fee of five hundred pounds when they became full professionals at the age of seventeen. The new chairman of the Club sent for me: 'Do you realize we've got *sixteen* players coming up to their seventeenth birthday?' he asked. He was red-faced with excitement. 'Sixteen!' he repeated, 'That means ... um ... eight thousand pounds! *Eight thousand!* They'll have to go. We can't afford ...'

'What, *all* of them?'

'Maybe not all – but *most* of them. We've not got fancy money to throw about you know.'

'What sort of money *have* we got?'

'Not much,' he admitted. 'Not much to spend on ... um ... *footballers.* I suppose we might run to a few thousand ... say four ... yes, we might run to four. But *four* at the most!'

Two years' work – *my* work – went down the drain, just like that. I protested of course. I reminded him of the promises made when I joined. Plenty of support, the directors had said. I'd had *no* support. They hadn't even paid me my salary. *Not a penny had been paid to me in two years!* The chairman huffed and puffed, said he hadn't been chairman when I was appointed, things like that – but the plain fact was that the club didn't have the money, and the directors hadn't a clue how to raise it.

I went back to Jackie Mudie and reported the conversation to him. Our entire youth policy lay in tatters. We had no option but to decide which of our boys to retain and which to release. It was a heartbreaking job. Boys develop at different ages. They're up and down, you can't rush them, you have to nurse them along. Some need time to mature into their game, and others – perhaps brilliant as fourteen-year-olds – tragically burn themselves out by the time they reach seventeen. Above all, they need *time*. Take Alan Ball as an example. He started with a trial for Bolton. They turned him down. Then he had a trial for Wolves. They turned him down too. Then he had a trial for Blackpool and it all came right for him – he was a regular for England by the end of his career.

One of our lads was a boy called Ray Kennedy. Ray was one of the nicest boys in the squad. We all liked him. We knew he would make the grade *one day*. 'But not next season,' Jackie said, 'he needs another year yet, maybe more.' At the time Ray was a bit cumbersome and awkward, the way some boys are in their early years. He would develop for sure, if we were able to give him *time*. But under the new policy there was no time available. We *had* to let Ray go – along with some of the other boys. Subsequently of course, Ray joined Arsenal, then Liverpool, and finally established a regular place in the England side. For reasons which will become obvious later, I lost touch with Ray years ago, but I like to think that he drew *some* benefit from his days with Jackie and me. And I wonder what the transfer fee might have been a few years later, if the Port Vale Directors had managed to find that extra five hundred pounds!

Jackie Mudie resigned just after that. True, he received a good business offer, but I think part of the reason was he felt betrayed by the board at Port Vale. Jackie's departure was a great loss. Partly because we had shared so much – playing together at Blackpool and Stoke, tours in Canada, Port Vale, and all the rest of it – but partly because the board felt they couldn't afford a replacement. I was to soldier on alone.

It was the end of the season by then, so I spent the summer thinking about it. I suppose the truth of the matter is that I hate to admit defeat. I really *hate* it. So I encouraged myself to look on the bright side. By the start of the new season, some of my boys would be ready for the first team; I would have a far better side than the one I inherited; I would have proved *something* – and so on. So I decided to stay at Port Vale.

The carrot juice never did make a product, but in July I got a call from Irving, now a co-director of our agency. 'Stan,' he said, 'I've set up a tentative deal with Czechoslovakia for us to promote their football boots. Your name on each boot. What do you think?'

'Are they any good?'

'Stanley! Czechoslovakia is probably the *biggest* maker of boots and shoes in the world. Ever heard of Bata? *He* was a Czech!'

Typical! One day facts and figures about the drinks and beverages business, now he was blinding me with science about shoemakers. Still I listened, and was pleased that I did. Irving had arranged for us to go to Czechoslovakia the following month to negotiate a sponsorship deal on their football boots – and, he added casually, I could take my whole team if I wanted. We would play one match – possibly two – all expenses paid. A match – right at the start of the season! The best possible thing for my young boys – and the board at Port Vale wouldn't even have to find the money for bus fares. I grabbed the chance, gave Irving a choice of dates, and that was that.

When the boys reported for training, they were delighted about the trip to Prague. I told the board that I had decided to stay on for a while longer, and settled down to prepare for the new season. This is it, I told myself, the *third* season – this is when my patience will earn its reward.

The team worked out well in their practice matches, and two weeks before the season opened we all went down to Heathrow to meet Irving for the trip to Czechoslovakia. We were all keyed up, and I was getting excited about the sponsorship deal. After all, royalties are royalties, and what I had not earned on carrot juice, maybe I would get from football boots. Anyway, we were in with a chance. It was not for me to be discouraging Irving at this point and reminding him about the carrot juice fiasco.

Mila

Ask anyone and they'll tell you, Prague is out of a fairy tale. A place full of dreamy spires and cobbled streets, and gracious squares enclosed by the finest Baroque architecture in the world. It is a city of theatres, concert halls, opera houses and art galleries. Gourmets can dine in some of the best restaurants in the world, or talk and argue for hours in the sidewalk cafés. It is a cosmopolitan city, at the crossroads of Europe. Western Europeans used to call it 'Little Paris' and although I love Paris, to me Prague is more beautiful. Perhaps because Prague was 'home' for so much of my life.

And life was good in 1967. Czechoslovakia was the most liberal of all communist countries, and becoming more so every year. Dubček was Prime Minister and governed with a light touch. A spirit of optimism swept the country from end to end. Even for 'ordinary' Czechs life was improving, and for me life was often spectacular.

I suppose I was part of what would be called 'the jet set' in the West. Every society has its élite and, invariably in communist countries, such an élite includes painters and film directors, writers and other practitioners of the arts. Such people, in those days, retained a remarkable degree of independence, but they were literally a handful. For instance, in 1967, only about two hundred people in the whole of Czechoslovakia were allowed to work on this freelance basis: everyone else was employed by the State. And my husband was one of the two hundred.

George Winter was one of Czechoslovakia's most prominent artists. His work hung in exhibitions all over the world. His drawings and cartoons appeared regularly in Czech newspapers. His books were published in Frankfurt and translated into several languages. His film cartoons drew crowds at the cinema. George was wise, talented and successful – and I had been his wife since 1961.

And I suppose George was rich. Not rich on the Paul Getty scale, but comfortably off. For instance, in those days he earned perhaps ten times more than the director of a large factory, or six times more than a lawyer, or fifty times as much as a clerk. We lived in an elegant house in Prague and often went out to parties at Mecenas, or dinner at the Alcron Hotel, or lunch at the Brussels overlooking the Vltava river.

We also travelled a lot – to attend exhibitions in Italy, to promote cultural treaties as guests of foreign governments, to perform private commissions. And we holidayed all over Europe: Paris, Cannes, Switzerland – the elegant watering-holes of the rich and famous. Sometimes we wandered off the beaten track. I remember going to Sicily once and meeting an Englishman who offered to take me across to Malta on his yacht. I had no idea what Malta was like and I was tempted to go, except for some doubt about my travel documents. But what really put me off was a warning from some Czech friends: 'Go over there and you'll be sold into slavery,' they said, with such conviction that I believed them – or at least harboured enough doubt to decline the invitation. Malta meant nothing to me then – yet a few short years later it was to mean 'home'.

George was a truly cultured man with friends all over the world. He held a doctorate in Fine Arts and for a hobby collected oriental art, to such good effect that by 1967 he had assembled the largest collection in Middle Europe. He was an authority on the subject, consulted by visiting professors and scientists, and invited back to view their collections in return. And he knew *so many* people. When Julius Katchen the concert pianist was in Prague he visited our house, and we visited him in Paris. Steinbeck was a friend, and Isaac Stern another. In fact our home was 'open house' for so many that often on Christmas Eve more than two hundred people would stop by for a drink, or just to wish us the compliments of the season. Life with George was crowded with incident, and there was never a dull moment.

And I worked as well. Not that George wanted me to. 'Why bother' he would ask, 'when I earn more in an afternoon than you do in a month?' But I had worked before I married and was happy in my job – and it was all very well for George to be dismissive about my salary but most people thought I earned an outrageous amount. One day I committed a minor traffic offence and the lady judge was horrified to learn that I earned twice as much as she did – and she fined me accordingly.

My job was at the American Embassy, where I was a Cultural Assistant, which meant, among other things, that I looked after visiting VIPs.

It was hectic and demanding, and a great deal of fun. Most weeks found me organizing two or three cocktail parties – and sometimes a good many more. And the people I met! Randolph Hearst, Adlai Stevenson (what a charmer he was!), Elmer Rice, Francis Lederer the actor, Eric Leinsdorf the conductor, Ginsburg the poet. Ginsburg was a man-sized headache, always getting mixed up with the wrong sort of people and arriving at parties dressed in a sweat shirt and tennis shoes, but he was fun too in an oddball way. I remember meeting Kim Novak at the Karlsbad Film Festival, and persuading 'Satchmo' Armstrong to play for a group of friends in a small avant-garde theatre. And Kirk Douglas and his wife were over for quite a long time. I took them to every theatre in Prague – sometimes two in one evening – *and* the theatre work-shops, *and* the actors' studios. Kirk wanted to go everywhere and meet everyone, anything and everything connected with acting and the theatre. One evening I took him to a party where I introduced him to Milos Forman, the film director. The two of them got on like a house on fire. Later, when Milos went to the United States, he met Kirk again and the two of them got talking about a book for which Kirk had bought the film rights. It was agreed that Milos would direct the film, which was called *One Flew over the Cuckoo's Nest* – and I've forgotten how many Oscars it eventually won.

But to go back to Prague in 1967 – life was exhilarating then. George was a big fish, and I suppose even I was a medium-sized one, in our own small pond. We met our crowd at the Park Julius Fučik to watch the ice hockey, or joined them to go to a boxing match at Lucerna. It was always the same select group of friends, and we were always in the best seats, just as our crowd were the only people who could be sure of getting a table at the Cinska Restaurace, Prague's famous and very expensive Chinese restaurant. George and I attended every first night – the opening of the ballet, the beginning of the opera season. Sometimes we went together but often apart, for our *circuits* didn't always overlap. In fact, frequently three or four days might pass without us even *seeing* each other.

Our home life – when we were there – was casual and relaxed. On the evenings when neither of us was committed elsewhere we would have dinner together, and afterwards I would sit in his studio while he sketched ideas for his cartoons. He would tell me about his day and I would talk about mine. He was a good story-teller, humorous and amusing, and the time would pass swiftly until bedtime. *My* bedtime. George generally worked at night, often until four or five in the morning.

Then he would sleep late and surface long after I had left for the Embassy.

George was everything I have described – and something more. He was perhaps the most patient man I have ever known. After six years our marriage was still unconsummated and, as far as I was concerned, it never would be. We shared the same house, and much of the same life – but not the same bed. Our separate rooms were foreign territory to each other, and if George had thoughts about changing the relationship he rarely expressed them to me. 'It is enough that you are here,' he once said – and if that sounds remarkable then the credit must be his, because he was a remarkable man. For my part I loved him without being *in love* and I enjoyed every minute of *my affair of the mind* with a man considered to be a genius.

Not being *in love* never troubled me. How could it, when I had never experienced it? And reading about it never convinced me that it was such a wonderful state to get into. It was something best left for others, dreamy young girls and romantic lady novelists. I rarely thought about physical love. By 1967, I was into my forties. I had kept my figure and, without being vain, I knew some men found me attractive. It was flattering and I would be less than human to deny that the attention of men pleased me at times, but I never had the desire to do anything about it. And perhaps that explains it: I never had the least *desire*.

That, then, was 'my' Prague in 1967. We lived in Czechoslovakia, but not the life of the Czechs. My life was busy, happy and stimulating, and I would have been more than content for it to be the pattern for the rest of my days.

Then we had a letter from Irving Toorchen. We had been introduced to Irving by the Czech Embassy in London. One of Irving's large industrial clients was doing a lot of business in Czechoslovakia, and they made a point of introducing him to visiting Czech artists. Our hope was that George would obtain some freelance work in England. We soon got to know both Irving and his wife and spent a good deal of our time in England at their home in Farnham.

Now Irving wrote to say he was coming to Prague, and would we meet him at the airport; and – of all things – he was bringing an English football team with him.

On the way to the airport at Ruzne, George asked: 'What was the name of this football team?'

I rummaged through my handbag for Irving's letter. 'Port Vale.'

George frowned, then shrugged – which I took as a sign that he was not impressed. George *knew* about football in the way George knew about so many other things. I closed my handbag and lit a cigarette.

'Wasn't Irving bringing someone else with him?' George asked.

'Yes,' I said. 'A Sir someone or other. Irving will introduce him.'

'But what's his *name*? You know I'm hopeless at introductions.'

I sighed and opened my handbag again. It took me a minute to find the appropriate part of the letter, and I hate reading in a car anyway because it makes me feel sick. Finally I found it: 'Sir Stanley Matthews,' I said.

George hooted with laughter. 'Only you could forget a name like that! Don't you know – he's the most famous footballer in the world!'

I flushed. Love George though I did, at times his laughter really *irritated* me. Generally he was more tactful when repairing gaps in my knowledge. So I wriggled in my seat and told him to concentrate on his driving. Then I said: 'How on earth would I know something like that? I've never even *seen* a football match!'

But George continued to chuckle until I was thoroughly discomforted. So I changed the subject by saying '*Anyway* – it will be nice to see Irving again.'

'And it will be nice to meet Stanley Matthews,' George said happily.

Stan

Irving was in good form on the flight to Prague. I suppose we all were really. The start of a new season is always exciting. It is all there to be won; promotion, the Cup, fifty matches ahead of us – everything to play for and to get excited about. Besides which I was determined to turn the 1967–68 season into something special. It was my third year at Port Vale. The younger players (or those I had left) were beginning to fulfil their promise, and I was sure that my youth policy would be vindicated in the months which lay ahead.

So it was a happy flight. The boys were keen to play and excited by a trip abroad, Irving was full of the sponsorship deal as well as looking forward to a reunion with some friends of his in Prague. One way and another everyone was brim-ful of optimism.

I had never been to Czechoslovakia. I played against them once, at Tottenham before the war. The Czechs were rated the best side in Europe then, so we knew it would be a battle even before we started. The balance of our side was upset by early injuries to George Mills and Jack Crayston, so we shuffled our forward line a bit and I played inside-right for most of the game. We were 3–2 up at half-time and hanging on by our finger-tips, until the Czechs scored an equalizer minutes after the interval. Then we got another which should have wrapped it up – but the Czechs fought back and, just minutes before time, made it 4–4. Most people thought it would end there, but with seconds to go I scored again and it was all over. 5–4 to England! The Press went mad! I had scored a hat trick so there was a lot about me in the headlines, which is one of the absurd things about newspapers. Sometimes reporters forget that football is a team game. Who scores the goal is irrelevant – so long as the ball hits the net at the right end.

But to get back to Irving and the football boot deal. It all sounded good to me, *too* good I suppose, but he was so confident that by the time we landed even I was convinced. My name was to be used on Czech football boots for a fee of twelve thousand pounds a year, and the contract would run for six years. Seventy-two thousand pounds seems a lot of money even now, let alone then. I was leaving all the negotiations to Irving, who was representing me on a commission basis, but I was a little concerned about his pricing of my worth.

'Look, Stan,' he said, 'these boys make boots by the thousand. But they need a *name* to sell them. *Your* name. Spread across their production run the fee might add a penny to a pair of boots. *A penny a pair!* And that's *too much*?'

Well, put like that it sounded very reasonable, so of course I agreed. Anyway, *he* was the businessman – who was I to argue? Besides the money would be handy, what with Port Vale not paying me a penny for two years.

It was raining when we landed. Not a downpour but a steady drizzle which cloaked the airport in a grey mist. But the welcome awaiting us was warm enough. The Czechs had arranged a special reception and within minutes of our arrival we were whisked off to a VIP lounge to meet everyone. Irving seemed to be everywhere, doing his thing – shaking hands and making introductions – which was just what was needed since I tend to hide in a corner at official functions. *Somebody* has to break the ice, and Irving could have thawed glaciers – so within fifteen minutes he was discussing our itinerary, replanning this and altering that. Then he introduced the friends he had mentioned.

'Stan, meet George and Mila Winter.'

We shook hands and said hello. Mila Winter was a blonde, well dressed and attractive, with a look of amused tolerance in her eyes. She spoke good English, which was a relief. Receptions are bad enough when everyone speaks the same language, but they can be unbelievably painful when you have to communicate with smiles and nods for most of the time.

When it was over we left for our hotel, with a free afternoon ahead of us. The Czech Chamber of Commerce was giving a dinner in my honour that evening, and I was nervous in case I should be called upon to make a speech. But Irving thought that was unlikely, which was reassuring enough for me not to spend the afternoon on tenterhooks. Instead I spent it drinking innumerable cups of tea while Irving briefed me on the programme for the next few days.

We were to go to Gottwaldow the next morning, to be shown over the factory where the football boots were made. Then we were to play our match there on the Wednesday, return to Prague on the Thursday, and fly back to England on the Friday. It seemed a sensible programme to me, and Irving's only worry was to find the 'decision makers' in connection with the sponsorship deal. Several committees were involved and Irving wanted to meet all of them during our visit. But as some were in Gottwaldow and others were in Prague he was a bit anxious about fitting them all in, so it was beginning to look as if a second visit might be necessary.

Dinner that evening with the Chamber of Commerce turned out to be a relaxed informal affair, and I was very glad about that. Irving and I spent most of the time with the Winters. George was a tall, heavily built man, who laughed a lot and seemed to know everyone. Unfortunately, however, although he spoke German and French he didn't speak English, so we had a communications problem. But Mila interpreted and the evening slipped past without any of those long silences which can make meetings with strangers a bit of a strain. Not that *they* were strangers of course. Irving and George had done some business together in London, and indeed some of the talk concerned further commissions which Irving was trying to arrange for the future. For my part I told them about the football boot deal and asked their advice. Mila listened carefully before confirming what Irving was already beginning to suspect – that with so many committees involved there was no chance of a quick decision. But she spoke confidently and knowledgeably, and she also mentioned a few people who might be able to help, so we were not totally despondent. Irving made notes in that little black book of his and from his expression I could tell he was as impressed as I was. Mila Winter was a lot more than just a pretty face.

Afterwards they took us round Prague, showing us the sights. Mila made a fantastic guide – but could she *talk*! I've never known such a chatter-box. But most of it was amusing and some seemed outrageously funny, so we had a whale of a time – just walking the streets while we were shown this and that. The odd thing was I was talking nearly as much as she was. In fact we were both so busy chattering that at one stage we walked down a street thinking that the others were behind us, only to discover when we turned round that they were nowhere in sight. But we found them eventually and returned to the hotel at well past midnight. Then Mila had her idea.

'Why don't I arrange a party for you?' she asked, when you get back to Prague on Thursday?'

Her suggestion was to assemble a few people who might help the football boot deal along. The British Cultural Attaché was a friend of hers and she felt sure he would help. Then there was so-and-so, and somebody else, so that within minutes she was mentioning all sorts of people. Well of course, Irving and I jumped at the idea. I promised to telephone her from Gottwaldow to confirm the details, and we all had a nightcap together before Mila and George went on their way.

As we went to our rooms, Irving remarked: 'Quite a lady, our Mila, eh?' When I agreed, he said, 'Tell you what Stan – I think it may take a while to put this deal together. Problem is I won't be able to get over to Czechoslovakia for all the meetings, but Mila might act as interpreter for you, if you ask her. How would that suit you?'

And I went to bed thinking that might suit me very well.

Mila

I *liked* Stan from the moment I first saw him. Meeting VIPs was no new experience for me. They come in all shapes and sizes, and some are so conceited that you end up thinking their only claim to fame is their hat size. Others are so rude and demanding that they regard whatever is done for them with infuriating condescension, as if it is no more than their due. And some can't *live* without being in the limelight. But Stan wasn't like any of them. In fact he wasn't like any VIP I ever met. He was actually *nervous* at the airport, and would have escaped altogether given the slightest opportunity. He slipped into the background whenever he could. Naturally he was polite and friendly, but you could see he wasn't *enjoying* it.

And two other things struck me. The first was that although I had never heard of him, other people had. The Press turned out in force and Stan's face was all over the sports pages the following morning. But the most uncanny thing was his resemblance to my father. They could have been brothers. My father was a sportsman too. He raced his speedboat in the Czech championships and could still beat people half his age at tennis. I felt *sure* they would like each other. Then I laughed at the thought – why on earth was *that* so important? The two of them would never meet.

Stan and I barely said hello to each other at the airport, but I got to know him better over dinner that evening. He was quiet and shy, full of British reserve, but beneath it there were occasional signs of a dry sense of humour, and enough of a twinkle in his eye to suggest he might be a lot of fun if he ever let himself go. We talked and joked a lot – especially when we went sightseeing afterwards – and by the end of the evening I decided that, all in all, I rather liked Sir Stanley Matthews, in fact I liked him quite a lot.

I had lunch the next day with Eva. 'Of course, he's only a footballer,' I said, 'but he's very nice.'

Eva and I were old friends. We were two of five girls who grew up together and who had remained close ever since. There was Inge, who was quite, quite beautiful and one of the best skiers in Czechoslovakia. Like me, Inge was married and, also like me, she worked at an Embassy, in her case the British Embassy at the Thun-Taxis Palace. Then there was Vera, the daughter of a famous Czech writer. Vera had spent the war years in England (where her father had risen to the rank of General with the Czech forces), and she had studied at a drama school there. Once back in Prague she became an actress and had subsequently married, but by 1967 she was divorced. Whereas Kveta was still married – to one of the most successful film directors in Czechoslovakia. But Eva was my best friend. She was divorced by then, with one daughter who is my godchild, and in 1967 she too worked for an Embassy – in her case the Mexican one. So between the five of us we knew most of what went on in Prague. And we were closer than sisters. Hardly a week passed without us meeting for coffee or lunch, or drinks at one of our houses. Not that I drank anything stronger than tomato juice or the occasional glass of wine. That was another thing I had noticed about Stan – *he* didn't drink either.

On the Tuesday I got busy organizing the party. Not a big affair, just a small cocktail party at which Stan and Irving would have a chance to meet a few people who might help their negotiations. But when I told the British Cultural Attaché about it he got very excited. In fact he was so enthusiastic that he wanted to take the whole thing over, turn it into a big reception, that sort of thing. I felt sure Stan wouldn't like that, so in the end we compromised: the British would give the party and I would select the guests. So it was quickly organized and I waited for Stan to telephone to confirm the details.

But there was no call, either to me at the Embassy during the day, or to my home in the evening. Oddly enough, it annoyed me. Having made all the arrangements it was understandable that I should want to tell him about them, so perhaps *some* irritation was justified, but not the really foul temper I found myself in. So I went off to bed in a bad mood, convinced he would phone in the morning. But he never did – neither did he phone in the afternoon nor in the evening.

The next day was Thursday and the cocktail party was planned for that evening. I fumed all morning, and then – just before lunchtime – Stan phoned. He and Irving, together with the football team, had just returned to Prague ... so Stan was cheerfully calling to see if I had managed to arrange anything? I could have wrung his neck! As it was I was a bit short with him. I said George and I would collect the pair of them from their hotel later, and left it at that. Then I put the telephone down and tried to concentrate on other things. But it was difficult, and it was a relief when it was time to go home, to bathe and change for the evening.

Stan

Had it happened to anyone else I would have said he was drunk ... or *she* was drunk ... or *they* were drunk. But I don't drink, and neither does Mila, so there had to be another explanation for our behaviour that evening.

It began quite normally. Mila drove us to the cocktail party in her car. 'Us' being Irving and me, and George of course. During the ride we brought each other up to date. Irving and I reported on our negotiations in Gottwaldow (not very productive), and Mila on who would be at the party. It was to be held at a house which had belonged to a Czech film star by the name of Lida Baarova, who had been Goebells's mistress during the war.

It was certainly some house, and when we got there about sixty or seventy people were waiting to greet us. I was introduced to all and sundry, and it seemed to go very well. Various Czech officials promised to help the football boot deal through the committee stages, Irving and I both did our bit, buzzing around like bees at a honey pot – except that I never strayed far from Mila, as if she were my own personal honey pot. She took me round, making introductions, translating, joking, talking and talking and talking.

When it was all over a whole crowd of us went to dinner together at a big sprawling place, set deep in its own grounds. It was an old hunting lodge, but a big one, big enough to be a castle. Inside was a superb restaurant and a little dance-floor, and a very festive atmosphere – as if it were Christmas or something like that.

After dinner, Mila offered to show me the grounds. George was in deep conversation with some Czech friends, and Irving was giving the British Cultural Attaché some guidance on how to arrange a sovereign loan to Czechoslovakia, so we just slipped away.

There were acres of gardens. Rose gardens and terraces, lily ponds and fountains. We walked down one path and up another, deep in conversation and oblivious of everything and everyone else. I've forgotten what we talked about, but I remember laughing a lot and being fascinated by her personality. She was the *warmest* person I'd ever met – warm and amusing. And I was matching her story for story – that was the most amazing part of it all. I'd never felt so witty, so man-about-town, so assured and confident. It was a warm, moonlit night and we walked and talked for much longer than we intended.

'We ought to go back,' I said without meaning it.

'I know – but I love your dry sense of humour.'

Then we fell into the swimming pool! Not fell, we actually *walked* into it! I stepped out, with Mila on my arm, and we were both looking into each other's eyes – and suddenly I was walking on air. I'd been doing that all night, I suppose, but this was different. Especially the landing. A huge water spout shot ten feet high into the air and then fell all over us. By the time our feet touched bottom we were standing in three feet of water. Mila shrieked and lost her balance, while I splashed about like a half-drowned rat. Then we were blinded by floodlights and deafened by alarm bells, and waiters and staff were running to the poolside, closely followed by George and Irving and the rest of the guests.

It was all very embarrassing. And freezing cold in that water. About eighty people lined the sides of the pool, stretching out their arms and shouting advice. 'Is this a private party?' Irving called, 'or can anyone join in?' All very funny – even worse when he yelled: 'George will go off the deep end about this!'

Luckily George did no such thing, and everyone treated it as a joke. Mila and I stood in the foyer, dripping pools of water everywhere while we thanked everyone for a splendid evening. Then she drove us back into Prague, squelching and giggling all the way.

She saw us off the following day. As smart, as attractive and as talkative as ever. I thought she was one of the most remarkable people I had ever met. Then I boarded the aircraft and we all flew home.

It was only a week to the start of the season when we returned from Prague, so all thoughts of the football boot deal were set aside as I concentrated on getting the team ready. The game in Czechoslovakia had been useful but the boys were still terribly short of experience so I arranged a couple of friendly games to help knit the team together. It was a busy time, but I liked the way they were shaping up, and my enthusiasm grew each time they played.

And then I arrived at the ground one morning to find young Smithers and his mother waiting to see me. Smithers wasn't his real name but it will save embarrassment all round if I call him that. I had seen him play for his school the year before and, there was no doubt about it, Smithers was good, *very* good. Half a dozen big clubs were after him but his mother fancied he would learn more with me – and of course I agreed. They were a Geordie family and ever since I can remember the north-east has been the breeding ground for the best players in the country. Mother and son had travelled down the day before and here they were, with the request that I take the boy on as an apprentice.

'He's finished school, Sir Stan,' said Mother, 'and I'd like you to take him under your wing.'

I was delighted. So I fixed the boy up with digs nearby, had a word with his landlady, sent Mother off happily, and that was that. Boy apprentices were paid five pounds a week, plus their lodging, and although not a fortune it was enough for a lad to live on comfortably.

So the season kicked off. Our early matches went quite well, and I was pleased with the way some of the lads were shaping up. Young Smithers settled in and began to shine in the junior side, so all in all I had reasons for optimism. Then I had a letter from the football boot factory in Prague. Could I go back for another meeting? Well, like most people, I'll go almost anywhere for seventy-two thousand pounds, so I wrote back saying yes, and I wrote to Mila Winter at the same time, asking if she would act as guide and interpreter.

Then Smithers's landlady came to see me. It was the day before I left for Czechoslovakia. The landlady was very upset. The boy had been misbehaving – wetting his bed, making a mess in the bathroom, using the telephone for long distance calls, all sorts of things. Naturally I had a word with him. I tell you, it's not easy being a football manager; you're a Dutch Uncle one day, physiotherapist the next, and psychologist the day after. So I had a long talk with young Smithers and tried to find out if anything was worrying him. I went on to say how pleased I was with his game and that he had a good future – *if* he behaved himself. In the end the lad promised to mend his ways and I persuaded the landlady to give him another chance, so the problem was resolved. I breathed a sigh of relief and sent them both on their way. Losing a boy prodigy as gifted as young Smithers was the last thing I wanted. Then I tidied my desk and called it a day, and the following morning I caught the first flight to Prague.

Mila

I took a few days' leave for Stan's second visit to Prague. He arrived on the Tuesday and was staying until the Friday morning, so we had the best part of three days together. Meeting the committees involved with the football boot deal would take up most of the time, but in the time not spent with them I planned to show Stan more of Prague and the surrounding countryside. But what else to do with him? Films and the theatre were obviously out of the question because of the language problem, so I booked a box at the ballet and tried to think of other things to amuse him.

Naturally I told George. I even invited George to join us, but he was busy on some project or other and couldn't spare the time. Besides Stan and George couldn't actually *communicate* with each other without me interpreting, so conversation between them tended to be stilted and awkward. I was glad in a way, about George being busy. Stan and I had got on so well before that I was curious to find out how we would react to each other. Curious and a bit apprehensive – as if I were afraid of being disappointed.

Not that I need have worried. We were relaxed and happy together from the moment we met at the airport. I took him to his hotel and we had lunch, after which we went to see his committee.

In the evening I took him to the ballet, or at least I *tried* to take him. We went sure enough, but Stan was asleep in his seat before the intermission. 'Jet lag,' he said, when I woke him. Jet lag, my foot – he was lively enough afterwards, when we went out to dinner and later dancing. But any irritation I felt was quickly forgotten in the pleasure of being with him. He was so amusing and we had such fun – arguing, talking, joking – that we might have known each other for years.

The following morning we had another committee meeting, and in the afternoon I took him to a football match, which at least kept him awake. I bombarded him with questions, just to prove how interested I was. After all, it was the first game of football I had seen in my life. I had so many questions. What were they doing? Why does the referee whistle all the time? Suddenly I asked what he did for a living? 'I play football,' he said. That amazed me. A grown man being *paid money* to play football! (There is no professional sport in Czechoslovakia.) So Stan took a long time to convince me that he had made his living playing football.

We went out to dinner in the evening, then dancing and sightseeing again, and more sightseeing the whole of the next day when we drove for miles through southern Bohemia. And on the Friday morning we said goodbye. Except by then I was sure it wasn't goodbye. It *couldn't* be.

Stan

I called myself all sorts of names on the flight back to England. Well, it was *ridiculous*! The way I was behaving you'd think I was nineteen, not fifty-two. You read about men of my age chasing chorus girls – I'd always had a good laugh about them. Well, there had to be *something* wrong with them. A man is a bit of a fool if he doesn't know what's what in life by the time he's fifty. By then a man has developed a sense of responsibility, his own values, experience with which to judge life – he's not a daft lad any more.

And yet reading the Riot Act to myself didn't alter the way I felt. It did nothing to change the fact that I was more relaxed, more comfortable, more alive with Mila Winter than any other woman I had ever known. Besides, Mila *wasn't* a young chorus girl. She was a sensible, mature, attractive woman with her own life to lead. Married, too – even if she and her husband seemed to go their separate ways.

It had been funny about that ballet though. Made her really *mad* – she almost slammed the door in my face on the way out. Still it had been all right afterwards, over dinner and at that place we went dancing. *Me – dancing?* I *never* danced. I *hated* dancing. And me having fun? That was the really daft part about it – I can't remember when I last had so much fun.

I forget if it was during the flight home or sometime the following day that I decided to write to her, but I certainly sent her a letter on the Monday. *And* a bunch of roses – not a dozen, but eleven, to represent a football team. It was the least I could do, to thank her for showing me round and for helping at the committee meetings. Or so I told myself.

When I returned to Port Vale I found I had a new chairman to contend with. He had been on the board for years, but it was his first spell in the chair. He was a local businessman and we had known each other for a long time. I never expected his appointment to bring about any changes, and I was right: money was as tight under him as it had been with his predecessor. But I struggled on, running the club on the proverbial shoe-string. It was my third season and I still hadn't been paid a penny – not since the day I started. I wasn't too worried. I had enough to live on and I felt that I was proving something with my young squad of players. And all of the directors at Port Vale promised that I would be paid – eventually.

So the weeks passed, and then I had another spot of bother with young Smithers, or rather with his landlady. The boy was still bed-wetting and making a general nuisance of himself, and she wanted to be rid of him. But after a long talk I persuaded her to keep him, although this time she made conditions: four weeks, that was all she would give him, and if he was no better then, out he would go. So I had another chat with the boy, and while I was talking to him I realized something – or at least I guessed it. The boy was *younger* than fifteen. He should still be at school! And when I put this to Smithers he broke down and admitted it: he was only fourteen.

Apart from anything else, we had broken the law. All boys should attend full-time school until their fifteenth birthday. *And* we had broken the FA rules. Clubs are *not allowed* to sign a boy as an apprentice until he leaves school at the age of fifteen. So, one way and another, young Smithers was causing a few headaches.

I had a word with the club secretary about it. Paperwork, after all, was his problem, and he should have sorted this out at the start. But it was too late for recriminations – we had a difficulty and we had to solve it. I was still loath to lose the lad, and it was obvious that he desperately wanted to stay, so I had a chat with a local headmaster and I thought afterwards that I had found the solution. Young Smithers would attend school locally, we would pay him pocket money for doing odd jobs at the ground, and he could continue to train with the players in his free time. The club secretary felt none of the rules prevented the idea, so I wrote to the boy's mother and everyone seemed happy with the new arrangement – or at least as happy as they could be under the circum-stances. I had half a mind to write a few hard words to the mother for misleading me about the lad's age, but I decided against it. As far as I could make out the family was hard-up, and no doubt the mother thought she was doing the best thing for the boy. Besides, no great harm had been done because we had remedied the situation as soon as we found out about it. So that's how matters were left.

Meanwhile Mila answered my letter, and I replied to her answer –

and I sent her more flowers. In fact we both wrote every day, and I sent flowers once a week. I just couldn't get her out of my mind. I even telephoned her every third day, and it was during a telephone call that she gave me some very good news. She and George were coming to England for a week, thanks to our old friend Irving Toorchen, who had commissioned George to work on a magazine cover. It seemed too good to be true, especially when I suggested that Mila come to Stoke for a few days – and she accepted. After that all I had to do was curb my impatience ... until she arrived.

Mila

There was no way of accepting Stan's invitation to go to Stoke without first telling George, and without past experience of that kind of thing I had no way of predicting what George's reaction would be. But he had to be told. I sat in my room for an hour after Stan's call, rehearsing my impending conversation with George, and then I went to his studio. He was sketching furiously and surrounded by enough crumpled paper to indicate it was one of those nights when ideas were hard to come by. I changed my mind about telling him and turned to go, but he insisted that I stay to talk. And somehow, during the conversation, I just blurted it out: 'George, I think I'm in love with Stan.'

His hand slipped and a black line shot across the paper. He looked at me in astonishment: 'You think *what?*'

My cheeks burned, but I managed to nod my head as he stared at me.

'With *Stan?*' He sounded horrified, then with a flash of sudden insight he added: 'But he's *English.*'

'I know that, but – '

'A Slav like you? Cosmopolitan. He's – '

'Travelled a lot,' I ventured, quickly and stupidly.

George boggled: 'And he remains as English as ... as ... that stuff they eat. That doughy mess with meat – '

'Yorkshire pudding?'

He nodded fiercely, 'That stuff. You've *nothing* in common. Language, art – '

'It doesn't matter – when you're in love.'

'*In love!*' He threw his arms in the air: 'Stop talking like a schoolgirl and *listen to me!*' He pushed his work to one side, then rubbed his face as he stared at me. Charcoal dust from his fingers left a grey smudge on his chin. He wasn't angry, just staggered. George was *never* angry – impatient sometimes perhaps, but never angry. And like most cartoonists he had a strong sense of the ridiculous and could reduce any situation to an absurdity when it suited him. I braced myself.

He sighed heavily, and shifted his position on his stool: 'Mila, my dear,' he said more calmly, 'you're an intelligent woman. Educated, well read – what do you find to *talk about* with a man like that?'

'We laugh a lot and – '

'*Laugh?* What's to laugh about? You took him to the ballet. What happened?'

'He fell asleep,' I admitted.

George pounced: '*The Slavonic Dances* and he fell *asleep?* All that leaping about in national costume – thumping across the stage in cossack boots – '

'There's no real story to it,' I said hastily, 'probably something like *Swan Lake* – '

'*SWAN LAKE!* He would have snored in the overture. The English *hate* ballet. The English have always hated ballet – '

'I don't understand – '

'This isn't love. At the most it's some mild infatuation. Love is sharing, life, experience, common interests – '

'Perhaps we *do* have common interests.'

'Such as? Such as laughing like hyenas? Such as walking into swimming pools? Those are *interests?*'

'More than that.'

He pretended to be impressed by crossing his arms and cocking his head to one side: '*More* than that,' he said, raising his eyebrows, 'Something *more than that* would be truly remarkable.'

I tried to ignore his sarcasm: 'George, this is serious – '

'Who's joking? My wife's in love with a footballer. You think I find that funny?'

He climbed down from the stool and crossed to the sideboard for a drink. It was going badly, but I had started now, so I had no choice but to finish. I said: 'He's invited me to go to Stoke during our visit to England. For a few days – '

'You don't even like football. Why?'

'Why Stoke?'

'Not why Stoke – why *Stanley Matthews?*'

'I don't know. I can't explain. We make each other laugh – '

'What's with all this laughing? To laugh is so terrific? You are telling *me*? Suddenly a footballer is funnier than a cartoonist?'

'Please George – '

'Laughter can be a prelude to tears. You remember that.'

'I'm sorry, but it's the way I feel.'

'Infatuation,' he snorted. He finished his drink at a gulp but stayed at the sideboard staring at me. Then he shrugged: 'Why not? Go to Stoke if you want to. Get it out of your system. See how bored you get when you stop laughing,' he shook his head. He sounded more bewildered than hurt, 'Mila Winter,' he said, 'with a footballer. An *English* footballer. Even a footballer like Stanley Matthews.'

And so I went to Stoke.

It was November. George and I travelled to London together and journeyed without incident. In fact he was full of amusing stories during the flight. He was looking forward to the Irving Toorchen commission, and as convinced as ever that I was merely infatuated with Stan. He was sure we would be sick of the sight of each other after a few days. Looking back from here I don't think he even minded that much – after all, we had always gone our separate ways, though never to this extent. But most of all he was convinced that he was right, and that it was just an infatuation.

Irving met us at Heathrow and took us into London. Then he carried George off to his home in Farnham and I caught the first train to Stoke. Neither George nor I told Irving. We just said I was visiting a friend who lived in the Midlands.

Stan had booked two single rooms at an hotel in Burslam – called The George. His face was blank when I said it was a tactless choice, then embarrassed when the penny dropped. But after that, of course, we laughed about it.

The five days and nights passed as if by magic. Stan showed me the countryside, took me to Buxton and various other places – and, as always, we had fun. Naturally he was recognized wherever we went, especially in Stoke, but I was never introduced so there were no embarrassing moments. We were lucky really, looking back. To have spent five days anywhere near Stoke seems the craziest thing to do. Perhaps George was right and we really were mad.

George was certainly right about another thing – laughter being a prelude to tears – because all too soon it was over and time to return to Prague. But Stan and I had enjoyed five precious days together and the memories would have to last until next we met. And neither of us knew when that would be.

Of course we continued to write to each other every day – sometimes twice a day – and Stan telephoned me most nights. He even telephoned on New Year's Eve. There was a huge party going on at my house, but when Stan's call came through at eleven o'clock I rushed to my room – to emerge again a whole hour later. There were lots of questions and curious looks, but only George knew for sure who had telephoned, though I think some of my friends guessed, even then.

Stan

A new year – 1968. So much happened in 1968 that it's difficult to believe the year had only twelve months, the same as any other. Had someone predicted what was to happen to me I wouldn't have believed it. I would have laughed and rejected it out of hand. But at least *some* of the signs were there in January, had I looked for them.

Young Smithers was the start of it. His landlady was up in arms again, and this time she was adamant! The lad had to go – be out of her house by the end of the week, never to darken her doorstep again! I was sorry to lose the boy because of his potential, but the more I thought about the matter the more I came to the conclusion that the problems would continue – even in fresh digs with a new landlady. He needed a strong hand, and more time and attention than I could give him. Maybe if Jackie Mudie had stayed? But as things were I was running the club single-handed and there were never enough hours in the day. So when the local headmaster added *his* doubts about Smithers, I made up my mind. The boy had to go – back home to Mum. I broke it to him as gently as I could. Then I wrote to his mother explaining the circumstances. I left the door open, with a lot of talk about when he had grown up a bit, maybe in a year's time, that sort of thing ... and I was sorry to see the lad go, I don't deny it.

But if losing Smithers was a disappointment, something else happened in January which filled me with excitement. I was invited to South Africa for two months in the summer, to play in some exhibition games. And a week after receiving that invitation I had another one – this time from Canada. They were both good offers, but what excited me most was this idea which I'd had: that Mila should come with me – to give us a chance to find out what we really felt for each other. People never *really* know each other until they live together, and it seemed to me that two months was enough for us to be able to decide about the future:

whether the attraction would last, or whether George was right and it was just some kind of delayed adolescent infatuation.

It's funny how attitudes change. It was the swinging sixties then, and newspapers were full of the permissive society. Divorce had become almost respectable, in fact *totally* respectable to some people. But not to me, at least not when I *thought* about it, and I had never even contemplated it until then. Divorce was something which happened to other people. Usually there was some scandal attached to it – unpleasant headlines in the papers, dirty jokes in the dressing-room – and it was certainly something best avoided.

Of course, my upbringing coloured my attitude. My parents had been happy together. Divorce had never touched anyone in our family, and like everyone else most of my thoughts on *life* had been developed during my formative years. After that I had been too busy playing football to think about it.

When I was young, certainly, divorce was invariably associated with scandal. I was playing for England long before the Abdication Crisis was resolved, and although that was the biggest scandal of all there were lots of others making the headlines. Even after the war 'a good juicy divorce case' could be relied upon to sell a lot of newspapers. So the prospect of having the details of my private life splashed all over the place frightened me to death. Not just for my own sake, but for the sake of my family: too many people would get hurt.

I married when I was nineteen, so by 1968 my wife Betty and I had shared good times and bad together, just like any other people. Our two children had grown up by then, so at least I didn't have them to consider, at least not directly – all I had to worry about was a thirty-three-year-old marriage which had run out of steam. Ours wasn't a *bad* marriage, and certainly Betty was in no sense a *bad* wife. We had our share of rows, but who doesn't? I doubt that we were any less happy than thousands of other people who had been married that amount of time. Our marriage was something we never thought about. We took it for granted – it was *there*, catalogued in the family photograph album, stuck together with shared memories but by little else. Warmth and affection had once been part of it, but that was long ago. By 1968 it was a sort of peaceful coexistence, with each partner troubling the other as little as possible.

We drifted along, neither actively happy nor positively unhappy. I cannot recall Betty actually calling me 'Stan' once during those last ten years. She had a habit of speaking to me through other people: 'Ask your father if he'd like another cup of tea,' she would say to the children – and I'd be sitting opposite her, close enough to touch her! Daft, isn't it, the things which irritate? I bet I had a hundred little habits that annoyed her just as much – more, probably. Habits like that spring up when people stop talking to each other – *properly* talking, I mean. Perhaps we had said all there was to be said to each other? Perhaps the marriage had simply worn itself out and neither of us would ever have known – had I not met Mila.

I couldn't get Mila out of my mind, especially after her visit to Stoke. Until then she had been the most charming woman I had ever met – fun to be with, interesting, different, and *alive*, so alive that everyone else seemed drab by comparison. But then I found out about her relationship with George, that they could each go their separate ways if they wanted to, and it seemed Mila *might* want to go her separate way with *me*.

So I telephoned Prague and put the idea of Canada to her, and a few weeks later I went to Czechoslovakia to talk to her about it.

Mila

The prospect of going to Canada with Stan was so exciting that I could hardly sleep at nights. The minute he phoned I knew I would go – *if I could*. But going was not to be easy. I would have to apply to the Ministry of the Interior for an exit visa, and *George* would be required to counter-sign my application. Meanwhile, in case that wasn't obstacle enough, the organizers of Stan's trip would have to send the return air tickets directly to me, together with a letter saying they would be responsible for all my expenses while I was in Canada. This latter requirement was to satisfy Czechoslovakia's stringent exchange control regulations.

Of course, I told the girls about it. They would have to know anyway, for I could hardly disappear for two months without them asking questions. In some ways telling the girls was even more difficult than persuading George to sign the visa application. To become someone's *mistress* was almost unknown in Prague. It just wasn't done, certainly not in our circle. In fact I cannot remember even *one* woman who lived as a man's mistress in peacetime Prague. Anyone foolish enough to do so would certainly have been ostracized.

The reason was less a moral one than a practical one: divorce was quick and easy and carried no social stigma whatsoever. The State believed that families were the bricks in the wall of society – unhappy couples made weak bricks, and weak bricks made weak walls – therefore if a couple were unhappy living together the State made it easy for them to divorce, and to re-marry other partners if they wanted. As a consequence many of our friends had done just that, so to be someone's mistress was unnecessary, as well as unthinkable. Perhaps because of this it took the girls some time to accept the idea of me going to Canada with Stan. The subject of whether we would travel as man and wife was studiously avoided, but from the things they said I know they were as concerned for me as I would have been had one of them been involved.

George, on the other hand, was no real problem. I can't say he was overjoyed with the idea, but he accepted it, despite remaining as convinced as ever that I would grow out of my *infatuation*.

So when Stan came over to Prague at the end of January, I took him to Karlsbad for three marvellous days, where we discussed the project non-stop. Karlsbad is a spa town about a hundred kilometres north of Prague. It is quiet and peaceful, and a bit off the beaten track as far as most of my Prague crowd were concerned, so we were undisturbed. We stayed in separate rooms at an hotel, but apart from when we slept we spent every minute of the three days and nights together.

People go to Karlsbad for the mineral waters. Not just one sort, for there is a cure for everything at Karlsbad – lumbago, gout, rheumatism, the lot. You sip cups of this or that water as you stroll up and down the promenades. There was nothing much wrong with Stan, but of course he insisted on trying everything – so I let him, but I should have warned him about the one for constipation. Never has the famous Matthews burst of speed been needed more.

By this time I had told my father about Stan. We discussed it on Christmas Eve. Father and I always went to Midnight Mass together, and afterwards, as we walked home arm in arm, I found myself telling him all about Stan. Father had been an officer in the Czech army and lived his life by a very strict code. He was shocked and upset, as I had known he would be, but I steeled myself and forced the words out somehow, knowing I would far rather he heard about it from me than from somebody else. We had always been close, much closer than my mother and I, and I was terrified he would have a bad opinion of me. He listened carefully, without interruption, while I sang Stan's praises and tried to explain how it had all happened. And when I finished he said: 'He *sounds* to be a good man. Let us hope so, and let us pray that God will forgive both of you for what you are going to do.'

Father never had the slightest *doubt* about what I would do. And neither, I suppose, did I.

Stan

When I returned once again from Prague, it was time to prepare the team for the next round of the League Cup. We were drawn against Chester, and although we were playing away I felt we had a good chance. The boys must have thought so too, because they asked for a bonus if we won.

Footballers can earn fabulous sums of money today, and I am glad they have the opportunity. After all, a career in football is fairly short compared with most, and there is always the danger that injury can compel a player to retire at the height of his powers. So in a high-risk business it is only right and proper that the rewards should be correspondingly large.

Not that it was always so. I remember when I first joined the Player's Union in 1932. I was playing for Stoke then, and a Mr Fay called at the ground every week to talk to the lads about the benefits of joining the Union. The club management never objected, but they obviously thought the Union would never amount to much. Understandably, perhaps, because less than half the players joined up. Subscription was two shillings a week then, out of a wage of five pounds, so it was never really expensive – but you could buy a few pints of beer for a couple of bob in 1932, and some of the boys thought more of their pint than of Mr Fay's arguments. Perhaps they were right, too, because although the Union achieved some benefits it was years before the big breakthrough came, when Jimmy Hill took over and negotiated the abolition of the maximum wage. That was the real turning-point. Within months of Jimmy's settlement his old partner Johnny Haynes was being paid a hundred pounds a week by Fulham, and things have never been the same since.

Not that Port Vale were paying anyone a hundred pounds a week in 1968. The club's finances were still badly in the red, and the players' wages were modest to say the least. So whenever the chance of a bonus arose they jumped in with both feet. And the League Cup match against Chester was such a chance – at least so they thought.

I raised the matter at the next board meeting: 'Mr Chairman,' I said, 'the boys have asked if they can have a win bonus if we beat Chester?'

The chairman turned to the secretary: 'Anything in the rules to say we can't pay a bonus?'

'No, Mr Chairman.'

'Very well then,' said the chairman to me, 'Okay Stan, tell the boys they are on a ten-pound win bonus – and good luck for the match.'

The decision was properly recorded in the Minute Book, and when I told the boys they were suitably pleased. Morale rose and a bit of an edge crept into training sessions, with every player anxious to win a place in the team. In the event we lost at Chester, so the boys never got their bonus, but the matter was to have unforeseen consequences which were not long in coming. In fact the trouble started only a few weeks later.

We had been training at the Keele University Ground in the morning. When the work-out finished I was due to catch the train to London and go on to Brighton for a sponsorship appearance. I showered and changed, then got into my car and drove to Stoke station. I switched on the car radio and listened to the midday news on the way. That was the first I heard of it. Even then I couldn't believe it. The Football League had announced an enquiry into the affairs of Port Vale Football Club! I was staggered. What sort of enquiry? What affairs were they talking about? There was no time to telephone the club from the station, because the train was due when I parked my car, so I clambered aboard and stewed silently all the way to London.

The midday editions of the newspapers were out when I reached Euston. Placards and headlines screamed from all sides: 'Football League to probe Stan Matthews ... Sir Stan on the mat ... Matthews in illegal payments scandal.'

I grabbed a few papers and searched for the story, but none gave any real details – just that the League had announced an enquiry into the affairs of Port Vale, with specific reference to payments to players. What did that mean? I telephoned the club from the station. It was true. The League had sent for the club's books. I asked a lot of questions but was given very few answers –or none that satisfied me, anyway. But there was nothing I could do about it, so I continued on my way to Brighton to fulfil my engagement. The next day I travelled back and the real extent of the problem became obvious at the very first board meeting.

We were charged on two counts. The first was that we had made payments to amateur players, and the second was that we had sanctioned illegal bonus payments to members of the playing staff.

My heart sank when I listened to the explanation offered by the club secretary. For reasons best known to him he had not filed the paperwork relating to all the apprentices with the Football League. Effectively this meant that some of the boys were not *registered* professional players. By definition therefore they were amateurs. Yet we had certainly paid them! So we were guilty as charged. I had no doubt about that.

It was news to me, and I wondered how the League had learned about it. Then I remembered young Smithers. When I sent him back home I had written to the headmaster of his local school in the north-east. Naturally I wanted to let the lad down as lightly as possible, and do what I could to ease him back into his home environment. So I had written to his old school saying I still thought the boy had a future in football and I would be obliged if they would let me know how he progressed. My guess – and it's only a guess, even today – is that the headmaster there, who had never wanted the boy to leave the north-east, had written to the League. Not that it mattered of course: what was done was done. And in the case of young Smithers I had acted as soon as I found out his real age.

We were also guilty on the other issue, that of sanctioning illegal bonus payments. It arose from the incident prior to the game against Chester in the League Cup. Apparently a bonus was *not* allowable under the rules. Yet there it was, in black and white in the Minute Book: we *would* have paid a bonus had we won.

What I could never understand was why *some* of the paperwork had not been properly filed? There was no rhyme or reason to it. A few apprentices who had joined quite recently *were* properly registered, whereas the paperwork for others, some of whom had been with us a good twelve months, had not been filed at all. It made no sense to me. Clearly it was an administrative foul-up, but it was hardly the end of the world. Obviously the secretary had been inefficient, everyone could see we had broken the rules – but we had committed sins of *omission*, not sins of *commission*. It was up to the secretary to shoulder the blame and put things right. Nobody is perfect. I've always found that if you admit to an honest error most people will help you out of the difficulty. It's facing up to it that counts.

But it became clear at the very first board meeting that *facing up to it* was the last thing the chairman had in mind. And the same went for the secretary. They even refused to meet the crowd of reporters who lay siege to the main gates. We stayed in the boardroom until it was dark, then crept out of the back door and into the car park, sneaking away from the ground like schoolboys caught cheating in an exam.

The following weeks were a nightmare. Not making a statement to the Press was like an admission of guilt. The headlines continued: 'Matthews in Port Vale Scandal' – as much as saying I had been cheating or fiddling. The innuendo was I had been caught with my hand in the till. That was a joke! Quite apart from the fact that it rankled, it was downright ludicrous. The club was as good as broke! There was *no money* to fiddle, and I hadn't even had a penny in salary since I joined.

Further board meetings were held during the following weeks. The pressure from the Press for a statement continued and I remember time and time again suggesting: 'Mr Chairman, let us meet the reporters. We are making things *worse* by remaining silent. I will face the Press, but not alone. Either you as chairman or the club secretary should be with me to explain the full circumstances.'

But it was to no avail. The chairman and secretary were adamant. No statement should be made to the Press. And after every meeting we sat in that boardroom until it was dark – then we sneaked out the back way to avoid the reporters on the front gate.

By now the Football Association had called for an enquiry, as well as the Football League, so we had *two* investigations to face. It was getting me down. I don't cheat; it's not even a question of principle – I just don't see the point. If a game is worth playing, it's worth playing well. In thirty-three years of playing professional football I was never so much as booked for a foul, let alone sent off. So it hurt when the Press and others implied I had cheated as a manager, and I don't mind admitting it. But I couldn't speak out without letting the chairman and secretary down – or so it seemed to me at the time. So I soldiered on.

The tension inside the club transmitted itself to the players, and our performance suffered accordingly. In fact the whole situation went from bad to worse.

Finally the FA held their enquiry, and we trooped down to London for the meeting. The club was fined £2,000. We returned to Port Vale in a gloomy mood. It was a swingeing blow for a club of that size, and the prospect of another heavy penalty from the League loomed large in my mind. Fines of that magnitude meant I would have even *less* chance of getting money with which to buy new players.

Then the Football League announced that their next meeting would

be held after a match between the English and Scottish Leagues, and that the Port Vale matter would be on the agenda. We braced ourselves for the worst. But nothing happened. Apparently the League Committee had been so bound up with other matters that they had not had time to deal with our case.

Meanwhile our ridiculous little board meetings continued – with the Press baying like hounds for the inside story, and us sneaking out through the car park under cover of darkness. Finally I telephoned Alan Hardacre, the secretary of the Football League. 'Mr Hardacre,' I said, 'I'm sorry to bother you, but I wonder if you could tell me when the League will conduct their enquiry?'

'I don't know,' he said in a most off-hand manner which suggested that he couldn't care less.

His attitude annoyed me. After all, the League had started this witch-hunt with their announcement of an enquiry. The very least they could do was to hold the wretched thing – get it over and done with. But I tried to keep my irritation from sounding in my voice. 'If you could fix a date I would be grateful,' I said. 'It's like sitting on top of a volcano here.'

Hardacre snapped: 'I've been sitting on top of a bloody volcano for years.'

That really made me see red. 'Don't talk to me like that,' I said. 'You are a *paid* secretary.' Then I put the phone down. I have no idea whether Hardacre answered or not – I was too angry to listen anyway.

And so the weeks drifted by. It was a depressing time for me, and the only patch of blue in the sky was Mila Winter. We continued to write to each other every day, and I slipped across to Prague a couple of times – from Tuesday to Thursday on both occasions – to discuss the possible trip to Canada. The most exciting thing was that she wanted to come, but for a Czech to make such a trip was far from easy. Mila explained about exit visas and meetings with the Ministry and all the other complications ... So although she *wanted* to, it was far from certain that we would see Canada together.

Meanwhile the football season limped to a close. The Football League finally held its enquiry and the club suffered another heavy fine. I came in for a fair amount of stick from all sides, but neither the chairman nor the secretary uttered a public word in my defence. Their attitude sickened me and made me take stock of the situation. Little of what I had hoped to achieve at Port Vale had been accomplished, and I could see little hope for the club's future while its affairs were controlled by the existing board of directors. So, thoroughly disillusioned with the entire business, I resigned.

Among other things, the matter of my salary had to be settled. In three years I had not received a penny piece, despite the fact that my contract entitled me to seventy-five pounds a week during the season, plus travelling expenses. Add that lot up and it comes to the best part of nine thousand pounds. I asked the board what they proposed to do about it?

The chairman hummed and hawed for a bit, then he said 'Stan, we haven't the money in the kitty. We can't *afford* to pay you.'

He let that sink in, then added: 'Not all at once, anyway.'

'Not for a long time,' the secretary chimed in.

Well, looking back, I suppose I *should* have created a fuss. Perhaps I ought to have really made trouble, perhaps even gone so far as issuing a writ. After all, it was yet another broken promise on top of so many others. But I hate unpleasantness. Besides it wasn't as if I was *desperate* for the money. I had my savings to fall back on, sponsorship earned me some more and I was being paid for my appearances in Canada. I reasoned that the game had been good to me; I had got a lot out of it so maybe it was time to put something back. I tried to do the fairest thing. So I said: 'Okay, tell you what we'll do. You can pay me a hundred pounds a month. How will that suit you? A hundred a month until the debt is paid off.'

Now I'm not saying I expected a round of applause, but I did expect to be thanked. After all, I was more or less offering them a seven and a half year loan – and interest-free at that! But not a word of it. Instead the secretary shook his head: 'Couldn't pay you in the summer,' he said. 'After all, we've no gates in the summer.'

'That's right,' agreed the chairman quickly, 'We couldn't pay you a penny in the summer. Be reasonable Stan, for heaven's sake!'

Be reasonable! They had already had my money for three years, now they were telling me they were going to take the best part of another *twelve years* to pay me my wages! Crikey, I tell you, football club chairmen are a race apart. Not all of them of course, but some are downright impossible. Anyway I was sick and tired of the whole business, and fed up with arguing about it. So that's how it was left. Port Vale would pay me a hundred pounds a month during the season, starting when the next season began. I told myself I had bent over backwards to play fair. I hoped they would reciprocate, but even then I had some niggling doubts, despite the chairman's vote of thanks and his promise to keep their end of the bargain.

And so I left Port Vale and ended my career as a football manager – hardly covered in glory, I have to admit. Frustrating too, sitting in the dug-out week after week and never allowed to play. I retired too early as a player, I am convinced of that now. I could have played for at least another three seasons by dropping back to mid-field and playing from there. Wingers were going out of fashion then anyway, and the mid-field role was just being developed. That would have suited me nicely, and just to think of all those *extra* games I could have played breaks my heart. So much more fun than being a manager.

As for managership – well, I'd had enough of that. I thought about it. Maybe my upbringing and background were against me. I had been taught that fair play was the be all and end all of sport. Come to think of it, I *still* believe that. But successful managers have to adopt a ruthlessness which I either couldn't or wouldn't acquire. And a good manager has to be good at *managing* things off the field as well as on it. For instance, not long after the Port Vale 'scandal', Manchester United were in trouble on a similar matter. But not for them anxious weeks of waiting for the League to conduct an enquiry. Not for Matt Busby headlines in the Press. Instead the whole matter was dealt with quietly. Just a brief announcement made *after* a meeting of the Football League: 'Manchester United fined five thousand pounds.' The whole thing over and done with. Don't get me wrong – that is no criticism of Matt, who, quite apart from being a very successful manager, is a very charming man. But Matt had a knack of getting his own way, and of course he was backed up by a very strong chairman in Louis Edwards. Edwards and Busby together were a formidable pair. Formidable enough, I believe, to have made the League officials think twice about tackling them in the way they dealt with Port Vale.

Anyway, that was how things stood in May 1968. I was out of a job and uncertain about the future, and felt bruised and battered after my experiences at Port Vale. But every cloud has a silver lining, and the day I resigned I had some marvellous news. Mila telephoned to say she could come to Canada! All the permissions and red tape and formalities had been completed in Prague – with barely a week to go! Suddenly none of the aggravation mattered – in fact *nothing* mattered. I was going to Canada with Mila, and the trip was less than a week away.

Mila

Maybe that's how Stan remembers it now – all that business about nothing else mattering and all the tension fading away. But it wasn't like that at all. When I flew into Heathrow Stan was as wound up as a watch spring. Tense wasn't the word for it – he was about as relaxed as a man in the condemned cell. He looked tired, strained and worried to death. There was I, bubbling with excitement and almost feverish about the trip to Canada and the prospect of two whole months together – and Stan looked as if he was going to the dentist.

We spent one night at the airport hotel to await our connecting flight to Toronto the next day, and Stan told me all about it. Of course I had heard *some* of the story, but not until I saw him did I realize just how much that business at Port Vale had got him down. It really had exhausted him and left him with a complete phobia about the Press. He was seeing reporters behind every potted plant and under every table. He was terrified that news of our trip together would leak out and there would be yet more headlines about a Stanley Matthews scandal.

It was all very understandable of course, and I *did* understand. But to begin with it was like being with a different man. Where was the warm, amusing, nice, funny, considerate man I was supposed to be going to Canada with? Not with me, that's for sure. Instead I was saddled with this nervous, twitching wreck who looked as if he regretted the whole thing. Did he know what I had *been through* to get here? Half the officials in the Ministry of the Interior were recovering from arguments with me – and the other half had collapsed from nervous exhaustion. Now the great day was finally here, but from the look on his face Stan might have changed his mind.

By the end of dinner I had made him laugh. I don't know *how* I did, but I did. Boy, it was hard work! But I persevered and gradually the *real* Stan began to emerge. Even so I was one very worried lady when I went to my separate bedroom at the end of the evening. I sat up in bed thinking about it. Naturally I had agreed that we should be careful about being seen together in public. Naturally we should be discreet. *Of course* it was important not to let the Press find out about our relationship. But talking about something and doing it are two very different things, and I was beginning to realize just how difficult it was to be discreet.

The following day we flew to Toronto. It was a very nice flight – until we landed. Then there was a battery of flashbulbs and a forest of live microphones, and Stan disappeared into the middle of a mob of reporters who wanted to know everything from who would win the cup to the state of play in South America. I was left standing there, open-mouthed and petrified until the organizer's representative found me. Now I don't want to say anything bad about that man. I'm sure he is kind to his wife and a credit to his local community – but he will never earn a living as a greeter in a night club. In fact I swear he was trained by the FBI, or whatever they have in Canada. He almost threw me over his shoulder in his hurry to get me out of there. Then we took a separate car to my separate room in Stan's hotel. When we arrived I expected a blanket to be thrown over my head before being smuggled upstairs in the dumb waiter.

'Sir Stan has explained all about you,' he said knowingly, as he closed the door in my room. 'We gotta keep you under wraps.'

I felt like a witness in a murder trial. And my face burned bright red at that remark about Sir Stan explaining *all* about me.

'Here's the itinerary,' said the man, taking a sheet of paper from his pocket. 'Reception lunch – grand banquet tonight – Press conference in the morning – first game in two days' time – '

'I know all that,' I told him.

'Problem is,' he said, scratching his head, 'what are we going to do with you?'

The penny dropped. 'You mean I'm not *allowed* to any of these things?'

He went white: 'Lady, you ain't *allowed* within a hundred miles of them.'

What was I doing there? I had travelled thousands of miles to *get to know the man* and now I would be lucky even to see him! I was still boiling about that when I heard a muffled knock at my door half an hour later. I quite expected to see the organizer's representative back with a false nose and a forged passport to Mexico – but it was Stan.

'Does that man know you're in my room?' I demanded.

'It's only for the first week. Just while we're in Toronto. Then we go to Winnipeg for a game there, and after that we're on holiday.' Stan smiled appealingly – appealing to me to be reasonable. 'After that,' he said, 'we'll just slip quietly away – anywhere you like – do whatever you want to do, and . . . ' I knew what was coming so I joined in: *'we'll just get to know each other,'* we chorused.

So that was our stay in Toronto. Actually I did get to see Stan play – even the organizer's representative conceding that I might not be *too* conspicuous in a crowd of twenty thousand people. But as for getting to know each other! The only man I got to know well in Toronto was Steve McQueen. I got to know him *really* well. Well so would you if you watched ten of his movies in one week. Meanwhile Stan was hitting the town: lunching here, having dinner there, meeting this one, having his photograph taken with that one. I suppose I *did* see something of him – after all he was on television twice.

But at the end of the week we left for Winnipeg – by train. The train was Stan's idea. It was a two-day trip and it would give me a chance to see the countryside. Maybe he thought I would get to know *that* instead of him. Mind you, there was another reason. We were less likely to run into reporters at railway stations than at airports. At least that was the theory . . . Then Toronto decided to give Stan a civic send-off *at the station*. Everyone was there – Press, television, radio, and *me*. The organizer's representative almost had a coronary but recovered enough to smuggle me aboard the train – with the threat that one of his pals would smuggle me off at the other end. Quite frankly I was beginning to feel like Mata Hari by then, and to my mind the trip was turning into a disaster.

However the train journey made up for it. We had a compartment to ourselves, the countryside was marvellous, and *at last* we really settled down to get to know each other. It was all great fun – except for meal-times. We ate separately, sitting at adjoining tables in the dining-car and doing our best to avoid the other's eye. It was a crazy way to carry on, but I have to admit it worked and the trip passed without incident – until the last morning.

The train was due at Winnipeg at about midday, at which time another organizer's representative would involve me in a further incident straight out of the Spy's Own Annual. But at half past ten we were ready for coffee. Stan had discovered a little snack bar further down the train, quite separate from the main dining-car. He scouted it first, made sure the coast was clear, then came back for me. We were the only customers so it couldn't have been better. The steward served us and retired behind his little counter, and Stan and I were talking casually about this and that, when I felt someone watching us. The steward was the only other person there, and, sure enough, when I looked up he was staring at Stan. I whispered, 'Don't look now – but I think you've been recognized.'

But Stan didn't believe me – or if he did he wasn't bothered. A day and a half on the train had relaxed him completely. In Toronto he would have jumped a mile. Whenever he opened a paper he expected scandalous headlines about our relationship. But forty-six hours of privacy had dispelled his worries completely. In fact he was so confident that he ordered another coffee, and that was his – our – undoing.

'I know that badge,' the steward said when he came to our table. His accent was unmistakably English, even to my ear. He stared at the gold badge in Stan's lapel. I could almost feel Stan kicking himself under the table.

'Water Rat's badge, isn't it?' asked the steward.

Stan looked at the badge as if seeing it for the first time. He admitted it was a Water Rat's badge, then changed the subject by asking the steward which part of England he was from.

'Southport. But I've been here three years now. Smashing country.' He grinned happily. 'I knew I was right about that badge. Bloke here last year had one. Comedian he was. What *was* his name? Short, stocky feller – you *must* know him. Had that catch phrase, "Can you hear me Mother?" ... Sandy something ... Sandy ... '

'Powell?' Stanley suggested.

'That's him! Sandy Powell. You must know him.'

Stan nodded and was about to say something else, when the steward interrupted him. 'I know you too. You're in show business. I know your face from somewhere. I'll get your name in a minute – you see if I don't.'

Stan had relaxed so much by now that he had taken my hand across the table and was gazing at me with undisguised fondness. I was loving it. As far as I was concerned the trip was improving by the minute. But the moment the steward said '*I'll get your name in a minute*' a look of alarm leapt into Stan's eyes. But what could he do? He could hardly pretend not to know me – not when he was holding my hand.

'It's on the tip of my tongue,' said the steward, fairly bursting with concentration.

Stanley looked panic-stricken. Then he gambled: 'We're a double act,' he said in a rush. 'This is my wife. We do a knife-throwing act.'

I spluttered on my coffee but the steward was delighted. 'Knife-throwing,' he said with approval. 'You'll do well with that here. They love acts like that. Wish I could see it.'

Apparently Stanley also wished the steward could see it, because he went into a lurid description of some of the tricks we did – ending with our finale in which I place a cigarette between my lips and Stan chops it in half from twelve feet away, throwing the knife over his shoulder. The steward's look at me was positively awe-struck. I had recovered from my choking fit by then and had just started to breath normally when the steward said: 'Could you do one of your tricks for me, now?'

'Wish I could,' Stan said airily, 'but our knives are packed away and these aren't properly balanced.' He pointed to the knives on the table.

The steward looked crestfallen and went away. I sighed with relief but Stan was jubilant: 'Got out of that well, didn't I?' he asked.

'Didn't you just. But I think we ought to go now – '

'Oh no, there's no need. Not now. We'll be all right here for the rest of the trip.'

Then the steward came back – with a crowd of kitchen staff. 'This is Harry the chef,' he said. 'He's brought you some knives from the galley.'

'How about these?' asked one of the men. Then he put all sorts of knives on to the table – long knives, short knives, wide blades and stilettos – and Harry himself carried a meat cleaver.

I was ready to pass out at the prospect of anyone throwing *anything* at me when Harry took one look at Stan and said: 'Knife thrower be buggered! That's Stanley Matthews.'

And so the secret was out. Once Harry said it, they all recognized Stan. Most of them were English and they had all seen him play. Stan dropped my hand as if it had caught alight. But the boys from the galley weren't interested in me. Their questions about football came so thick and fast that I doubt they even noticed when I slipped away five minutes later. And Stan arrived back at the compartment some time later saying, 'We're okay, they'll keep quiet about it.'

But it had been a close call and we both knew it. In fact we remained snug in our compartment for the rest of the trip.

Then we arrived in Winnipeg. 'Winnipeg welcomes Stanley Matthews,' said the banners. The crowd cheered and the brass band thundered a greeting. Stan waved from the window, while I hid in a corner. Then the door opened: 'Psst,' hissed a man as he beckoned to me. By now I recognized an 'organizer's representative' a mile away. We made our escape down the length of the train, alighting from the very end coach as Stan stepped down from the front of the train. I sighed as I watched him, and wondered if any *new* Steve McQueen movies were showing in Winnipeg.

Stan

I knew it was difficult for Mila to begin with, but I could do nothing about it, except hope that things might become easier as the trip progressed – and in fact they did. Winnipeg was less formal than Toronto, and maybe I was more relaxed. The train journey had helped me unwind and the Port Vale nightmare already seemed a long way away. And the organizers of the trip were helpful, bringing Mila to functions as their guest and always including her in *our set*. We were not obviously together, but at least we saw a lot more of each other. And the parties were fun. At least most of them were. But one night I was trapped in a corner by a real bore who insisted that the way to learn any sport was to watch it, not play it, because 'the spectator sees most of the game'. If he said that once he said it a hundred times. In the end I had to tell him about something that happened to me – just to shut him up.

Years ago I owned a racehorse, a four-year-old called Parbleu, and Billy Hammit trained it for me at Beverley. My racing colours were a mixture of the Blackpool and Stoke City colours; tangerine, and red and blue. Parbleu was a great little horse but it never won when I watched it – always came second or third instead. Finally Billy Hammit banned me from the course whenever he was racing, and it did a lot better after that.

Anyway one Saturday Parbleu was running at its home course of Beverley. Billy phoned me on the Monday beforehand, full of enthusiasm for its chances: 'Check with me on Friday though,' he cautioned, 'just to make sure.' Well I couldn't wait until Friday, so I telephoned on Thursday, and he was as confident as ever: 'Stan, the horse has never looked better.'

'But what about this six-pound penalty?'

'Forget it. Parbleu could win carrying twice that.'

Now Billy Hammit was a good trainer, and generally trainers are a bit wary when talking to owners about a horse's chances, but Billy threw caution to the winds. According to him it would be a one-horse race. So of course I backed Parbleu to win. Not only did *I* back it, every player in the Blackpool side backed it. We put a small fortune on – spreading our bets all over Blackpool so as not to alert the bookmakers.

We were playing the last match of the season on the Saturday, up at Newcastle, so I couldn't have watched the race even if Billy had given me permission – which was probably why he was so confident. Anyway we travelled to Newcastle on the Friday and booked into the County Hotel, and in the evening Jackie Milburn and some of the Newcastle players came to see us.

'What about the horse, Stan? It's running tomorrow, isn't it?'

Well, naturally I *had* to tell them what Billy had said. They were a bit dubious at first: some of the other horses in Parbleu's race had useful form and certainly Parbleu would not start as favourite. So I telephoned Billy Hammit, just for the benefit of the Newcastle boys.

'It's raining cats and dogs here,' he said cheerfully. 'Soft going tomorrow for sure. Just how Parbleu likes it.'

'Soft going *and* a six-pound penalty?' Jackie Milburn was more doubtful than ever.

But after a long chat Billy convinced him, and Jackie and his boys left to spread the word to the rest of the Newcastle team, so that by the time we met at the ground the next day, *every player* on both sides had backed Parbleu to win. The only one not to bet on the horse was Johnny Lynas, our trainer. Johnny wanted no part of it. As far as he was concerned we were in Newcastle to play football, and nothing else mattered. He made that quite clear in the dressing-room: 'Stop talking about that bloody horse and concentrate your minds on football.'

Which was easier said than done. It was the last game of the season and nothing depended on the result. Both sides were in the middle of the League table, so neither was threatened with relegation nor had a chance of winning the championship. The most the players stood to gain was the two-pound win bonus, and that paled into insignificance next to the money we would collect from the bookmakers if Parbleu won.

Billy Wardle was our twelfth man that day. 'The Count' we used to call him because of the way he held his cigarette and various other mannerisms. Just before we ran out on to the pitch I took him to one side: 'Listen Count, you're on the bench. Parbleu's race is the three-thirty – keep your ears open – you might hear the result on someone's radio.'

And with that we went out to play football. Newcastle were one up at half-time and Johnny Lynas was furious at the interval: 'You've all got your minds on that damn horse,' he said. 'Forget about it. Roll your sleeves up and get stuck in.'

Nobody knew the result of Parbleu's race and the Count hadn't been able to get at a radio – so out we went again. Twenty minutes later Newcastle scored a second goal, and 2–0 was in fact to be the final result. But just after they scored, the newspaper vendors started to mingle with the crowd, selling the early sports editions. I was pacing down the right wing, watching the game which was mostly going on at the other end of the park, when suddenly someone in the crowd shouted, 'Eh, Stan Matthews – your 'orse won.'

I took a quick look down the field to make sure the ball wasn't coming my way, then I nipped over to the touchline: 'What were the odds?'

He scrambled back into his newspaper, then shouted, 'Hundred to eight.'

A hundred to eight! I tell you, we had really cleaned up. So I started running back and forth across the pitch, telling the players on both sides. 'Lads – we've won! We've won at a hundred to eight!'

Everyone was delighted, but I heard the funny side of the story later. The broadcasting box was high up in the stand and the commentator was going into raptures: 'Matthews is everywhere at the moment – on the right wing, on the left wing – calling for the ball – shouting encouragement to his team-mates – dashing all over the place. Only twenty minutes to go, Blackpool are two nil down, *but remember the Cup Final*! Matthews is rallying his side for a last ditch onslaught. The Newcastle players are shouting at each other ... pointing to Matthews ...'

Meanwhile I'm running up and down shouting '*A hundred to eight! We won at a hundred to eight!*'

So whenever I hear that corny old line about the spectator seeing most of the game, I remember Parbleu. And I'll never forget Johnny Lynas's face either.

Mila

Life got better and better after Winnipeg. Stan had no further engagements (except one last game in Toronto at the end of our stay in Canada, and that was weeks and weeks away), so we toured aimlessly across that vast country, stopping here and there as we pleased. It was wonderful. Then we found a place called Clear Lake which was too beautiful for words. An admirer of Stan's put a cabin at our disposal, right at the edge of the lake itself, so we settled there for a few days.

Stan was right – you need to live with a person to get to know him. Everyone in the world is different. We've all got *some* quirks which take getting used to, just as I believe we all have our own personal clocks inside us to regulate our day. Now take me – I'm a night person. That's when I really come alive. I *hate* the mornings. But Stan is the opposite. Unless he is out training by six o'clock his whole day is ruined – I mean *really* ruined, for without that exercise he is lethargic and ill-tempered all day. So at Clear Lake we began to hammer out the ground rules for this difficult business of living together without driving each other mad. Of course it helps when you are in love, but even then there can be problems. Like breakfast, for instance.

By the time I sit down for breakfast, Stan has been up for hours. And I like to move *slowly* in the morning – have a cup of coffee, take a bath, decide what to wear, you know the sort of thing – whereas Stan does a million and one press-ups and takes a five-mile run. *And* he collects the newspapers. At Clear Lake I found out all about the newspapers.

'It's a lovely morning,' I said cheerfully. (At least I am cheerful in the mornings.)

Stan murmured something quite unintelligible from behind his newspaper.

'What shall we do today, Darling?'

'Mmmm.'

'What shall we do today?'

'Mmmm – if you say so.'

'What do you mean – if I say so?'

'Yes.'

'Yes *what*, Stanley?'

He put the paper down and blinked, as if surprised to see me. 'Good idea,' he said, then disappeared behind the paper again.

Now I admit we weren't on a traditional honeymoon, but it had all the trimmings. A lakeside cottage for two, blue skies and warm sunshine, the fresh invigorating air of the Rockies. But I may as well have stayed in Prague – at least at breakfast time.

'Stanley, I asked what you would like to do today?'

'No thanks.'

'*Stanley* . . .'

There was a hissing sound like escaping gas as he re-emerged from his paper: 'Mila,' he said sternly, 'Mila, you *never* interrupt an Englishman over his morning paper.'

'Never?'

He shook his head.

'I thought we were getting to know each other?'

'Exactly,' he said, and went back behind the paper. I fidgeted for a minute, then buttered some toast and said brightly: 'Personally, I like to talk over breakfast.'

Silence. Not even a 'mmmm'. I fumed. When you think of all the things we *had* to talk about. I went out on to the verandah and looked down at the lake. But it was silly to be irritated. Or so I told myself. Especially on such a lovely morning. The lake stretched for miles, fir trees on the far shore looked an inch high. Then I heard the 'phut-phut' of an outboard motor. I watched some men put out for a day's fishing. Then I had my idea. That's what *we* would do – go fishing. I would prepare a picnic lunch, we could hire rods and lines from Sam's shop, and then we would spend the day on the lake. It would be perfect. The more I thought about it the more the idea appealed to me, and when Stan came out ten minutes later I was full of it. But I contained my enthusiasm long enough to ask if there had been anything interesting in the papers.

'No,' he shook his head, 'nothing.'

'Then what was all the fuss about?'

He gave me a long-suffering look: 'You don't know what's *in* a paper until you've read it – do you?'

There was no answer to that. Anyway I told him my fishing idea and he was as enthusiastic as I was, so five minutes later he went off to the little shop to hire the fishing tackle while I put a picnic basket together. Then we locked up and went fishing.

My father has always owned a boat so I've known them from a child: sailing boats, dinghies, motor boats – all sorts. I've fished a bit too, but boating and riding are the only sports I'm any good at – certainly they are the only sports I am better at than Stan. I didn't know it then, but he had never been out on a boat in his life. It was soon to become obvious.

'How do you start these things?' he asked, pointing to the outboard.

That should have been warning enough. But Stan can beat me (and most other people) at tennis with one arm tied behind his back, and the same goes for golf and every other game, so I was too busy showing off to be concerned about his lack of knowledge. I pull-started the outboard, cast off and steered us out towards the deep blue yonder.

It took half an hour to find a likely looking spot for fishing. And all the while I was giving Stan the benefit of my knowledge on the sport. Finally I cut the engine and settled down to show him how to thread a fly, how to cast, how to handle his rod, all sorts of things. I was having a lovely time. Then we began fishing – with a lot more chat from me on how he would have to be patient and why he couldn't expect to be as good as me to begin with. Then – damn me – if he didn't get a bite within the very first minute.

'Mila! Mila! I've got something. Look!'

Sure enough, his rod bent almost in half. It *had* to be a big fish – one look at his rod told me that.

'Mila – it's getting away. Quick! *Do something*!'

I'm not sure what he expected. Me to jump in and wrestle the fish? Anyway I clambered down the boat and helped support his rod, until both of us were huffing and puffing and pitting all of our strength against that fish. It broke the surface once. It was *huge* – the biggest trout I've ever seen. And it fought like a wild thing. Twice I thought we had lost it. Once it nearly had us overboard. But I can be stubborn too. The battle seemed to last forever. Five minutes, ten ... it took us twenty minutes to bring that fish alongside. Then Stan said, 'Mila, I don't want it.'

'What do you mean, *you don't want it*? We came fishing, didn't we?'

'Yes, but it's so big – '

'Big nothing. Hang on to the rod while I get the keep net.'

But there was no keep net. Stan either didn't know about such things,

or hadn't bothered to get one at the little shop. That proves how
optimistic he was. Still I refused to be beaten – so I got an oar and tried
to lever the fish out of the water, fighting against time because Stan kept
shouting: 'It's getting away – it's getting away!'

Eventually, with a tremendous heave from Stan and a helping whack
with the oar from me, we landed the fish. The three of us lay in the
bottom of the boat, gasping for air and looking at each other. Then Stan
shouted, 'It's still alive!' He sounded horrified. 'It's still alive I tell you.
Mila, what do we do now?'

Now this next part will offend people with a queasy nature – I know
that. Just as I know that fishing purists will shudder when they read it.
But put yourself in my position. There I was, with the love of my life,
feeling that I had to *prove* myself. After all, he was the one going on
about it being some sort of trial period. I didn't *need* a trial period. I
knew I could live with him. I was in love with him, wasn't I? But he kept
going on about this trip being to decide if we could live with each other
– so much so that I felt I was sitting some kind of exam. I *had* to prove
myself.

'Mila,' he shouted again, 'it's alive!'

That settled it. I looked that fish straight in the eye, then bashed it
over the head with the oar. It was a very big fish and enormously strong.
But I was bigger – and stronger. And what that fish never knew was that
it was him or me. So I really laid into him. There was blood everywhere.
Stan was wearing white trousers and white socks, and by the time I
finished he looked like something out of an abattoir. But finally the trout
rolled over and lay still, with its big fat stomach up to the morning sun
and its mouth open – like the original capitalist on a beach somewhere.

I sat down and took a rest. After that I needed it. Then I dipped my
hands overboard to clean them, dried them on a towel and lit a cigarette.

Stan stared at the dead fish. Then a quite remarkable change came
over him. 'It's big, isn't it?' he said in awe-struck tones.

I was still getting my breath back.

'My very first fish,' Stan said.

There was a note of pride in his voice which was difficult to ignore.
I watched him carefully, sitting at the other end of the boat in his blood-
splattered clothes. Every now and then he threw an approving look at
the fish and repeated, 'It's big isn't it?' over and over again like a
catechism. Then he asked, 'Did you bring the camera? You could take
a picture of me holding my fish.'

Apart from the fact that he should have been taking a picture of *me*,

I had forgotten to bring the camera. He was very displeased: 'Crikey, *I* catch a fish that size and *you* forget the camera. Nobody will believe me when I tell them.'

Very sweetly I said: 'Sure they will. We'll take a photo when we get back. Then we'll take the fish up to Sam's and get him to cook it for supper.'

Stan pointed at the fish: 'But we can't spend the day with – with a corpse. Won't it start to smell or something?'

Now that was really my cue to tell him all about keep nets, but I decided against it. Instead I emptied my string shopping bag of its contents and, *after* removing the hook from its mouth, started to wrap the fish in a towel.

'What are you doing?' Stan asked.

'When I've got the fish in the towel we can put it into the shopping bag. Then we'll trail that in the water until we get back.'

If he thought it was a good idea he said nothing about it. Nor did he help me wrap the fish, which weighed a ton. But once it was covered by the towel and there was no chance of him being touched by it, he did hold the mesh bag open while I finished the job. Then we tied it to the boat with a length of line and lowered it into the water.

Stan decided that was enough fishing for one day. Well, as he said, any fish after *his fish* would be an anti-climax. So we pottered around the lake, exploring various creeks and inlets, stopping for our picnic and generally enjoying the sunshine until it was time to go home.

'I can't wait to see Sam's face,' Stan chortled, 'How big would you say that fish is? Three feet? Bigger?'

'About four feet,' I nodded.

'And it weighed a ton. I wonder what the record is for a trout caught in Clear Lake?'

'Sam will know.'

'You get the camera as soon as we get back. I'll take the fish straight up to Sam's.'

'Okay.'

So I took the boat into the jetty, cut the engine and tied up. Then it was time to retrieve Stan's fish. Now most people won't believe this. I'm not sure *I* would believe it, but I was there so I know it is true. The mesh bag was there with the towel still inside it – but the fish had *gone*! Honestly it was a mystery. The mouth of the bag had been tied together, so the fish could not have escaped that way. And the mesh was so fine that to poke a finger through a hole was a squeeze. And the fish had been wrapped inside a towel inside the bag. Besides, it was dead! I had killed it. *Brutally* I had killed it! It *had* to be there. But it wasn't.

Stan's face was a picture. Not just sheer disbelief – I shared that, after all – but outrage that his fish had cheated him. Plus the suspicion that it was all my fault. As if I had organized it out of professional jealousy. We were speechless – apart from a few stifled exclamations like 'How – ' and 'But – ' and 'It's impossible!'

Eventually, in a despairing effort to cheer him up, I said, 'Don't worry Darling, we'll find it. All dead fish float to the surface.' I knew full well that it takes three days, but then hardly seemed the time to tell him.

Stan was back in the boat before I finished speaking. 'Cast off,' he yelled. 'Come on, we must start a search.'

Now Clear Lake covers some thousands of square miles, but by night fall we had covered a good part of it. Of course we never found the fish – nor were we likely to – but it was not for want of trying. Stan would have sent frogmen down if they had been available. But it taught me a lesson: never to go fishing again.

Stan

We had a great time at Clear Lake, apart from Mila's carelessness in losing my fish. Then we moved on to another place called Lake Louise. The weather was warm and every morning dawned blue and clear. We played golf and tennis, and took an occasional dip in the pool. Then we met an old pal of mine, Bert Moseley, who used to play for Derby County and England. Bert had emigrated to Canada some years earlier and he invited us to Calgary to see the famous stampede. That was a lot of fun, and although the rodeo and the famous stampede were the central attractions, all sorts of other activities take place in the parklands surrounding the town. For instance we met Rocky Marciano the former world heavyweight boxing champion there. He and I were asked to kick off at a game of American football. The idea was that he stretched full length on the ground, while I kicked the ball out of his hands. Even then his fists were insured for a million dollars, and he expressed some doubts before we started. 'You ever kicked a ball before?' he growled. I managed.

But the big events are the stampede, the rodeo and the horse-racing. I dare say it was not horse-racing in the English style, but there were enough bets flying around to remind me of the time I nearly won a fortune on the horses. It was in 1953, the year Blackpool won the cup.

I had accepted an invitation to go over to Ireland at the end of the season to appear as a guest player. Ernie Taylor, Blackpool's inside right, was invited as well. All expenses paid and a hundred pounds a match! Cash money too. Not to be sneezed at when Blackpool were paying me about twenty pounds a week.

We flew into Dublin a week after the Cup Final and were given a right royal welcome. Everyone in Dublin wanted to shake our hands. Even the Mayor invited us to his parlour for a glass of Guinness. Anyway after the hospitality we were taken out to Darymount Park to play the first game. The opposition was West Bromwich Albion and a crowd of thirty thousand turned up. It was all very successful and after the match Ernie and I went back to the Gresham Hotel where we were staying. We walked into the Grill Room and who should I see but an old pal of mine, Duggie Page the jockey. So naturally we spent the evening together and brought each other up to date, especially about what we were all doing in Ireland.

At that time Duggie was number one stable jockey to Dick Kerr the trainer, and was over to ride at the big meeting at the Curragh that week.

'Stan,' he said, lowering his voice, 'There's a horse of ours running in the big race on Wednesday – called Sea Lion. It's got a very good chance.'

'Are you riding?'

Duggie shook his head: 'I slipped up on it last time out. Came second when the Guv'nor thought I should have won. He's hired Rae Johnson for the ride.'

Rae Johnson was the very successful Australian jockey who lived in France and raced all over the world. Johnson was good, very good indeed.

Well by the time dinner ended Duggie suggested that Ernie and I drive out to the stables the next day, to meet the Guv'nor Dick Kerr himself. So that's what we did. When we arrived Rae Johnson was there, with another chap by the name of Willy Sattinoff. Willy was a wealthy manufacturer of raincoats from Manchester and a fervent United supporter. We had met before and I knew enough about him to respect his opinion of horseflesh, for he owned horses in England and France as well as in Ireland. So we were introduced all round and I tried to pump Rae about Sea Lion's chances in the big race. Rae was quietly optimistic, but mostly he wanted to talk about South American football. (It goes like that – sportsmen everywhere prefer to talk about the other fellow's game. Whenever I have coffee with Bobby Locke in Johannesburg he insists on talking football instead of telling me how to improve my back-swing.) Anyway we all had a good chat, and Ernie and I took a hard look at Sea Lion. Duggie Page was as confident as ever, and I must admit I have never seen a fitter-looking horse in my life.

The next day was the day of the big race at the Curragh. Ernie and I were playing again that evening in Dublin but we had the afternoon off, so naturally we went to the races. We had been paid that day. Four hundred pounds in crisp five-pound notes for the four games we were booked to play. And on the way to the race course I had my big idea:

'Ernie,' I said, 'we'd be mugs to miss an opportunity like this. Here we are, with four hundred pounds in our pockets and a chance to turn it into a fortune. If Duggie is still as confident about Sea Lion, I'm going to put the lot on.'

Ernie was a bit taken aback and suggested another conference with Duggie Page. So we parked the car and hurried round to the paddock in search of Duggie and Dick Kerr. Dick was nowhere to be found, but we caught Duggie on his way to the dressing-rooms. He was as sure as ever. Sea Lion would walk it according to him. More than that – he had *another* tip. The horse he was riding in the following race. 'Don't even bother to back it each way,' he said, 'I'm going to win.'

Two red hot tips! Ernie and I seethed with excitement. The first race came and went, not a penny left our pockets. The same with the second, no bets until the big race. We were like soldiers – 'Don't fire until you see the whites of their eyes.' Ernie fancied a horse in the third but we were resolute – not even the mildest flutter until the big race. The horse Ernie fancied won, but that didn't matter: it was a good omen, that's all.

Then it was time for the big one. We rushed down to the paddock and who should we bump into but Willy Sattinoff. I took him aside: 'Sea Lion looks good,' I whispered.

Willy nodded, but somehow he lacked the enthusiasm I expected. Then he said, 'Sea Lion is a very good horse – but King of Tudors will beat it.'

I went cold. Ever since I arrived I had been screwing up my courage to make a really big bet. The biggest bet I'd ever made in my life. And the signs were so right. Duggie was positive and Dick Kerr had hired Rae Johnson for the ride. It was the hottest tip I had ever had. Not only that but Sea Lion looked tremendously fit. But I had to admit that Willy knew a thing or two about horses.

'King of Tudors,' he repeated in a confidential whisper. 'Been flown over from England especially for this race. Mark my words, Stan, that's the winner.'

Ernie and I slipped away for a conference. We were in a bigger muck sweat than the horses. What to do? I watched Rae mount up on Sea Lion. Rae seemed as quietly confident and the horse looked as good as ever. But Willy's words rang in my ears.

'What do you think?' I asked Ernie.

He shrugged: 'You know more about horses than I do. I'll back whatever you choose.'

Fat help that was. We hummed and hawed a bit, then I reached a decision: 'Back them both,' I said. 'But I still fancy Sea Lion the most. I'm going to put three hundred on that and the rest on King of Tudors – just in case.'

Ernie took a deep breath, then agreed to do the same. Off we went to see the bookmakers. Then we hit a snag. The first bookie refused to take the bet. So did the second – and the third. I waved my money under his nose, but he was adamant. He looked at the wad of crisp new fivers in my hand and shook his head: 'Sorry, there's a lot of forged notes about. I'm not taking that lot.'

'These are perfectly good fivers,' I protested. They were the old-style five-pound notes, the big white ones which looked like the deeds to a bank vault.

But the bookmakers would take none of them. Ernie and I jumped up and down. The odds on King of Tudors shortened to six to four, but Sea Lion was still at ten to one. *Ten to one!* Three hundred to win would earn three thousand! You could buy a new house for three thousand pounds in 1953!

I was desperate. I tried fifteen bookmakers. Not one would take my money. Meanwhile the horses were leaving the parade ring and cantering down to the start.

'Where's the General Manager's office?' I asked in final panic.

One of the bookies pointed to the far end of the grandstand. I set off like a rocket, with Ernie hard on my heels. The General Manager recognized me: 'Stan Matthews isn't it? That Cup Final was a grand game. How about an autograph while you're here?'

I was still catching my breath. Ernie arrived and explained what had happened, and we emptied our pockets of the suspect fivers.

'Nothing wrong with these,' said the General Manager.

The horses were down at the start! A commentator was calling the names over the public address system.

'Will you change these for one-pound notes?' I asked, 'Just to be on the safe side.'

He agreed – but it took him forever to count the notes, then to replace them with packs of one-pound notes held together with elastic bands. I seethed and hopped from foot to foot, while Ernie looked out of the open door. 'They're being called into line, Stan,' he shouted. 'They will be under orders in a minute.'

I stuffed the last pack of notes into my pocket and sprinted back down the grandstand. I reached the Tote just as the loudspeakers blared, 'They are now under orders.'

I dashed up to the counter, pulling notes from every pocket. The voice on the loudspeaker shouted, 'King of Tudors is well drawn on the inside.'

'King of Tudors,' I gasped. 'This lot to win.'

To this day I don't know why I did it. Panic, I suppose. King of Tudors was the favourite and the name was on everyone's lips. Especially on the lips of the commentator. The name came across the public address just as I staggered into the Tote. I put the whole lot on. Ernie's money as well. Eight hundred pounds on King of Tudors – to win.

Sea Lion walked it. Absolutely walked away with the race. Won by about five lengths, I think. It was still going away from the rest of the field as it passed the post.

I've never been so sick in the whole of my life. Poor old Ernie took it a lot better than I did. Perhaps being responsible for losing his money was partly why I felt so bad, but I felt dreadful. We went off to get a cup of tea and Ernie tried desperately to cheer me up. 'Come on Stan,' he said, 'remember Duggie's tip for the next race. Let's have ten pounds on – maybe we'll get some of our money back.'

Ten pounds! We were reduced to making bets of *ten pounds*. I had planned to put half my winnings on Duggie's mount. That would have been *fifteen hundred* pounds. And here was Ernie talking about ten pounds!

I was disconsolate. Nothing Ernie said cheered me up. It was all my fault. We sat there, letting our tea get cold, looking gloomily out across the Curragh. Then the results of Duggie's race were announced. He had won – at seven to one!

I sat there working it out. Fifteen hundred pounds at seven to one. Ten and a half thousand pounds. Plus the rest of our winnings. We would have won more than twelve thousand pounds. Instead of that we – *I* – had lost the lot!

Ernie was very good about it. He never said a word.

We had arranged to meet Duggie after the last race to have a drink together. But I felt too sick for that. I just slunk away, got into the car and drove off. I've never seen Duggie to this day. He must think me a pretty poor sort. After all, when you give a pal a couple of red hot tips the least he could do is buy you a drink from his winnings. But there were no winnings – and Ernie and I played our four games in Ireland for nothing that year.

Mila

And so the weeks slipped by. It was a marvellous time. I wished it would last forever. We went right across Canada, dodging the Press now and then, meeting some of Stan's old friends, sightseeing and generally enjoying ourselves. As for deciding about making the relationship permanent, well I had no doubts. And neither did Stan, I'm happy to say – even if there had been times when I felt I was competing for some kind of seal of approval. But all too soon we were back in Toronto, and boarding the plane for the return flight to London.

Parting at Heathrow was a kind of exquisite torture. I was to catch the flight to Prague, and Stan was to return to his home in Blackpool. Naturally we had *talked* about the next steps, but talk is easy. All sorts of nettles had to be grasped before we could have a future together. And Stan's divorce was likely to be the most painful nettle of all. I knew that but there was little or nothing I could do about it – other than to encourage him and tell him how I felt.

So we said goodbye at Heathrow and I flew back to Prague, while Stan went home to Betty.

Stan

In fact I went *home* to Stoke first. To my mother's home, where she lived with my older brother Arthur. I know why I went: it was to tell them about Mila. I had made up my mind about the future, and Mila *had* to be part of it. How we did it, how we got her out of Czechoslovakia, how I arranged a divorce, how I told my children, were all unanswerable questions at that stage. All that mattered was that I had made a decision and felt I had to tell my mother about it first, before she read about it or heard the news from somebody else.

We were always a close-knit family, us Matthews. There had been six of us when father was alive, him and mother, my older brothers Jack and Arthur, me, and young Ronnie. Four boys. It must have been hard work bringing up a family like that during the depths of the depression, but if so there were no signs of it – or at least none I remember. All I recall is the support they gave me, all the help and encouragement a kid could ever wish for, especially from my father. It was father who made me into a sportsman – in fact it was father who turned me into a *professional* sportsman at the age of five, although I never found that out until years later.

Father owned a barber's shop in Hanley, at No. 7, Market Square, about five minutes' walk from where we lived. He was a good barber but he was more than that: he was a boxer too. The Fighting Barber from Hanley they called him. And he was more than useful at that too; three hundred and fifty fights all over the country – quite a few of them at the National Sporting Club at Covent Garden in London. Naturally being a boxer made him a keep fit fanatic and all of us boys were taught the benefits of personal fitness at an early age. Not that he forced us to do things – father was strict but there was nothing of the sergeant-major about him. Instead he *encouraged* us, in all manner of ways. Like when he bought me a pair of running spikes for my fourth birthday.

I ran everywhere as a kid – never walked when I could trot, and never trotted when I could run flat out – and half the time I'd be kicking a stone along the gutter as I went. That's probably why father bought me the running spikes. There was no talk about it beforehand. No 'What would you like for your birthday?' and no talk after. There were the spikes and I was left to get on with it.

I used to run round the track at Finney Gardens, sometimes with other boys but as often as not by myself. Finney Gardens was a recreation ground near where we lived. I never knew it then but father would sometimes slip away from his shop and time me with a stop watch. Not that he ever said a word about it. In his book that would be 'making a fuss', and he was never one to do that.

After the gift of the running shoes, not a week went past without several visits to the track at Finney Gardens, and when the lighter evenings came in April and May I was at Finney Gardens every night. I practically lived there. The months passed and when summer arrived father decided to take me to the August Bank Holiday Sports Meeting at the Victoria Ground in Stoke. That was a huge affair in those days. Thousands of spectators and hundreds of competitors. I trotted along on father's heels, carrying my running spikes in a paper bag. Everyone knew father. Not just because of his shop but from his days as a boxer. It seemed that hundreds of people wanted to shake his hand and talk about his days in the ring. I watched with eyes like saucers and thought he was the most important man in the world. I was very proud of him, I can tell you.

Then the racing started. Father let me watch a few, then suggested I have a go. I burst into tears. It was all so different from Finney Gardens where a kid could run his heart out in peace and quiet. There were thousands of people watching here. The roar from the crowd was deafening when a race was on. I wanted no part of it. Father wiped my tears and bought me an ice cream, and said no more about it. There was no disapproval in his voice, no scolding, and above all, 'no fuss'. If I wanted to run that was fine by him, but if I didn't want to run that was fine too. So we watched the racing and then went home – but we went back on the Bank Holiday Monday to watch the rest of the meeting.

A whole year passed, and it was August again. Time for the Bank Holiday Sports Meeting. I looked forward to it. In fact whenever I ran at Finney Gardens I pretended it was the Victoria Ground. Pretending was enough for me – but not for father.

We went with a friend of his – the man who kept the pet shop down

the street from the barber's shop. I took my running spikes again and
we sat on top of the bus from Hanley to Stoke. My big brother Jack was
with us. Jack was a good sprinter and was down for the hundred yards.
Of course he was very grown up and had been to these things often
before, whereas it was only my second time on that Saturday in August
1920.

The crowd inside the stadium seemed bigger than ever. The Bank
Holiday meeting at Stoke drew contestants from all over the country.
Even members of Britain's Olympic team competed, so it was a 'big do'
as folks used to say. The people in the crowd were good-humoured and
excited, buying programmes and toffee apples and sweets for the kids,
while they sorted out where they wanted to be on the terraces. It was
hustle and bustle wherever you looked. And they had bookmakers in
those days – which is why father's friend from the pet shop was there.
Unbeknown to me, he had been out at the Finney Gardens with father,
timing me on that stop watch.

When we arrived we went to the competitors' enclosure with Jack.
Then the man from the pet shop turned to me: 'What about it, lad?' he
asked. 'Fancy a run today?' My eyes filled with tears, and I was shaking
my head when father said, 'We'll give you an ice cream – *afterwards*.'

That's what I mean about father. There was never any *pressure* – but
he encouraged me in all manner of ways with the occasional bonus –
like an ice cream on a hot August Bank Holiday.

So of course I agreed to run. Father went off to see the officials and
came back rubbing his hands. 'We've got forty yards!' he said to the pet
shop man. 'They've given him forty yards' start in the hundred yards.'

Pet shop man and father held a conference about that. They were
both excited about something – even I could see that. Then father handed
the man some money – one-pound notes, which were a rarity in those
days – and the man went away. I wondered what he was going to buy
– it was an awful lot of money for an ice cream.

Meanwhile I changed into my running spikes. Jack was in my race.
He was fourteen. So were all the other lads – big, lanky boys who looked
like giants to my five-year-old eyes. I remember standing next to one of
them. His *legs* were taller than me. But I did have a forty-yard start.

The Victoria Ground at Stoke. How well I was to come to know that
place. It was different then, for it had a running track round the edge of
the football pitch – a four hundred and forty-yard oval circuit of brick-
red cinders. To my eyes each straight looked a mile long and the terraces
seemed higher than mountains. And all those people!

An official paced out forty yards and father led me to my marks. He squeezed my shoulder as he turned away. The crowd hushed. My heart was pounding so fiercely that I was sure everyone could hear it. Then the starting-pistol cracked and I jumped like a startled hare. But I ran as if the devil himself was chasing me. The crowd erupted into an explosion of noise. I thought my lungs would burst and my eyes pop out of my head. But I won.

Pet shop man was doing a little jig when I got back to the competitors' enclosure. He grinned hugely at me and started towards me, but father caught his arm: 'No fuss,' he said – and that was that. But I did get my ice cream.

We watched the other races and then went home. I was sent out to play while father told mother about it. Not that I needed much sending. And on August Bank Holiday Monday we went back to the Victoria Ground – for the finals.

'How are you feeling?' pet shop man asked on the bus. He kept throwing me anxious looks and would have discussed the race with me if father had let him. But father seemed more interested in the weather, or the cricket scores, or the price of haircuts – anything, in fact, except the race.

For the final the handicappers reduced my start to thirty-five yards. Father and pet shop man had a talk about it. They were beyond my hearing but I guessed they were talking about me because pet shop man kept looking my way. Then he took some more money from father and disappeared into the crowd.

Jack was in the final too. I think he was favourite. Father led me to my marks again. Thirty-five yards might sound a long way, but those big lads looked awfully close. Close enough for them to reach out and touch me. That's how it felt. And when the pistol cracked I expected that to happen. I imagined a hand reaching out to my shoulder and pulling me back. I thought I would be passed at every stride. But I ran like a fox with all the hounds in the country baying at its heels – and I won again.

Pet shop man was shaking hands with everyone in sight when I got back. Father smiled and ruffled my hair. I don't remember him saying anything. Not 'Well done' or anything like that. It wasn't his way.

I won a prize for coming first. A silver watch. Jack won something too, for coming third. We sat on top of the bus going home. Father sat up front, next to the man from the pet shop who was smoking a big cigar and talking in a loud voice about 'the coup of the century'. Every now and then he burst into fits of laughter and slapped father across the back. Jack must have been in on it too – I realize that now – because he was in high good humour and full of funny remarks. When we reached Hanley we went to the pet shop and my father's friend presented me with a bowl and two goldfish. My, I was proud of those goldfish. They died two days later but I'll never forget them. I thought more of them than the watch.

I ran at the Bank Holiday sports every year after that, but not until years later did I learn of 'the coup of the century', and how father and the man from the pet shop cleaned up from the bookmakers.

Growing up. It was another world then. Not much money about but people seemed to enjoy life. When they left school Jack and Arthur became assistants in father's shop. I went sometimes too, usually on a Sunday morning, to help out. Not that I did much work – I was too busy listening to the talk for that. Men in barber's shops talk for hours, and most of it was about sport then. Football and boxing mainly, but cricket and horse racing featured as well. Sport was the great escape in those days, and the hours spent on the terraces on a Saturday afternoon was the high spot of the week for most men. And to me, sport was life itself.

There was school of course. I worked enough to stay in the middle of the class, but the real joy of school was to play football. I was in the school team when I was eight, and playing for England schoolboys a few years later. I loved every minute of it.

Meanwhile there was the future to think about. I wanted to be a builder. Father took me to see a friend of his, and at fourteen I became a builder's apprentice. It was hard work but I enjoyed it. Not that it lasted long. Father came to watch me one day. He took one look, then shook his head: 'Come on Stan, let's go home. We'll spend another twelve months building you up. Health and fitness come first. This work will kill you.'

Health and fitness! Crikey, ever since I can remember father had me doing deep breathing exercises in front of an open window. Every morning, and a session with the chest expanders after that. Jack and Arthur did it too. We all grumbled like mad, especially when father pulled the sheets back at six on a winter's morning, but we did it just the same. Yet there were compensations – like steak for breakfast when father was building me up.

It must have been about then that Tom Mather came into my life. *Mr* Mather to me. He was a character. I don't think I ever saw him without his bowler hat. He affected an amiable, easy-going manner for most of the time, but he could be as stubborn as a mule when it suited him. *Mr Tom Mather.* At the time he was manager of Stoke City and he called at the house with a proposal for father. That I should go into the Stoke City office as an office boy and play in the Stoke junior side as an amateur.

So that's what happened – though I think father played hard to get for a while. I got a pound a week at Stoke for my wages. In the office I licked stamps, answered the telephone, made the tea and – most important of all – I began to breathe the atmosphere of a professional football club.

On Saturdays I played for the junior side, and twice for the reserves when I was fifteen. The following year I had more than twenty games in the reserves, so things were looking up. When we won, each of the older boys in the side chipped in two shillings of their bonus for me, so I went home feeling like the man who broke the bank at Monte Carlo.

The fun and games really started in February 1932 – just before my seventeenth birthday. Rumour had it that some of the big clubs were interested in offering me professional terms. Certainly Aston Villa expressed interest, and there was even talk of Arsenal wanting to sign me. Not that I knew anything about it. Father kept the news from me, as determined as ever that there should be 'no fuss'. But I did know that Stoke were interested, though it was years before I found out what really happened.

Apparently poor Tom Mather had been threatened with the sack by his directors if I didn't sign for Stoke. (I tell you, even then a manager's job was far from easy.) So, as January slipped towards February and my birthday drew nearer, Tom became more and more agitated. He was at father's shop for a shave every morning, and often back for a trim or a massage in the afternoon. Then he would be round at our house for a cup of tea in the evening – using any excuse he could think of to explain why he 'just happened to be in the neighbourhood'. Of course the persuasive pressure was aimed at father far more than me, because it was father's consent which was needed for me to sign as a professional. But father played his usual cautious waiting game and refused to commit himself. Poor old Tom became desperate. Father was a marked man – especially with about a week to go. Tom's idea was to spot any other club managers who might call at the shop or our home. Consequently Arthur Sherwin, the Stoke chairman himself, took up guard in the pub opposite the shop and stared across the road all day – while Tom positioned scouts all over the place, checking the number plates of cars arriving in Stoke in case they bore a Birmingham registration and hence might be from Aston Villa. What would have happened then I've no idea.

Anyway, my birthday finally arrived and father ended our misery by saying it was all right by him if I wanted to sign for Stoke. There was considerable relief all round. So I became a professional footballer. Ten pounds for signing on, five pounds a week in the season (plus a pound bonus when we won), and three pounds a week during the summer. That was good money for a lad of seventeen in 1932. Not that I spent much. Father insisted that I open a bank book and half the signing-on fee went in for a start, and half my wages every week after that. Which about sums up life with father. I've made him sound strict, and he was in a way – very strict by today's standards. But it was all for my own good and the lessons he taught me have stood me in good stead all my life.

Settling in at Stoke City was not much of a problem. Working in the office and playing for the reserves had helped ease me into the ways of the club, and of course I knew most of the players. But I was still treated as a kid in a man's world, even when I made the first team. A word out of place and I was set upon. Often I was thrown into the big bath just for the hell of it, fully clothed or otherwise, it made no difference to them. Most of the first-team players were in their middle to late twenties, so I suppose it was an understandable reaction to a seventeen-year-old joining their ranks. But I was certainly taught to mind my 'p's and q's'.

Football, like everything else, was different in those days. Football clubs were different too. They had a much bigger playing staff for one thing – most had a squad of at least forty professionals – and for a club to field the same team two weeks running was almost unknown. Even when a side won by a hatful of goals, you could guarantee team changes a week later. Perhaps managers and trainers justified their salaries that way – though in my opinion they earned every penny they got.

Take the matter of club discipline, for example. Every player at Stoke had a rule book, and you were in trouble if you didn't abide by it. There were rules for everything. Like having a few drinks, for example. During the season players were only allowed to drink beer on very special occasions, and even then only in moderation. That was the rule, but applying it involved a constant battle of wits between at least half the squad on one side, and Tom Mather and the trainer Jimmy Vallance on the other. This was in the early thirties, remember, when private cars were nothing like as commonplace as they are today, so we went every-where by train. To and from the station we walked in single file, with Tom Mather at the head of the column and Jimmy Vallance bringing up the rear. It was Jimmy's job to make sure none of the lads slipped out of the line and into the nearest pub for a swift half pint on the way. That was relatively easy. Keeping check on the lads in their free time was much more difficult, but Tom and Jimmy must have had every publican in Stoke on their payroll, because whenever a player trans-gressed he was on the mat the following morning. Tom knew exactly where he had been, who had been with him and how much he'd had. But even that didn't stop some of the lads from trying it on.

The drinking crowd had a much better chance when we were playing away. I remember one occasion, when we were playing at Plymouth. I was sent to bed at half past nine as usual, but some of the lads slipped out the back door and went into town. (Tom Mather used to patrol the front lobby, and Jimmy generally sat guard at the back door, but the boys gave him the slip that night.) Anyway it was past eleven when the boys returned, and about six of them piled into my room. We slept two to a room in those days; no bathroom of course, and the chamber maid delivered hot water to the rooms in the mornings. That night the boys settled down for a game of cards and a few more beers. Bottles were produced from under jerseys and out of pockets. I watched slit-eyed, pretending to be asleep, as the boys realized they had neither bottle openers nor glasses. But they overcame that: the necks of the bottles were smashed, and the beer poured into a chamber pot drawn out from under a bed. Then the pot was passed from mouth to mouth as the game of poker proceeded. The chamber pot must have added potency, I think, because four of the boys passed out an hour later and were still flat on the floor in the morning – when Jimmy Vallance found them.

And so I grew up. Football was my university and it began to open more doors for me than I would have ever dreamed possible. It enabled me to travel the country, and even abroad when I was selected for England at the age of nineteen. And football cushioned me against the stark miseries of the depression. I earned five or six pounds a week, at a time when an unemployed man with a wife and children to support was drawing less than thirty shillings on the dole. They were hard times for some all right, and to escape the tedium of their lives people flocked to places of entertainment. The cinema boomed: forty per cent of the population went once a week and twenty-five per cent went even more often. New events like speedway and greyhound racing drew big crowds,

and established sports like football and cricket attracted enormous fol-
lowings. Sports stars leapt to the public eye and became a constant
source of newspaper headlines. Inevitably the publicity went to the heads
of some players, though surprisingly few considering the acclaim they
received. Perhaps the general level of discipline helped most players keep
their feet on the ground. It was so much tighter then – and of course I
was particularly lucky.

First of all, there was father with his determination that 'no fuss'
should ever be made of me. He went to amazing lengths too: for instance,
when I first joined Stoke as an office boy, father insisted that I walk to
and from the ground every day. That was eight miles a day, and I did
that until I became a professional at seventeen. Until then my only
chance of getting bus fares was if it was snowing. And it was years
before I learned that father never missed a game at Stoke when I was
playing. He slipped away from his shop on a Saturday afternoon and
watched the game from the terraces, but there was never a word of it
when I got home for tea. Not a word – and Jack and Arthur were warned
to keep quiet too. And if father wasn't enough to teach me a sense of
proportion, being the youngest lad in the side was. The general attitude
that I was a boy in a man's world continued even when I played for
England. 'You can answer when you're spoken to,' I was told. 'Mind
your manners and shut up!' Plus the threat of being thrown into the
bath. And on top of all that there were the officials to contend with,
forever imposing rules.

Players were not allowed to talk to the Press. A player booked for a
foul automatically lost his chance to be selected for England. Players had
to 'look after themselves' in their off-duty hours, which involved all
manner of things. The rule which irked me most was the one about golf.
I fell in love with the game when I was nineteen, but the rule book
banned the playing of golf on Thursdays or Fridays for fear a player
might overtax his strength prior to Saturday's game. I thought it was
nonsense. I was the best judge of my fitness. So I often sneaked away for
a game on Thursday afternoon – until Tom Mather got wind of it –
then he soon put a stop to that.

Discipline was everywhere. I remember the old-style army pay parades
which the FA held at international matches. You were paid in cash in
those days, eight pounds a match I think it was, plus travelling expenses.
And the pay-out took place before the game. Officials in bowler hats
and with watch chains adorning their waistcoats would sit on one side
of a trestle table.

'Matthews,' one of them would shout.

I would step one pace forward.

'Expenses?'

'Return ticket to Stoke, sir,' I would say, then add how much it was.

A man next to the secretary thumbed a railway fares book, and if he found that you had added sixpence to your fare you were in trouble. The money would be counted and checked, then set down on the table. You picked it up and took a pace backwards. 'Lawton,' would come the shout, and Tommy Lawton would step forward for his pay. And so it went on.

None of us thought anything of it – it was the way things were done and that was that. Besides we were all too excited by thoughts of the match to pay much attention. And in my case I would be feeling sick.

I was always sick before a big game. No matter how fit I felt, no matter how often I told myself I would be all right, ten minutes before kick-off found me heaving up in the lavatory. I suffered agonies of nerves, especially in the early days. Daft, isn't it? There I was, doing what I wanted to do more than anything else in the world, but just before we went down that tunnel and out on to the pitch, I was as sick as a dog.

But to get back to seeing Mila off that day. I don't know why, but as I sat on that train after saying goodbye at Heathrow, all sorts of memories flooded through my mind. I suppose it was going back to Stoke which did it, and the prospect of telling mother and Arthur about Mila. They would be shocked – I knew that. Father would have been shocked too, had he been alive. But mother had to be told sooner or later, and I decided the sooner the better.

Mila

Parting from Stan had been painful, but for me to return to Prague was far less daunting than Stan's journey. The other people in my life knew about Stan. Stan would have to break the news about me.

Naturally I told George that I wanted a divorce. He sat at his drawing board in his studio, listening to me, watching me. Then he said, 'Why not wait a while? After all, you say Stan hasn't made a move to get a divorce. Why should you?'

'But he is *going* to get a divorce. He's gone back to England to see about it.'

George looked doubtful.

We spent an entire evening talking about it, but nothing much was resolved. He obviously preferred to await the outcome of events, and there seemed no doubt as to how he saw the matter ending. I screwed up my courage and told myself he was wrong: that Stan *would* get a divorce and that we would soon marry.

Of course, the girls wanted to know all about Canada. I showed them photographs and told them about the trip generally. They were excited and worried for me, both at the same time. And naturally they wanted to know what would happen next.

'Stan will get a divorce,' I said firmly. 'So will I – then we shall marry.'

But where will you live? In England? In Czechoslovakia? In the West? In the East? Will you be *Lady* Matthews? When will it happen? How long will it take?

So many questions. How I ached for the answers! I tried to appear confident and serene, but Eva saw it for the pose it was: 'Mila, are you *sure* Stan will come for you? After all, he will be giving up so much.'

The seeds of doubt which George had sown in my mind began to take root. I told myself that *of course* Stan will·come for me. He said he would. But that was in Canada. Now he was in England, going home to his wife. So far he had said nothing to her about a divorce. What would happen when he did? Would there be a reconciliation? But there was nothing I could do about it, except wait - and worry.

Stan

Mother was almost eighty years old in 1968. Despite crippling arthritis she was still one of the liveliest people I knew. A lot had happened in her lifetime: marriage, motherhood, widowed; the Depression, two World Wars. So much had happened, but nobody in the family had ever been divorced. I shuddered to think what her reaction would be, and hoped I would find the words to break it gently.

But I need not have worried. She heard me out, then said, 'It's been coming a long time, something like this. If you think this Mila will bring you happiness, then of course you must get a divorce. It's well past time you got some fun out of life.'

Fun? I had a face as long as a fortnight, what with seeing Mila off, worrying about mother's reaction, the prospect of going home to Blackpool – and mother talked about *fun*. But her attitude was a tonic. And the astonishing thing was she knew far more about divorce than I did. In fact it was from her that I learned how long it could take. Naturally I knew it would take time – I had expected a delay of months, even a year perhaps – but mother was talking of *years*: two years, three perhaps, even four conceivably. *Four years!* Once I recovered from that shock the next thing to strike me was that even getting Mila out of Czechoslovakia would be difficult. I remembered the problems she had faced to obtain an exit visa to visit Canada. By now I knew more about the system. For example I knew enough to realize that the authorities might give her an exit visa to get married, or for an occasional holiday, but they would never give her a visa to come and live with me until my divorce was finalized. And that might be four years away! I was in despair.

But not mother. She listened to the problem, and then said, 'The answer is simple. Tell her to get a visa for a holiday, then she must stay in England and not return to Czechoslovakia.'

But even that idea had a flaw. I shook my head: 'She will *want* to go back, to see her parents from time to time. If she leaves illegally she might never see them again.'

Mother understood that reason well enough, and even Arthur sympathized. I ought to explain about Arthur. He was almost sixty then and very set in his ways. Arthur was – and still is – one of the nicest, most straightforward people you could ever meet. Generous, humorous, quiet and modest – but he is also something else. Arthur is a confirmed bachelor. In fact he is the *most* confirmed bachelor you can imagine. So it was difficult for Arthur to understand the muddled state of my emotions, but he was doing his best, until mother had her idea.

'Let me get this straight,' she said slowly. 'This lady will be allowed to leave her country to get married.'

I nodded miserably.

'And if she is married she can go back to see her folks?'

I nodded again.

'And her divorce can be arranged quickly? From her husband George?'

'Yes, but – '

Then the answer is simple,' mother smiled happily. 'Mila must divorce George while you divorce Betty. But divorcing Betty may take a long time, so meanwhile Mila must marry Arthur.'

'*Arthur!*'

Mother nodded: 'Then Arthur divorces Mila and she marries you.'

I nearly fell over. Arthur went ashen: '*Me* get married?'

'Why not? Stanley can't,' mother said crisply. 'Neither can Jack or Ronnie. You are the only one free.'

'But I don't *want* to get married.'

'That's nothing to do with it. Stanley has a problem and it's up to the family to help out.'

I found my voice: 'But I don't want Arthur marrying Mila.'

'I've never even met her,' Arthur wailed.

'It won't be for long,' mother said firmly. 'Just until Stanley gets his divorce.'

'But that could be *years*.' Arthur shook his head from side to side. 'I'm sixty years old,' he said. 'Are you saying I've *got* to get married – at my age?'

'And divorced.' Mother wagged a finger at him.

Arthur shuddered and turned to me: 'There must be another way – '

'Well there isn't,' mother said, 'and I really can't see what the fuss is about.'

'You would,' Arthur said hotly, 'if someone forced you to get married.'

I wondered what Mila would say? She would be as horrified as Arthur. Crikey, *I* was horrified. But if we had to wait four years? It was a possible solution. It would mean Mila could come over to England while my divorce was going through.

Mother beamed proudly: 'Well Stanley, I suggest you put the idea to Mila. Meanwhile,' she added ominously, 'you can leave Arthur to me.'

Poor old Arthur was far from happy about it. I can't say I was delirious either, but the idea of waiting four years was appalling. And for the suggestion to come from mother of all people – that fair took my breath away.

We talked about it over a cup of tea until it was time for me to leave. Arthur was grumbling furiously when I left, but I walked back to Stoke station in a much better mood than when I arrived. I had expected an ordeal and instead – well, every time I thought of Arthur's face I burst out laughing. Mind you, there was no telling what Mila would say, but once she got over the shock I reckoned she would see the funny side of it too. And I told myself that it wouldn't really be necessary, that mother was wrong, that getting a divorce couldn't *possibly* take as long as that.

It was raining by the time I reached the station, but even that failed to dampen my spirits. I kept chuckling about mother and the look on Arthur's face. And I was so *relieved* to have told someone. I tell you, I felt like Gene Kelly doing that number from *Singing in the Rain* – more than even when it turned into a real downpour. The rain came down in sheets. Good football pitch weather. Heavy rain makes the pitch greasy, and a greasy pitch makes for a better game. It makes it more exciting, gives the forwards a better chance of beating defenders. In fact it reminded me of 1963, when Stoke won the Second Division championship.

I was forty-eight then, and had been troubled by an old knee injury for a few months. The physio worked on it every week but it was like patching a patch: most weeks it lasted the game out, but the following day it was back again, as sore as ever. It just would not get better. And to make matters worse it was my right knee, my favourite side for slipping a defender. When the knee functioned properly it gave me a half-yard start over most full-backs – and half a yard is all you need at times. And we figured that the knee always worsened when I played on hard grounds, and improved when the grounds were soft. So we developed our secret pitch technique.

Nobody knew about it, outside of the Stoke City squad and the City of Stoke Fire Brigade – and none of them would breathe a word to an outsider – but it was our secret weapon when we won the championship that year. I forget who came up with the idea. Tony Waddington was manager, and it might have been one of his, or the trainer's, or it may have just developed from a general natter in the dressing-room. But it was a winner of an idea, whoever thought of it.

We had some good ball players in the side then. Dennis Violet, Jimmy MacIlroy, Jackie Mudie and a few others, and we all liked playing on a greasy pitch – not a quagmire or thick mud, but just that sponginess which turf gets after a good downpour. So it wasn't just my knee that preferred it – we all did. We always did well on a pitch like that, and one day someone said, 'By heck, if we had a pitch like that every week we'd win the championship.' And that set us all thinking.

Winning the League is a long hard slog. It's not like the Cup, where an easy draw or one lucky game can set you on the road to Wembley. League championships demand consistency, every result counts, every match is important – and half of those matches are played on your own home ground.

So the question was how to get the pitch just right for us for *every* home match of the season. We couldn't leave it to chance and hope for a downpour every Friday night. We had to make sure. So we called in the Fire Brigade.

Those boys did a marvellous job. They were up at the crack of dawn whenever we were playing at home. Then they drove quietly through the empty streets to the Victoria Ground, where they hosed *thousands of gallons* of water on to the pitch. Then, just as quietly, they drove away again. So that even early in the season when the weather was still hot and dry, our pitch was greasy. Elsewhere in the country fields and football pitches were parched and cracked – but never at Stoke.

Referees arrived on a Saturday and went out to inspect the pitch. Their eyes popped. On a boiling hot day, under a cloudless blue sky, *steam* would be rising from the turf as it dried out. The ref would squat and pat the ground: 'It's *wet!*' he would say in astonishment.

And Tony Waddington would scratch his head: 'You know,' he would say, 'I *thought* it was. Must have been a shower, early this morning. Heavy too, by the look of it.'

'A *shower*? Must have been a bloody cloudburst!'

Then they would stand in the middle of the pitch and look up at the sky. 'English weather,' Tony would say, shaking his head. 'Amazing, isn't it?'

And that's what we did for a whole season. Nobody twigged, but it nearly went wrong on us once. The Fire Brigade left it a bit late one morning. Instead of arriving at six they appeared at nine o'clock. Apparently our usual Fire Chief had gone on holiday and his instructions had been mislaid. So his deputy arrived three hours later than usual and hosed the normal quota of several thousands of gallons of water over the pitch. But it really had rained heavily that night, and an hour later pools of water were lying over a pitch which looked like Blackpool beach with the tide coming in.

Panic stations! Scores of men were recruited from the local Labour Exchange and put to work spiking the turf, alongside players and groundstaff and everyone available. By noon most of the pools had disappeared and disaster was averted – but we played on an *extra* greasy pitch that day.

I remember, about a year later, being shown a photograph taken on the 18 May 1963. There's me at the Victoria Ground, scoring the goal against Luton which clinched the championship. I grinned when I saw it. The people with me thought it was because that goal made me the oldest player ever to score in a League game. But they were wrong. I was grinning at the sight of that pitch. It was the middle of May, and the pitch looked like a mud bath. If only people knew, I thought ... and now they do.

Mila

Stan telephoned me the next day from Blackpool. He still hadn't told his wife about wanting a divorce – and my heart sank. George's comments echoed in my ears, and I tried to shut my mind against the feelings of doubt. Then Stan told me about his mother and Arthur. I thought, thank goodness, at least he has told someone. That cheered me up – at least it did until he said I might have to marry Arthur. What kind of a crazy joke was that?

He said he was going away again – on a promotional tour to sponsor a health food. He would be travelling all over the north of England. Being away from Blackpool would give him a chance to decide what to do next.... I wanted to ask if he had seen his solicitor, taken advice and set the wheels in motion – but I bit my tongue. Instead I told him about the girls, and how pleased they had been with the presents I brought back from Canada. Then I asked when he would next come to Prague.

'In a few weeks,' he said. 'When I've sorted things out in my mind.'

And so I continued to wait and worry. Poor Stan. I knew the agonies he was going through, but there was nothing I could do to help. He telephoned often during the following few weeks – from some hotel room as he crossed the country on his promotional tour – and nine times out of ten he prefaced a remark by saying, 'You know, I remembered something last night. It happened a year ago. . . .' You didn't need to be a psychologist to understand what was going on in his mind. He was weighing the life he *had* against the life he *might* have with me. I don't say it was deliberate, but that's what he was doing. And I knew it.

Meanwhile life in Prague continued much as before. I saw the girls every week and met Eva most days for coffee. They all asked about Stan and when was he coming to take me away. We joked about it, and if it was a strain for me I think only Eva realized it. I kept remembering her words – about Stan giving up so much. She never said it again, but that once was enough.

Days passed. Days and nights – the nights were the worst. Worry turned to uncertainty, and uncertainty soured into doubt. Perhaps George was right after all? Perhaps Stan only wanted an affair? Surely not. Surely it was more than that? He had said it was. But that was in Canada. Now he was in England, while I waited in Prague.

He telephoned almost every evening, but there was no *real* news. I longed for something concrete – to hear that he had told his wife or seen his solicitor. But more and more his conversations began: 'You know Mila, I was thinking last night and I remembered ....'

Stan

It was true, that business of remembering. They say a drowning man sees his whole past life as he goes under for the third time. Well, it wasn't *quite* like that, but I suppose I was wrestling with the biggest decision of my life and all sorts of things came into my mind. And I was away from home a lot – alone in my car or in a hotel bedroom – so I had plenty of time to think, and to remember.

Mostly I remembered the thirties. Well so much happened to me then. I got married for a start – in 1934. I was nineteen. Betty was the daughter of Jimmy Vallance, the Stoke City trainer. It was through Jimmy that we met. Jimmy was a good golfer and he invited me for a golfing holiday in Ayrshire – and Betty Vallance joined us. It was a whirlwind courtship and we married within the year. Jimmy was such a keen golfer that the wedding ceremony was actually held in the club house at Bonnyton Golf Club near Glasgow – the place where Rudolph Hess landed after his fantastic flight from Nazi Germany in 1941.

I nearly met Hess once, when England played Germany in 1938 – the year before the outbreak of war. Europe trembled on the brink of hostilities even then. In March German tanks had entered Vienna as Hitler announced the union of Germany and Austria, in open defiance of the Treaty of Versailles. The name Sudetenland was on everyone's lips and people held their breath to await a reaction from England and France. But nothing much happened and two months later – in May – England actually sent her football team over to play Germany in the infamous Berlin Stadium. What a trip that was! It took two days in the train to cross Europe, and once we entered Germany every other field seemed to contain an aerodrome. We had never seen so many aerodromes, or so many aeroplanes and gliders. And uniforms, of course – everyone seemed to be wearing uniform – in the streets, the cafés, the railway stations – everywhere.

We arrived in Berlin two days before the game and I went on a sight-seeing tour with Bert Sproston, the Leeds full-back. We did all the usual things and we were having a cup of tea in a café when suddenly everyone rushed to the exit. Women waved handkerchiefs and men stood stock still in the open doorway. Bert and I pushed our way through the crowd onto the pavement to see what was happening. A column of SS motor cycle outriders appeared, followed by a couple of large black motor cars. It was Hitler. And wherever we went after that people wanted to tell us about him. There was no doubting the sincerity of the people we talked to – they wanted to talk about Hitler for hours: how he was a man of peace and how what he was doing was for the greatness and good of Germany. And how wrong the English were to be suspicious of his motives. The people we met were absolutely mesmerized. 'A truly historic man,' they said. 'He will change the face of the world.' How right they were.

A dinner was given on the evening of the big match – ostensibly in our honour. The German team arrived from their secret training quarters in the Black Forest. After ten days spent preparing for the game they looked like Greek Gods – bronzed, super-fit and very, very confident. We looked washed out by comparison. The English soccer season was as arduous then as it is now, *and* we had just made the two-day train journey to Berlin, so I suppose we had reason to look tired. But there is no doubt that the Germans used that dinner to 'psych us out'. I spent most of the evening studying Muensenberg, who had given me a night-mare of a game when we played Germany at White Hart Lane two years before. He was one of the most effective full-backs I ever played against and had been recalled to their side with specific orders to take me out of the game. So it was hardly a jolly evening as far as we were concerned. In fact we were thankful when it finished and we were allowed to escape back to our hotel.

The German 'psyching out' process continued the next day when we went to the ground. It was Hitler's showcase – the Berlin Stadium which had been built for the 1936 Olympic Games. Certainly it was magnifi-cent, but the shock came when we were shown to our dressing-room. It was right at the top of a huge stand. We had to climb two hundred steps to get there and it seemed to take forever. We went up and down those steps six times that afternoon and believe me climbing steps can be hard work when the muscles are tired and cramp is setting in after playing on that lush turf. But, in the perverse way of the English, instead of being angry at the obvious gamesmanship, we all found it funny. It became a

The eleven-year-old centre-half of the Wellington
Road, Hanley football team.

Forty years on, Matthews the manager with a new
generation of footballers at Port Vale, 1966.

December 1938: Stan watches groundstaff at Stoke City using braziers to thaw out the pitch. Wheeling the barrow is apprentice Doug Bròwn, who later was to play for Stoke.

The RAF football team. Back row (*left to right*): Rowe, Mullen, Busby, Ellderson, Carter, Swift, Macauley, Barnes, Mortensen, Welsh, Scott. Front row: Matthews, Joy, Lawton.

February 1938: the *Evening Sentinel* reports the protest meeting of Stoke City fans, which produced a resolution demanding Stan's retention.

May 1947: Stan signs for Blackpool, watched by (*left to right*) Ernest Henshall (Stoke chairman), Joe Smith (Blackpool manager), Bob McGrory (Stoke manager) and Harry Evans (Blackpool chairman).

Above: April 1948: Stan takes a corner kick from which Ricketts scores for Blackpool.

Below: Cup Final day, 1953. At the end of an unforgettable match, known ever afterwards as 'the Matthews Final', Stan receives from the Queen his winner's medal.

England's attacking trio of 1956: Stanley Matthews, Tom Finney and Johnny Haynes.

Above: May 1963: on a waterlogged Stoke pitch Stan pushes the ball past Luton goalkeeper Ron Baynham to win the Second Division championship and promotion.

Right: Two great strikers. With Jimmy Greaves in the dressing-room before Stan's 'Farewell Match' on 28 April 1965.

Below: There weren't always thousands of cheering fans. In this bleak, wintry scene Stan is proving his fitness in a reserve match against Manchester United.

It was a proud and emotional farewell to first-class soccer when Stan was chaired off the pitch by Russian goalkeeper Yashin and Puskas of Hungary and Real Madrid.

Back in the dressing-room, Stan hangs up his boots.

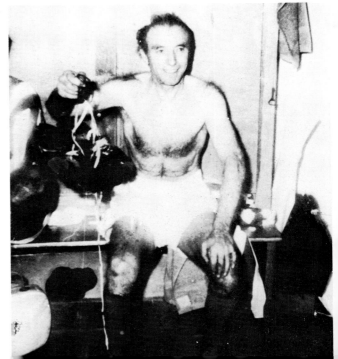

joke. The Germans had overplayed their hand – and it backfired on them.

But a much worse shock was sprung on us just before kick-off. The FA decided that we should give the Nazi fascist salute during the German national anthem. We were appalled. I've never known such an atmosphere in an England dressing-room. Apparently the British Olympic squad had restricted themselves to the 'eyes right' salute at the 1936 Olympics, and the Germans had taken it as a deliberate snub to their beloved Führer. Sir Neville Henderson, the British Ambassador to Germany, came into the dressing-room, on the face of it to wish us good luck, but rumour had it that he had been involved in the FA's decision so I am inclined to think it was more than that. The official view was that an 'international incident' was to be avoided at all costs. Goebbels, Hess and Goering would be watching the game from the Distinguished Visitors Box. I looked at the other players. There could be no mistaking their feelings, but we were virtually under orders. Finally Eddie Hapwood the skipper shrugged and the decision was accepted – but it was a team of angry players who made that long walk down the steps and on to the pitch.

The stadium was a mass of blazing red swastikas, thousands upon thousands of them – and the roar which greeted the German team was earsplitting. We gave the Distinguished Visitors Box their precious salute, and then settled down to play football. I shall never forget those opening minutes. We were forced back into defence and subjected to immediate pressure. The Germans forced a corner. Then, just behind our goal, in the middle of masses and masses of swastikas, two Union Jacks unfurled and a voice piped, 'Let 'em have it England!' What a moment! Football supporters come in for a lot of stick, and certainly some are far too rowdy. But I can assure you that those few piping voices lifted us that day. We tore into the Germans. Cliff Bastin scored, Jackie Robinson got another, Frankie Broome got a third and I added a fourth. The Germans hit back, but we were 4-2 up at half-time. We almost soared up that long climb to the dressing-room. In the second half Robinson got another and Goulden scored the sixth – and we finished comfortable winners by six goals to three. And yet, but for those few shrill voices shouting 'Let 'em have it England!' and the feeling of bloody-mindedness caused by being made to give the Nazi salute, it could so easily have gone the other way.

It was a satisfactory end to what had been a traumatic season for me. Earlier in the year I had been unhappy with things at Stoke and had requested a transfer. Nobody could have foreseen the repercussions. The board rejected my application, but somehow news of it leaked to the Press. Within days it was headlines. All sorts of clubs were rumoured to be interested: Everton, Bolton, Derby, Manchester City.... In fact both Aston Villa and Leicester made official approaches to the Stoke board to discuss terms. Not only that, but my very first boss, Tom Mather, who had left Stoke to go to Newcastle, travelled down overnight with a blank cheque in his pocket. Dear old Tom, he was a sight for sore eyes.

But the publicity took my breath away. I couldn't leave the house without being stopped and asked why I wanted to leave Stoke. People seemed horrified. Arguments raged on street corners. In the end I asked for a week's leave of absence and fled to Blackpool to get away from it – hoping that the furore might have died down by the time I returned.

But not a bit of it. In fact it was worse. Hundreds of placards had been printed. Posters were on every hoarding: 'Matthews must not go.' And a group of leading industrialists had called a public meeting at the King's Hall. Three thousand Stoke City fans packed into that hall, and hundreds more paraded outside, all waving placards and banners: 'Stanley Matthews must not go!' It was the most astonishing display of public loyalty I have ever seen. I was amazed and very touched by it.

The businessmen who called the meeting said that the controversy was undermining output throughout the whole of the Potteries. It seemed crazy to me, but there you are. Nobody could doubt the astonishing sincerity of those supporters. The public meeting was presided over by Ashley Myott, the chairman of the Wages and Conditions Committee of the British Manufacturers Federation, an experienced man when it came to settling a difference of opinion. The meeting decided to send deputations for separate meetings with the Stoke directors and me. I was torn. I had made up my mind to leave Stoke, but I was bowled over by the obvious warmth and affection of those people. To have left then would have been so ungrateful, so lacking in feeling, so ... well all I know is I just couldn't do it. If people like that thought enough of me to go to all that trouble and expense – well it seemed to me I should respond by staying at Stoke for the rest of my life. So I patched up my differences with the club and settled down to spend the rest of my life there. But it was not to be. The following year the country, and then the whole world, were plunged into war.

The war changed everything of course. Organized sport and sportsmen's lives changed along with everything else – but not everything altered overnight. Some games were still held, but with very small gates compared with 1938. For instance, as a result of the bombing, a government order was made to limit the size of crowds to fifteen thousand in 'safe areas' and eight thousand elsewhere. And the whole League format was changed. A system of district competitions was devised, with eight Leagues in England and Wales, and two in Scotland. Eighty-two of the eighty-eight leading clubs took part, but it was a poor substitute for what had gone before. People's minds were on other things, and spectators often seemed listless and bored.

Many grounds were damaged by bombing and even more suffered from neglect. For instance, it may seem hard to believe now but trees six feet high were growing on the terraces at Old Trafford by the end of the war.

Spectators had to be a pretty dedicated lot during the war. Matches often started two hours late because of air raids, and some were abandoned half way through, the score when the siren sounded counting as the final result. Even worse for the fans was the unpredictable behaviour of their favourite team. Many players had been called up, and their places were taken by anyone available, including spectators. So results like 'Brighton & Hove Albion 0, Norwich 18' started to crop up. The Brighton team that day consisted of five Brighton players, two Norwich reserves, and four soldiers recruited from the crowd.

I joined the RAF and spent most of my war at Blackpool. Betty and my baby daughter Jean were there with me, so all in all I had a comfortable billet. I ran the sports store on the pier and organized boxing tournaments and other activities for the troops. And of course I played football whenever I could: for Blackpool and the RAF, for Glasgow Rangers when I went to Scotland, for England in wartime internationals – in fact anywhere and everywhere I could get a game.

But finally the war ended and life struggled back to normal. The Football League didn't open shop until the 1946-47 season, but the crowds started to return to football in 1945. Especially when the Moscow Dynamos arrived in Britain in November of that year.

England had been the citadel of world football before the war, and most of us wanted to keep it that way. But the Dynamos created a sensation when they arrived. In their opening match they held Chelsea to a 3-3 draw in front of eighty-five thousand spectators at Stamford Bridge, then they hammered Cardiff 10-1 at Ninian Park. Newspaper headlines shrieked: 'Dynamic Dynamos', 'World Beaters', 'The finest football machine ever seen'.... Then they ran follow-up stories demanding that something be done about it. English prestige was threatened, and the Dynamos had to be beaten. And the Press decided that Arsenal was the club to do it.

Which was easier said than done. As I said, like everything else in the country, football was still struggling back to normal. Many players were overseas in the Armed Forces and lots of clubs were hard pushed to get a decent side together. Arsenal were no exception. At least three of their first-team players – Leslie Compton, Bernard Joy and Reg Lewis – were on service in Germany, so players from other clubs rallied round and offered their services. In the event Bernard Joy was able to get back for the game, and along with Bastin, Halton, Drury and Cumner, was one of five 'genuine' Arsenal players in the side. The others came from all over the place: Stan Mortensen from Blackpool, Griffiths from Cardiff, Ronnie Rook, Joe Bacuzzi and Laurie Scott from Fulham, and me from Stoke. And that was the *Arsenal* team.

We struggled into London from all points of the compass – and a compass was something to treasure that day because the city was enveloped in fog. A real old-fashioned pea-souper. We went to the ground, expecting the game to be cancelled, but various officials made optimistic noises about the fog lifting in time for kick-off. So we fidgeted around while they made up their minds. Eventually they decided the game was on, so we got changed and went out.

Instant disaster! The Dynamos scored in the very *first* minute. Not that many in the crowd of the fifty-four thousand *saw* the goal. Come to that, most of the players missed it. Visibility was down to twenty yards and the fog was getting thicker by the minute. After that it was a nightmare. 'Your ball Stan,' someone would shout, and I'd spend the next minute looking for it. It was like a party game for kids, except nobody shouted 'You're getting warmer' if you got near the ball. And if you did find it a Russian full-back ripped the shirt off your back before you as much as moved. It wasn't football, it was a sort of maniacal blind man's buff. You saw the whites of a player's eyes before you saw the colour of his shirt. If you glimpsed a silhouette that resembled an England player you passed the ball, if not you hung on to it. By some miracle we were 3–2 up at half-time and we groped our way off the pitch and down the tunnel.

The talk in the dressing-room was all about the shirt-pulling tactics of the Russians – and the fog, of course.

'Bells round our necks – that's what we need in the second half.'

'Bells on the ball.'

'What bloody ball? I haven't seen it in half an hour.'

'Hey Skip, we gotta do something about this shirt-pulling lark.'

'*Shirt pulling!* That centre-half's had my shorts down twice. Be different if I fancied him.'

But out we went again and the fog was even worse in the second half. I could hardly see my feet, let alone the ball! After about ten minutes word filtered through that the Dynamos had equalized, and just after that came the best moment of all, though it's been a secret until today.

The Russian goalkeeper had been nicknamed 'The Tiger' by the Press, though it was hard to understand why, for there was nothing tigerish about him that day. He had an infuriating habit of getting the ball, dropping it to the ground, then falling on top of it and just lying there, shouting his head off and not getting up until four or five Dynamo players made a ring round him. Then he would jump up and kick the ball out.

George Drury really lost his rag. He stood over the Russian and shouted down at him: 'You hatching that or something? You're a duck, not a bleeding tiger!'

Anyway, just after that one of George's more robust attempts to relieve the goalkeeper of the ball resulted in him being sent off by the Russian referee. 'OFF – OFF – OFF!' shouted the ref, pointing to where we all assumed the tunnel to be. George looked disgusted, said 'Quack, quack' to the goalkeeper, and disappeared into the fog.

Ten minutes later I had the ball on the edge of their box and was trying to find one of our boys to pass it to. '*Stan!* Stan! – inside,' came a shout ... and George flitted into sight about a yard away. I was so surprised that I miskicked and the ball spun off for a goal-kick.

'George,' I hissed, 'you were sent off.'

'I know, mate, but I couldn't find the way,' he grinned – and disappeared back into the fog.

Nobody ever found out, and George played out the remainder of the game along with the rest of us. Even afterwards nobody twigged – not the referee, nor the linesmen, nor any of the Russian players. Not that it mattered. The Dynamos won 4–3 in the end, but it was a farce of a game.

Mila

George was being difficult about the divorce. He was adopting 'let's wait and see' tactics – meaning let Stanley get divorced first. Obviously he still thought nothing would come of it, that Stan would stay firmly married in England and forget all about me. It was a ridiculous attitude in face of the evidence. Stan continued to send flowers and to telephone me several times a week. But George was being stubborn.

Eventually I called a 'council of war' among the girls and brought them up to date. I even explained that I might have to marry Stan's brother. When they stopped laughing, Eva made the point that British divorce laws were as fascinating as tribal rituals, which just about summed up my feelings too. But meanwhile there was the problem of *my* divorce to contend with.

As I said earlier, divorce in Czechoslovakia is quick and easy, as long as both parties agree. Complications set in, however, if one party drags his feet, and clearly George was dragging his. So something had to be done.

Then Kveta had her idea: 'George must be compromised,' she said brightly. 'Then you can divorce him for adultery.'

I thought she was joking at first, especially when she added, 'And I know who will do it for us.' Then she mentioned the name of a very famous Czech film star. Now this lady is as famous in Prague as, say, Sophia Loren in Rome, or Bo Derek in Hollywood. So what Kveta was suggesting was breathtaking to say the least. But Kveta was closer to the film crowd than to some members of her own family. She really knew her actors and actresses. She spent most of her life with them, and one look at her face said that she certainly wasn't joking.

'You mean it?'

'Of course I mean it. And I *know* she will do it, if I ask her.'

It was an astonishing solution, but when I got my breath back some perverse sense of loyalty to George made me say, 'George wouldn't do it. I just know he wouldn't.'

Kveta said nothing. She just raised an eyebrow and looked at me.

I thought about it. The actress concerned really was very beautiful, I had to admit that – and very sexy, if you like that kind of woman. And most men did. Half Czechoslovakia dribbled whenever she appeared on the screen – the male half. In fact, now that I remembered it, there had been a seduction scene in her last film. I closed my eyes and imagined George in the role of that actor. That did it! My eyes sprang open. 'He would do it!' I said.

Kveta nodded knowingly: 'Do you want me to ask her?'

She really was *absolutely serious*! I couldn't get over it. The other girls thought it was a good idea, but I was still struggling to take it in. My mind overflowed with questions: 'How – I mean, when –'

Kveta frowned: 'When is Stan coming over to see you?'

'Next month – sometime in August – I hope.'

'For a few days?'

I nodded.

'And you'll take him to Karlsbad again?'

'Yes.'

Kveta smiled: 'Well, that's the time. While the cat's away the mouse will play – and George will play with. . . .' She repeated the name of the actress.

I sat there shaking my head: 'She *really will* do it?'

Kveta nodded.

I savoured the idea for a minute. Then I was smitten by a guilty conscience. It seemed so unfair. Planning George's downfall like . . . like a military campaign. I hesitated, then said: 'It seems a dirty trick somehow.'

Eva burst out: 'Are you kidding? George would give his eye teeth to take her to bed. *Any* man would. And look at the result. You get George where you want him, and he gets to enjoy himself. What's so bad about that?'

But I was still doubtful.

'Look at it this way,' Kveta suggested, 'You are going to divorce George anyway. We all know that. It will take longer if he drags his feet, but you will still divorce him eventually. He gets nothing out of it doing it your way. This way at least he gets a little bonus.'

'Some bonus,' Eva said emphatically; 'Think of the memories he'll have. That's if he doesn't have a heart attack.'

'And it speeds everything up,' Kveta pointed out. 'You can be divorced within a couple of months and free to marry Stan.'

'Or Arthur,' Eva said drily, '– whichever the case may be.'

Life was getting so *complicated*! All I wanted was to be with Stan. Now I was faced with marrying his brother and George was going to romp with an actress.

'So we do it?' Kveta wanted to know.

I took a deep breath and nodded my head.

'Your troubles are over,' she said triumphantly. 'I'll make all the arrangements. Just let me know when Stan is due and leave the rest to me.'

Stan telephoned that evening. He would be coming to Prague on 20 August – for three whole days. I was too excited to tell him about Kveta's idea. Besides, I was beginning to have second thoughts about it. Discussing it with the girls had been funny, but alone in my room it seemed a mean thing to do. After all, I was very fond of George. I had never been in love with him, but that didn't mean I wasn't grateful for his many kindnesses and his consideration. Maybe he would be reasonable about a divorce after all? It seemed worth trying again, so I went downstairs to tell him about Stan's intended visit.

'Has he got his divorce?' was the first thing George asked.

'Not yet – these things take time in England –'

'Has he told his wife?'

'No,' I admitted, 'No, I don't think so, not yet –'

'*Not yet*,' George echoed sarcastically. 'Not yet means never. Mila, he will *never* tell her. Can't you understand that? Forget about him. You are better off married to me.'

I wanted to avoid a discussion along those lines so I changed direction, thinking I might be able to joke him into a better mood: 'You never know,' I said, 'but perhaps you will change *your* mind? Perhaps you will want to divorce me?'

'Me? Do I ever look at other women?'

'You might,' I said, 'if you weren't always so busy –'

'It's not busy that matters. It's maturity of outlook. I am too mature to be distracted by women.'

Now I had gone down to the studio with the best of intentions, anxious not to hurt his feelings. But I had feelings too, and he was trampling all over them. As calmly as I could I asked, 'Are you saying you wouldn't be attracted by *any* other woman?'

'That is *exactly* what I am saying!'

He was so smug about it – that's what got me – so infuriatingly smug! He really was behaving like a 'male chauvinist pig'. 'That's nonsense,' I said. 'Of course you would be –'

'No I wouldn't. Never! Never, never, never –'

'Don't be perfectly ridiculous. You know very well that given the opportunity –'

'*Opportunity!* I get the opportunity every day of my life. But I have the will power to –'

That did it. That bit about will power. I really saw red. 'George,' I snapped, 'you are being insufferably pompous.'

'Pompous! Me? Because I can resist –'

'And I say you can't. Not if the opportunity presented itself –'

He was red-faced with indignation: 'If *I* had an affair? Is that what you mean? Well let me tell you something. The day *I* have an affair will be the day I give you a divorce. Until then you stay married to me!'

That was a declaration of war. I stormed back to my bedroom and telephoned Kveta. Operation Seduction was very much on. It couldn't happen fast enough. George would jolly well have his actress – whether he liked it or not. Then we would see how righteous he felt!

Stan

I was becoming more and more agitated about the future. It was now four weeks since I had returned from Canada and I still hadn't said a word to Betty about the divorce. Neither had I been to see my solicitor. The days passed and I continued to put off the evil moment. I shied away from inflicting pain and upset on Betty and Jean and Stanley Jnr, and I cringed with embarrassment whenever I thought of the publicity. But I had to tell someone, and finally I travelled up to Rhyl to see my old pal Charlie Chester. Charlie was appearing in a show there, and after his performance we went out for a meal together.

Charlie and I have been friends for more years than I remember: twenty-five years at least and probably longer. Doretta, his wife, and Betty are close friends, and the four of us have spent countless holidays together. Not only that but Charlie and I have worked together on numerous occasions all over the country. Mostly at charity football matches involving the Water Rats or various Show Biz Elevens – and we once staged a unique golf match for charity. I played with golf clubs and a ball, but Charlie used a bow and arrow. The match took place over the full eighteen holes at Lytham St Annes and crowds of spectators turned up to watch. Now you might think that a golfer would beat an archer hands down, but archery is one of Charlie's many talents. As it happened, I *did* win, but only by the odd hole, so it was a closely fought battle.

Apart from the fact that he is my oldest pal, I have a lot of respect for Charlie. I suppose he is best known to the public as a comedian and broadcaster, but he is a man of many talents. He writes and paints and never stops working for charity. He can be as funny in private as he is in public, and we've had some marvellous times together. And he can be generous: for instance, after he had organized my Farewell Match he offered to take a year off from his show biz career to stage similar farewell games for me all over the world. And it was Charlie who wrote my speech when I was elected to the Water Rats. So he and I were tremendous friends. But it was more than that. Charlie can be serious when he wants to be and very capable of giving good advice, so I suppose I was hoping he might give me some when I went up to see him.

But first of all he brought me up to date on what was happening to my many other friends in show business. People like Tommy Cooper, Dickie Henderson, Tommy Trinder, Ted Heath and so many others. Or dear old Ted Ray, for instance, who alas is no longer with us. When I knew Ted he was constantly involved in organizing Charity Football matches. He and I played at Stamford Bridge together, and in several games elsewhere. Then Ted had a bad motor accident which put paid to his days as a player. I remember going to see him in hospital with Charlie. Ted was stretched out in bed with both legs in plaster and one arm in a sling. He was in a very bad way indeed. But it took a lot to keep Ted down. Charlie and I were sitting at his bedside eating his grapes, when suddenly Ted said: 'The accident was nothing. I'll get over that. But what happened yesterday was worse. *Yesterday was terrible.* I shall never get over that.'

It was impossible to imagine anything worse than Ted's accident. Goodness knows how many bones had been broken – he was in an awful state.

'*Worse* than the accident?' Charlie asked.

'Much worse,' Ted said miserably.

Charlie and I stopped eating grapes and listened.

'It all started when I needed the toilet,' Ted began. 'I pressed the bell for a nurse to come and give me a hand.'

Ted was so encased in plaster that he could hardly move.

'Nobody came,' said Ted, 'I rang and rang and rang, but nothing happened. This went on for ten minutes. By then I was desperate, really desperate – so in the end I started to hoist myself off the bed. First one leg, then the other. The pain was agonizing. I thought I'd pass out at one stage. And I knew if I fell over I'd never get myself upright again. Anyway, finally I managed it, and I was just sitting down on the pot when the door opened and in marched Eamonn Andrews. "Ted Ray," he said, "This is Your Life!"'

That was Ted all over – he would make a gag out of anything. The trouble is I never see Eamonn now without imagining Ted on that pot, with Eamonn standing over him with his big red book.

But to get back to Charlie and when I saw him that night. We had a meal and talked of old times, and when I thought the moment right, I told him about Mila. I think Charlie was more sad than shocked. It had been obvious to him for a long time that things weren't right at home: he knew us all too well to be fooled by outward appearances. But it took him a while to realize how serious I was - that I really did want a divorce so that I could marry Mila. He tried his best to talk me out of it - understandably I suppose, for after all he knew Betty well and had never even met Mila. He even suggested that I keep Mila on as a mistress. Charlie himself was happily married, but to run a wife *and* a mistress was almost a status symbol with some of the showbiz crowd - like having a Rolls in the garage. But I could never contemplate that. The complications in my life were already bad enough, the last thing I wanted was to prolong them. I remember saying I would rather settle for a short time of happiness with Mila than spend the rest of my life without her.

Poor Old Charlie. He was like a Dutch Uncle that night. He even talked about the bad publicity and things like that. Just to hear me discussing divorce was painful to him. And it was a daft thing to do on my part. How can anyone advise a pal in circumstances like those? The feelings involved were just too personal. But it shows the state of mind I was in. So at the end of the meal I said: 'Thanks for lending an ear - but don't be surprised if I just up and go one of these days.'

Then I drove back to Blackpool.

Mila

Stan arrived in Prague on 20 August 1968. My father was with me at the airport. I was desperate for him to meet Stan. It was somehow important to me that they liked each other: perhaps I felt defensive about what I was doing, because I was eager to have the approval of both of them. In fact they took to each other from the first moment. I was relieved and delighted. We spent a happy hour having coffee together, and then I drove Stan to Karlsbad in my car. It had been eight whole weeks since that trembling goodbye at Heathrow. Now we had three marvellous days together and I was determined not to waste a minute.

First I told Stan about Operation Seduction. Kveta was planning to implement it while we were away. Stan was shocked. In fact he protested, until he saw a photograph of the actress; then he felt it might not be so rough on George after all.

'So what happens afterwards?' Stan wanted to know; 'When you get back from Karlsbad?'

'The actress will provide me with evidence of George's adultery: then I can get my divorce.'

'George will agree? Just like that?'

'He won't argue once he's been compromised. Don't you see? I will soon be free to marry you. In eight weeks at the most.'

'Eight weeks,' he groaned. 'It will take me eight months – and that's if I'm lucky. More like eighteen – and probably longer.'

'Longer than *eighteen months*?'

'It could take years,' he said gloomily.

'You mean I really will have to marry Arthur?'

'It looks like it – if that's the only way to get you an exit visa.'

It was daunting news. I don't suppose Arthur was exactly thrilled about it either. And I was disappointed to learn that Stan still hadn't discussed divorce with his wife – or his solicitor. But I closed my mind to all dark thoughts. We had three wonderful days ahead of us, and I was determined not to spoil them by worrying. For the present it was enough that Stan was there – with me in Czechoslovakia.

Karlsbad was full of holidaymakers – mostly Germans but with a scattering of Yugoslavs and other nationalities. The hotel echoed with sounds of laughter and gaiety, and guests were invited to this or that party in an atmosphere of relaxed informality. For days past the weather had been warm and sunny, with long evenings ended by moonlit nights, so that when we went down to dinner that evening I tingled with excitement. We were on the verge of a magical interlude, I thought – and so it was, but hardly in the way I imagined.

Stan

I was up at my usual hour the following morning, ready to go for my morning run. It was six o'clock, and outside the sky was blue and cloudless with the promise of another fine day. I trotted downstairs in my track suit, expecting the lobby to be empty, but instead it was packed tight with people, all talking excitedly while some listened to portable radios and others crowded round a television set. Mostly they were Czechs – members of the staff, waiters and suchlike – but as I crossed the lobby I noticed many of the German guests in the crowd. Then I opened the front doors and went out for my run.

When I returned the lobby was more crowded than ever. People were milling around, shouting and calling to each other, all very excited. The mob clustering around the television was bigger than before, thirty or forty deep, with those on the fringe having details of the pictures relayed back to them over people's shoulders. Everyone was talking at once, in Czech or German, which made no sense to me, and I couldn't get near enough to the television to see what was happening. Of course I asked, but nobody nearby seemed to speak English. Besides, by now the staff were rushing around with suitcases as if half the guests were leaving. I ran upstairs and knocked hard on Mila's door.

It took her half an hour to get bathed and dressed. Meanwhile I got rid of my track suit, showered and changed, and eventually Mila was ready.

'It must be something important,' I said on the way downstairs. 'Perhaps it's a football match.'

But it was more important than that. Much more important. The Russians had invaded Czechoslovakia! Russian tanks had crossed the border during the night. Russian troops were already in Prague. And not just Russian – East German, Rumanian and Polish troops, tanks and armoured vehicles had poured across every neighbouring frontier.

Prague airport had been closed to all normal traffic. Exit points to the West were being sealed tight. I was cut off in Czechoslovakia!

I was stunned. There had been no warning. I don't greatly interest myself in politics, but I *do* read the papers. There had been nothing to indicate this. It took a while for the news to sink in. Meanwhile every other guest in the hotel was throwing suitcases into his car and jumping in after them. Some Yugoslavs who had recognized me over dinner the night before asked what I was doing – was I leaving or staying? How could I leave? Prague airport was closed, and so was every other airport in Czechoslovakia. I gave the Yugoslavs my home address and asked them to cable my wife to let her know I was safe, but that was about all I did. I was dazed by it all. Besides there were other things to think about – like what would happen to Mila in a Russian invasion?

By noon we were the only guests remaining in the hotel.

The initial shock subsided. It was a funny feeling – to know that we had been caught up in an invasion. But what to do about it? There was *nothing* I could do, and once I accepted that I ceased to worry. Strangely, perhaps, neither of us was frightened. We were part of it, because it was happening, yet at the same time we were *apart* from it. It didn't concern us. And Mila had never been a political activist, so she felt she had nothing to fear personally. So we settled down to wait it out.

Mila

The truth is we were so bound up with each other that the rest of the world could have stopped for all we cared. And of course it very nearly did. But life in the hotel continued. Meal-times were a strange experience, having that huge dining-room all to ourselves. It had been crowded on the first night, full of laughing, talkative people, with waiters dashing from table to table. Now the guests had fled and the waiters were left with only us to serve.

In fact the waiters became our prime source of news. With so little to do they had time on their hands. Consequently a knot of them was forever crouched around the television, while others pressed radios to their ears, and at meal-times the latest bulletins were relayed to us.

The weather continued warm and sunny. The days passed. Stan and I confined ourselves to walks in the grounds of the hotel, and the occasional game of tennis. Prague Airport remained firmly closed, and all other routes to the West had ceased to exist. Stan *had* to stay, whether he liked it or not, and fortunately he seemed more than content with the arrangements.

We often saw Russian tanks on the distant roads, but no troops ever appeared at the hotel. A rumour reached us that Russian troops were being billeted in the hotels, and such things might have happened elsewhere – but not at Karlsbad. It was as if they too had decided we had no part to play, so we were left in splendid isolation.

The days slipped into weeks. It was like being marooned on a desert island, except we were cocooned in a luxury hotel, with more than fifty staff to cater to our every whim. If it sounds unreal I can only agree that there was an air of unreality about it. We knew it could never last, that soon it would end, but *how* and *when* were questions we preferred not to ask. The future had been uncertain before – now it defied contemplation. Obviously a time would come when Stan could return to the

West, but what about me? Would I *ever* be allowed to leave a Czecho-slovakia under Russian domination? We tried not to think about that. In fact we talked of everything under the sun *except* the future. We lived for then – each minute of every day – knowing it might be all the time we would ever spend with each other.

Then came the news. A train would leave for Nuremberg in Germany on the Sunday. It was Stan's gateway to England – and we both knew he had to go. I couldn't go with him; I had neither my passport nor a valid exit visa. But Stan *had* to go, just as I *had* to stay.

Stan

I had been in Karlsbad twenty days by then. Originally I had planned to stay for three. The inevitable happened – I ran out of money. I couldn't cash a cheque and even banker's cards were unacceptable. I hadn't even enough money to pay the hotel bill. Under other circumstances it would have been an embarrassing moment, but at Karlsbad it seemed just one more thing to laugh about.

Karlsbad. I shall never forget it. Or the twenty days we spent there. People were desperately afraid, the world trembled on the brink of war, an entire country was flooded with foreign troops – and to me none of it mattered. I was with Mila, and as far as I was concerned being in the middle of an invasion just about summed her up – it was just the sort of crazy thing she would drag me into. Not that Mila *is* crazy, but from the first moment I met her crazy things have happened to me. She doesn't set out to land me in trouble, but I tell you, the troubles I've had since I met Mila are nobody's business. And Karlsbad was one of them. We refused to worry about it when it happened. We just enjoyed ourselves – living each day as it came – until the very last day. And that was awful.

We had to face up to it then. We might never see each other again. It had always been at the back of our minds – but we had to say it aloud on that last day. *We might never see each other again.* Both of us were physically sick. I wondered whether to let the train go to Nuremberg without me? Perhaps there would be another one? Perhaps Prague airport would be re-opened to commercial traffic? Perhaps the situation would soon be *normalized*? I enquired. The Nuremberg train was a special train – for refugees cut off by the invasion. The authorities had no plans to run another one. Prague airport would certainly remain closed to non-military traffic. I was not a Czech citizen. I had run out of money. I was *advised* to be on that train, and there was no doubt that I was expected to take that *advice* – or else.

The business about running out of money was easily settled. Mila simply rang George who cabled enough cash to the hotel to meet our bill. I gathered that Operation Seduction had been abandoned. The much bigger Operation Invasion had occurred one night too soon. I couldn't decide whether to be glad or sorry for George, but it was decent of him to cable the money. And with the hotel bill taken care of I had enough cash to get back to England.

But the awful part of that day had nothing to do with money. The awful part was saying goodbye to Mila. We were both desperately miserable. It was the worst day of my life.

On the way to the station she told me about a friend of hers, a German dentist living in Frankfurt. 'Try to telephone me,' she urged. 'If I say I'm going to the dentist you will know I mean to escape – that I shall try to get to Germany.'

It was wild, despairing talk. Some of it registered, but only just – my mind was a jumble of confused and conflicting emotions. Even after kissing her goodbye, even when I went through the ticket barrier to go to the train – even then I was in two minds about leaving. Should I stay? *Could* I stay? Should I go back to Prague with her? Would the British Embassy help? I underwent agonies of indecision. But the train to Nuremberg was the *last* train. All other exits had been closed. No other escape would be possible. *I had to go.*

Mila

I have never felt so lonely in the whole of my life as when Stan went through that barrier. Lonely, empty, and desperately afraid. The station was alive with activity, jam-packed with soldiers, police, railwaymen, officials, while the concourse was thick with people. I was bumped from all sides by suitcases and luggage. The noise was deafening. The public address system blared, people shouted to each other, calling their good-byes and passing last-minute messages to friends and relations who squeezed paths between trucks laden with luggage. Others stood in little groups of four or five people, stamping their feet against the cold night air, while children sat shivering on milk churns or boxes, clutching their pitiful possessions and looking about them with wide, frightened eyes. Wherever I looked I saw people – yet I felt so dreadfully alone.

Stan was hanging out of a door, half-way up the train. His face turned in my direction as his worried eyes searched the crowd. I waved, tears streaming down my face, distorting my vision. Somebody pushed past me, I almost lost my balance, and when I looked back at the train Stan had gone. The carriage door swung open as before, but Stan was no longer framed in the opening. Then I saw him. He had climbed down on to the platform. I almost fainted with relief. He was *coming back*! Stan was not going to leave me after all. He had decided to stay!

But instead of walking back to the barrier he stayed where he was. He hopped from foot to foot, straining to see above the heads of the crowd. I stretched, making myself tall, waving furiously. I shouted, 'Stan! Stan! I'm here!' But the noise swallowed the sound of my voice. I could see the indecision on Stan's face, almost *hear* his questions. Shall I go? Shall I stay? Oh stay – for God's sake *stay*!

Suddenly the engine hissed steam and the wheels of the train spun on the rails. Guards up and down the platform were waving passengers on to the train – and Stan climbed back on board. He remained in the doorway, jostled and knocked sideways as others pushed past him. He craned his neck, turning his head back and forth as he scanned the concourse for sight of me. A guard slammed the door. Stan pulled the window down and leant out so far I thought he would fall. I waved and waved. The engine hissed again, wheels shuffled ominously as the brakes were released. Oh please God - stop it! Make the engine break down, make a signal fail, derail a train up the line - *anything*! Just let Stan stay here with me.

And then it was moving. The train was actually moving. Slowly, an inch at a time, drawing away, out of the brightly lit station and into the darkness. Stan waved from the open window, waved and waved and waved. He waved blindly, without seeing me. Then he was lost in the night. Red lights glowed on the end of the last carriage. The train was gone. Stan was gone. Stan was gone forever.

I was numb. The night air felt bitterly cold, chill, bleak, cruel. I turned and walked sightlessly back to my car. It took ages to open the door. I couldn't see the lock through my tears and my fingers wouldn't stop trembling. My teeth chattered with prayers for the train to return. I got into the car and just sat there, calming myself, smoking a cigarette while trying to come to terms with what I must do. Then I drove back to the hotel.

I might have driven to Prague that night, but for the people at the hotel. 'Stay off the roads at night,' they said. 'Listen to us, for your own safety listen to us.'

'Why? Is there a curfew?'

Shrugs, embarrassed looks, muttered warnings. I telephoned father for advice. He said, 'Stay there until morning.'

Stay *here* - in Karlsbad! Waste a night - when I *had* to get away. Did people realize what they were asking of me? Every hour was precious. With the passing of every night and every day the borders to the West would be sealed more tightly.

But I stayed. I felt drained and exhausted, my nerves jumped wildly and probably I would have ploughed the car into the first ditch in the dark. The hotel staff gave me some sleeping pills and promised to wake me in the morning. I went to bed.

It was another golden summer's day when I awoke. Like the last twenty days - except that Stan had gone. I packed my things, drank some strong black coffee, paid the hotel bill with George's money, and left for Prague.

The roads buzzed with military. Russian jeeps, open-backed lorries full of East German troops, tanks, armoured cars. Rumanian despatch riders on motor bikes weaved in and out of the traffic. Private cars were few, mine and perhaps half a dozen others – no more than ten during the entire journey. The sun shone on the fields in blissful ignorance of what was happening. After about twenty kilometres I realized that all signposts to Prague were pointing the wrong way. I smiled. Oh Czechoslovakia – is this the height of your resistance? The Russians sailed blithely past, not fooled for a minute.

The centre of the city was full of tanks. Czechs on the streets were outnumbered two to one by Russian soldiers. But there were no road blocks. Nobody stopped me to ask for my papers. I was allowed to finish my journey unmolested and without hindrance. My father was still at his apartment when I arrived. The television was on and the radio blared from the kitchen.

He clasped me in his arms as my mother appeared at the door. Her face was creased with worry and she dry washed her hands as she looked at me. 'The Russians...' she began, but I cut her short.

'Stan has gone,' I said. That was all that mattered. What a selfish thing love is. My country had been invaded, my parents were worried sick, people in the streets were angry and resentful. But all I could say was, 'Stan has gone.'

Predictably mother turned away: 'You made your bed,' she said. 'Now you must lie on it.'

Father's arm tightened around my shoulders: 'Come – have some coffee. You must need it after that drive.'

But I couldn't. I couldn't stay, talk, have coffee – there was no time for that – I had things to do. My parents were safe. At least I had been unselfish enough to make sure of that. I had seen them. It was enough.

I went to the Embassy and telephoned Eva: 'What's happening?' I asked.

Prague airport was occupied by the Russian army. It remained closed, except for aeroplanes from the Warsaw Pact countries. All exits to the West were blocked. The rumour was that Prime Minister Dubček had been taken to Moscow. Bulletins and announcements were being made on radio and television almost every hour.

'Stan has gone,' I said. 'I must follow him.'

Eva gasped: 'Mila, stop it! You are upset – disturbed. Don't do anything foolish. Things may calm down, sort themselves out. Stan may be able to come back soon.'

But I refused to listen. I left the Embassy and went on a tour of friends' houses and apartments, stopping at each only long enough to discover who was planning to leave and who was going to stay. And of those who wanted to leave I asked: 'How? How is it possible to get out of Czechoslovakia and escape to the West?'

Nobody knew. Or perhaps nobody was saying. Perhaps each was making his own desperate plan and was afraid to talk about it. I went home. Stan had promised to telephone – if he could get through. I did not expect to hear from him. After all, if all contact with the West had been severed, that would surely include the telephone lines? I remembered the code. The code was all I thought about – the code and being able to use it. *But how?*

George arrived an hour later. One look at my face told him that Stan had gone. Perhaps just my being there was enough. He knew that if Stan was in Czechoslovakia I would be with him.

We said little to each other. I thanked him for the money, we listened to the radio, watched television, telephoned friends – anything and everything to find out what was happening in the city.

'Will you stay?' I asked.

He smiled sadly: 'You think we will have a choice in the matter?'

'There's always a way.'

'Where there's a will, you mean?' He cocked an eyebrow at me, then he waved a hand at the room: 'This is my home. Prague is my home. Czechoslovakia is my country.' He shook his head, 'My country, right or wrong.'

I said nothing. There was no need. I would go if I could. George knew that, I had no need to tell him.

Then the miracle happened. Stanley telephoned. It had taken him twenty hours to reach Nuremberg – a journey normally accomplished in half the time. 'Are you all right?' he asked, over and over again. 'What is happening there? What's going on?'

As if I could answer such questions over an open line. We would be disconnected at any moment.

I was crying, choked up, not speaking clearly. I said: 'I am going to see my dentist.'

'What? Mila, I can't hear properly. Mila – *are you all right?*'

I bit back the tears. For a moment I couldn't speak at all. Then I cleared my throat and managed to repeat, 'I am going to the dentist.'

The line crackled badly. 'Stan,' I shouted, 'Stan, can you hear me?'

But the line was dead.

I sat up half the night, waiting and hoping he would call back. I rushed to the telephone whenever it rang, praying it was Stan. But it never was. Just friends, asking what we had heard, passing on what they knew, pooling information. Stan's call had been one of the last to get through from the West.

I was awake all night. Every minute I thought of a new scheme. Perhaps the Americans would smuggle me out? Perhaps my friends at the British Embassy would help? After all, Stan was British. Perhaps if I went to the Embassy and *explained*? Or perhaps if I went to the Ministry of the Interior? Maybe they would let me out. After all, why bother to keep me in Prague? I was hardly a threat. I was non-political – I had never been active in political matters. Why bother to keep me here?

The following day is mostly forgotten. I stayed at home for much of the time, just in case Stan managed to get through again. Friends called, people came and went – talking, angry, resentful. I do remember that quite clearly: people were more angry than afraid. They felt let down, betrayed, shocked. There was much talk of the Hungarian experience. It was a cold awakening after the Prague Spring. Many people were concerned about the safety of Dubček and other political leaders. Some of the talk registered with me, but not much. The day passed slowly and the night lasted forever.

Then in the morning I heard some incredible news. The radio had been on solidly ever since I returned from Karlsbad. It was the same everywhere. People conducted conversations against the background noise of radio and television for fear of missing an important news flash. And the announcement I heard that morning took my breath away. There was to be *another* train! One last train was to be allowed to leave for the West. To Vienna. Exit visas would be required naturally, together with entry visas into Austria, and only those people with a valid reason would be allowed to make the journey – but the astonishing thing was that some people were to be *allowed* to go!

I listened anxiously, trying to discover what constituted a valid reason. The reasons were listed: the re-uniting of families, travel on State business, the repatriation of foreigners stranded by the 'emergency', and various other reasons. None of them applied to me, not one of them. But a train *to the West*. I could hardly believe it!

My exit visa! The one for Canada. *It was still valid.* The morning paper arrived and I searched for details of the train. People wishing to travel should first apply to the Ministry of the Interior for an exit visa, giving reasons for wishing to undertake the journey. Then, if such a visa was granted, it should be taken to the Austrian Embassy where it would be counter-stamped for entry into Austria. But I *already had* a visa. If I went to the Ministry of the Interior and explained my reasons for wanting to leave I would be refused exit, but if I took a chance – if I used the visa I already had? What then would the Austrian Embassy do? Would they stamp *all* exit visas – or just special ones issued for the passengers of that train?

I drove to my father's apartment, not daring to discuss the matter on the telephone. Queues had already formed outside the Ministry of the Interior, and another line of people stood outside the Austrian Embassy. And that was within a few hours of the announcement! For a train not leaving until eight tomorrow evening. I checked my watch. It was ten o'clock. Thirty-four hours to go.

My father was out. I didn't dare discuss the matter with my mother. I turned in my tracks and headed for the Mexican Embassy to see Eva. On the way I passed the Austrian Embassy again. The queue had lengthened, people were standing six deep across the pavement and the line stretched half way round the block.

Eva was apalled: 'You're crazy. They will stop you at the station. Everyone's papers will be inspected before they get anywhere near that train.'

'But I already have an exit visa.'

She shook her head: 'Not for that train and you know it. Mila, you will be trying to leave *illegally*. You know the penalties. Don't do it.'

But I refused to listen and returned to father's apartment. The queue outside the Austrian Embassy was longer than ever.

Father listened and fell into a long silence. Then he said: 'Have you come to ask my advice? Or have you come to say goodbye?'

Oh bless you, father! No reproaches, no argument, no attempt to dissuade me. He just looked at me and asked simply, 'How can I help?'

I didn't know. How could *anyone* help? Besides it would be safer for all concerned if I did as much as possible by myself. It lessened the risk of them getting into trouble afterwards. But at least I calmed down enough to drink some coffee, and I stayed with father until I thought of my next move. Then I drove to the American Embassy and asked to see my old boss.

'I've come to say goodbye,' I said when I was shown into his office, 'I'm catching that train tomorrow night. I already have an exit visa.'

His eyebrows climbed into his hairline: 'Is it stamped – for entry into Austria?'

I shook my head.

'Have you seen the queue outside the Austrian Embassy?' he asked. 'Those people will be there all night.'

'I know – I'm going there now.'

'Wait a minute.'

I waited, hoping, and half knowing what he was going to do. Embassy staff are the same the world over. They all know their counterparts, and the world of diplomacy trains them to help each other where they can, knowing that a favour done today will be returned tomorrow.

He was back within ten minutes: 'Come on – we'll go in my car.'

We avoided the main thoroughfares and drove through the back streets. They were expecting us at the Austrian Embassy. A side door opened quickly and closed tight behind us. I produced my exit visa and trembled while it was examined. The man read every word of it – *twice*. Then he said: 'This visa is different from those issued this morning. No one in the crowd outside has a visa similar to this.'

I had my answer prepared: 'I happened to have a visa already,' I said. 'It is still current. The Ministry of the Interior said I could use that as it was still valid. It saved them making out a new one.'

He looked at me for a very long time. He had grey eyes, set quite deep, fair hair receding at the temples, flecked here and there with strands of silver. When he removed his spectacles there was a small indentation across the bridge of his nose where the frames had rested. He seemed tired, but not *too* tired to take an interest. 'They said that, did they?' he asked softly.

I nodded. My mouth was too dry to speak.

He polished the lenses of his glasses with a handkerchief, watching me carefully with a thoughtful expression on his face. Then he replaced his spectacles and resumed his examination of the visa. 'You will be staying in Vienna?' he asked, almost absentmindedly.

'No. I am going on to Frankfurt – I have friends there.'

At least that was true – not that my friends were expecting me. I pushed my hands deep into my coat pockets in case he noticed how badly I was trembling. Not that he missed much – with or without his spectacles.

Then, unexpectedly, he smiled – first at me and then at my boss. 'It is good to have friends,' he said in the same soft voice, 'in times like these.'

My boss said, 'It is good to have friends at any time.'

I smiled, or at least I tried to, but my face muscles were stiff with tension and I guessed the colour had drained from my cheeks. My voice had deserted me too, because I had to cough quite loudly to clear my throat. Then I said: 'My friend's name is Guenther Mueller. He is a dentist.' After which I volunteered Guenther's address. I don't know *why* I did. I just felt a compulsion to talk – to say and do anything which might divert attention away from the visa.

The man put a finger to his lips. 'It is not necessary for me to know that,' he said. Then he hesitated: 'If you will allow me to give you some advice? Just answer what is asked – that is enough. Anything else betrays your anxieties.'

I nodded and the colour flooded back to my face. 'Of course,' I stammered. 'Thank you. Thank you very much.'

He stamped my visa and handed it to me. 'Bon voyage,' he said with a smile.

I could have kissed him, but my boss had the good sense to take my elbow and lead me to the door.

'Thank you,' I said again over my shoulder, 'thank you very much.'

The man inclined his head in the faintest suggestion of a bow. Then I lost sight of him as the door closed and we hurried down the passage to the side entrance.

When we were in the car my boss said, 'He didn't believe a word of it.'

'I know.' I was close to tears again, a mixture of relief and gratitude.

'Remember his advice, Mila – and I'll give you some more if you will let me.'

I looked at him and waited.

'Make sure a few people see you off at the station,' he said. 'Not a big party – that would draw attention – but don't go alone. Individuals will be even more conspicuous.'

I knew he was right. I hadn't thought that far ahead, but as soon as he said it I knew it was good advice. I reached across and squeezed his arm: 'I'll remember, and thanks. It is good to have friends – in times like these.'

He smiled: 'It is good to have friends at any time.'

I went to see Eva at the Mexican Embassy and asked her to call at my home in the evening. One look at my face told her what I was going to do. She nodded sadly, and said she would call at about seven.

Then I returned to my father's apartment. With the exception of Stan, I loved my father more than anyone and anything in the world, and I was going away from him. I was leaving the country illegally, *if* I left at all. Running away to live with a married man – to become someone's *mistress*! Nothing could be more likely to incur his disapproval, or to break his heart. But he said not a word about his own feelings. We drank coffee and talked for an hour or more. He promised to come to the National Bank with me in the morning. Then I left for my home, and George.

George said a lot that afternoon, and most of it hurt. It was *meant* to hurt. He was in the sitting-room, waiting for me when I arrived, and I barely had a chance to sit down before he started – and once George gets started he is very hard to stop. He said everything possible to make me change my mind.

'You're a fool Mila. You know you're a fool. Stan will stay in England with his wife.'

'*No!* You don't *know* Stan. He will come.'

'Rubbish! He will *never* come for you. Can't you understand that? It would ruin him. Financially, professionally – his whole *life* is football –'

'He *will* –'

'You little idiot. Are you completely mad? To have an affair is one thing. For a man to leave his family, his friends, his position, his country – '

'George, *please*! I'm going – '

'Illegally! You're going illegally! And you will go to prison when you come back.'

'No – '

'For God's sake, will you *listen to me*. Do you know how much money you'll have? Do you know what you can take?'

'It – it was in the newspaper – '

'So? How much?'

'Nine dollars.'

'Nine dollars! That's all you are allowed to take. For heaven's sake – in Vienna a cup of coffee will cost you nine dollars! Then what will you do?'

'I don't know – not yet. Perhaps Stan – '

'Stan will damn well stay put. You'll starve! Can't you get that into your head? And when you've starved long enough you'll come running back – '

'George, *please*!'

I was on the verge of tears again – frightened I suppose – even, for a split second, frightened that he might be right. And frightened because I had never seen George like this: angry, desperate, he was scared too in a way. I tried to calm him but nothing I said would satisfy him, so I fled to my room. And when Eva came an hour or so later, George called up the stairs after her: 'Try to talk some sense into her.'

But Eva did nothing of the kind. In fact she sat in a chair and smoked the best part of a cigarette before she even spoke. Then she said, 'I've come to help you pack.'

Pack? I hadn't even thought about it. Packing, money, the invasion: nothing really registered. Only one thing was important – to be on that train tomorrow night.

Eva went through my wardrobe, suggesting this and discarding that, while my poodle sat on the bottom of the bed listening, watching me, wagging his tail. He was someone else I would have to leave behind.

Eva did most of the packing. Not that there was much to pack. Each passenger was restricted to two suitcases. Two suitcases and nine dollars. Not much with which to start a new life. Not much of a dowry for Stan. But without Eva even the two suitcases might not have been packed. I was nervy and jumpy after the scene with George; sick with worry, chain smoking, quite unable to concentrate on anything. I worried about the police checks at the station, worried about my visa, worried about Stan.

After Eva's departure the night dragged on interminably. I hardly slept a wink and was up at first light to run a bath – simultaneously dreading the day and yet anxious for it to start.

Father accompanied me to the National Bank. The precious visa had to be produced to obtain the nine dollars, which was the maximum foreign currency allowed to any citizen leaving the country. We queued for hours, inching steadily forward, not talking much, taut with nerves. Then it was my turn. I passed my passport and visa through the metal grill, together with my cheque for nine dollars. Father said something about the weather, making conversation, trying to make me relax, trying to appear casual and normal. I gripped his hand and tried to respond, but my knees trembled and I felt terribly sick. The bank official eyed me through the grill, then checked my face against the passport photograph. Then he gave me the nine dollars! Oh, the relief! I can't describe it. I stuffed the money into my handbag and turned to go.

'Stop! One moment please.'

I froze. Father shifted his grip to my elbow. We turned and walked slowly back to the counter.

The clerk smiled and held out my visa. 'You left this behind. Take better care of it. You will need it tonight.'

Father had to drive home – I was still shaking. George poured me a brandy when we arrived, but even so it took me twenty minutes to stop trembling. And that was just the *bank*! What would I be like tonight? I would never get past the police at the station.

George was different during those last few hours. More like the old George. He made no further attempts to dissuade me. It was as if he had reconciled himself to the idea of my going. But he was still convinced I would come back. He made jokes about it – not unkindly; perhaps he had saved the last reserves of his considerable patience to help us all through the pain of parting. And it did help – it helped a very great deal.

Eva arrived. It was almost time to leave. I went up to my room for the very last time. I had separated my jewellery earlier that morning. Two little piles – one, gifts from George; the other, family heirlooms or presents from other people. I left everything George had given me. It was the least I could do. If he had made a bad bargain with me, at least he would get his money back. Besides it would have seemed wrong to go to Stan, wearing gifts from another man.

I cuddled my dog goodbye. Father carried my suitcases down to his car. Then he drove us all to the station. I never looked back – at our house, at my home, or at my dog who I knew would be watching from the window. I kept my eyes front, and tightened my resolve for the ordeal which lay ahead.

Police and soldiers were everywhere. And those were the ones you could see. There would be others in the crowd – plain clothes men – listening, watching, noting this and remembering that. And the crowd was enormous. Far, far too many people to be able to travel on one train. Thousands of people, scrambling and shoving their way around the concourse; talking, shouting, waving, kissing, crying. We linked hands and arms, father carrying one suitcase, George the other, and fought our way through the scrum as best we could.

It was seven fifteen: forty-five minutes before the train was due to leave. We thought we had allowed plenty of time, but we knew we were mistaken before we reached the first barrier. Rumours reached us from all sides. The train had been overbooked! Everyone was saying the same thing. Even people whose papers *were* in order could not be guaranteed a place on the train.

'But I booked a sleeper,' I complained to an official.

He was answering a dozen questions at once, trying to stem the rising tide of panic, doing his best to reassure – but with little success. I could hardly believe it. After all this! *Not* to be able to get a place on the train.

Desperation overcame everything. George hurled my cases at an official. I slammed my papers down on a policeman's desk. 'Hurry, *please* hurry.'

'But this visa – '

'*Please*. Didn't you hear what he said? My sleeper will be taken and – '

'Everything in good time.'

'But there isn't time.' Suddenly I was knocked half-way across his desk, pushed by the crowd behind. People really were panicking. Another few minutes and the crowd would turn into a mob. Father fought to give me some space. Eva was in danger of being crushed against the barrier next to me.

'This visa is different – ' the policeman began.

'It's stamped, isn't it?' I demanded angrily. Hopelessness gave me courage. I glared at the policeman. I could *feel* his uncertainty. The crowd behind me shouted and pushed and screamed for attention. Then the miracle happened. The policeman handed me the visa and passport – and waved me on, to make space for the next passenger.

I was saying goodbye. Crying, kissing father, pleading with him to make mother understand. Hugging Eva, kissing George, collecting my cases and staggering down the platform, buffeted on all sides by other anxious passengers. My ticket designated a specific carriage, but one look told me it was hopeless. The train was packed tight. People were jammed together like animals in a cattle truck. *God, I was too late!* There was no space at all, not even room to stand.

'Mila! Mila – over *here*!'

I turned and saw Milos, a friend of mine, squeezed tight against a window. 'Give me your cases,' he shouted. 'Here – pass them through the window.'

He fought for elbow room inside the carriage, and lowered a window. I hoisted a case as high as I could. But it was too heavy – I couldn't raise it high enough. Suddenly stronger arms were lifting it, pushing it through the window. I turned and found Eugene, another friend, already hoisting the second case. Then he grabbed my elbow and pulled me into the carriage after him.

There were so many friends on that train. More than twelve hundred people made that journey – on a train designed to carry three hundred when full! My mind was a blur. Sorrow at leaving my father so hurriedly. I had meant to say so much to him – and most of it was still unsaid. I had planned to ask Eva to say goodbye for me to so many people. And I had wanted to thank George for his generosity and understanding.

The night wore on. The train stopped at every field. Usually the journey to Vienna is along a straight line drawn through southern Bohemia, but we made a huge detour to travel through Bratislava, the capital of Slovakia, to avoid Russian troops on the south Bohemian border. Whenever we stopped we expected troops to board the train, with orders to turn it back to Prague. But the miles passed and we drew steadily nearer to the Austrian border.

I spent most of the time wedged in a corner, standing on one leg. People sang and told stories to keep their spirits up. Not many wanted to talk about what we were leaving behind.

And then, at three in the morning, we reached the border. We braced ourselves for the inevitable officials. But none came. We were waved through by smiling Czech faces. Suddenly I realized something. Hardly any of my friends on board would have qualified for the *official* reasons to make the journey. None of them was on State business, none of them was a foreigner cut off by the invasion. On the contrary, many were writers and artists; many had spoken out on television or in the Press against the fiercer restrictions of communism. Most had supported Dubček's aspirations during the Prague Spring. *That* was the reason for the detour to avoid the Russian troops. It occurred to me that the whole train was a Czech conspiracy – a final thumbing of noses at the Russian invaders. But before I had chance to pursue the idea we were in Austria – and free.

Milos emerged from a ruck of people with a bottle of slivovice to toast the future. Excitement shone from people's faces. Further down the train a crowd of people broke into song. A shiver ran up my spine. I was an illegal immigrant. I looked out into the night and wondered what my new life would bring.

Stan

It took me twenty hours to reach Nuremberg. Then I caught another train to Frankfurt, where I managed to board a flight to Manchester. The first thing I saw upon landing was a newspaper placard: 'Stanley Matthews still trapped behind Iron Curtain.' It dashed my hopes of a quiet homecoming. But I scurried through Customs and managed to avoid the Press. Then I collected my car from the car-park and drove back to Blackpool.

I was worried sick about Mila. The interrupted telephone conversation just made things worse. I *thought* she said she was going to see her dentist – which meant she would try to escape. But how? I imagined all sorts of things. I saw a film once about the Berlin Wall, showing East Germans being shot on the wire. The scenes from that film kept going round in my head, until I could stand it no longer. Half-way to Blackpool I stopped the car and tried to telephone her again – but all lines to Prague were dead! So I continued the journey home. Even now I only remember part of that journey. I drove in a daze, and it was a miracle I arrived without having an accident.

I might have told Betty that night. I was screwing myself up to get it over and done with – say what *had* to be said – but friends were at the house when I arrived, so the opportunity was lost. By morning the moment had passed. I was a mess of nerves and the prospect of a scene sent shudders through me, so I left the house as soon as I could.

I took refuge in work and travelling. I sponsored a health food in those days, and my prolonged stay in Czechoslovakia had disrupted the tour which had been planned for me. So I plunged into the back-log of appearances to which I was committed. I was glad to be doing something. It occupied my mind and took me away from Blackpool and my home.

Then I heard from my brother Arthur. I was in Darlington of all places, staying at an hotel to make a sponsorship appearance the following morning. Arthur telephoned and said simply, 'I've heard from Mila. She is in Vienna.'

Mila

I telephoned Arthur as soon as I reached Vienna. It was a magical moment. I was free and in the West. I had two suitcases and nine dollars, and nothing else in the world, but I was *free* and on my way to Stan.

I think Stan had forgotten giving me Arthur's telephone number. It was in the rush during that last terrible day at Karlsbad. Funny, but when I spoke to Arthur I expected him to put me through to Stan there and then – as if Stan was waiting on an extension and Arthur was some kind of telephonist. Mad, I know, but I was light-headed enough to expect almost anything. I was giggly with happiness. I almost vamped Arthur on the telephone and was tempted to say, 'Hello Darling, this is your wife-to-be calling you.' But I restrained myself. After all, he *was* a sixty-year-old bachelor – there was no telling what the shock would do.

I was lucky in Vienna. Some other Czechs had borrowed a car and were driving to Germany, and they offered me a lift to Karlsruhe. It was a fantastically good omen. I spent some of my precious nine dollars on badly needed cigarettes and we set off.

Behind me lay my parents, my husband, my dog, my friends, my possessions – and probably the Czech authorities with a warrant for my arrest. As I saw it, if I was an illegal emigrant the converse must apply: I must also be an illegal immigrant in the Federal Republic of Germany. My Czech passport would almost certainly be on somebody's wanted list. I was a fugitive! But somehow, right at that moment, none of that mattered. It sounds corny and trite – like a teenager on her way to her first date – but all that really mattered was that I was on my way to a new life with, of all people, a footballer – a man I had never even heard of a year before.

Stan

Things happened fast after that. At least they did in Karlsruhe, due probably to a mixture of German efficiency and Mila's determination. By the time I went over to see her a week later, all sorts of things had happened. For a start she had a job – with the American Army. When I got over the shock of picturing her in uniform she told me it was an administrative job, dealing with schools for the children of American service personnel. But the job was just the start of it. She had also negotiated a lease on an apartment, and on top of that she was half-way towards getting a German passport. I had guessed she was the efficient sort, from what I knew of her job at the American Embassy in Prague, but to have accomplished so much so quickly took my breath away. I was speechless with admiration – I tell you, Mila at full steam is a powerhouse of organizational energy.

But the most important thing was just her being there – free and in Germany – safe and waiting for me. I was so relieved to see her that I very nearly stayed there for good. That's what I wanted to do. Make a clean break and start a new life with Mila in Germany. But we had to be practical. I had business affairs to settle in England, not to mention getting a divorce. So after a wonderful reunion, I returned to England.

Mila

I *did* work fast in Germany. Well, I had to – you can't live long on nine dollars. But I had other reasons, not that I discussed them with Stan. Fleeing from Czechoslovakia had been an act of desperation. Of course I was deliriously happy to be in Germany and closer to Stan, but on the other hand I had never *planned* to leave Prague in the way I did. In fact I would not have done so had the Russians not invaded. But once they occupied Prague it meant I might never see Stan again – and I couldn't risk that. However I could hardly claim to be a political refugee, nor did I seek to be labelled one. So as soon as I had caught my breath I wrote to the authorities in Prague, admitting that I had left illegally, but explaining why – and asking that my departure be given official blessing. It was to be the start of a long battle.

But that wasn't the main reason for organizing my life at such a furious pace. The main reason was Stan. After all, he still had not discussed divorce with his wife, or even with his solicitor. I knew how he felt about me, I knew he wanted a divorce, but he still hadn't grasped the nettle. And you have to *know* Stan to understand why. He can be painfully shy – much more so then than he is now – and his shyness showed itself in various ways. Perhaps the most revealing was that he abhorred (and still does) anyone making a fuss, either of him or in his company. It's not that he gets embarrassed, it's worse than that, he actually gets physically ill. Stanley is *exactly* what he appears to be, a quiet, modest and unassuming man. It is one of the many nice things about him – that none of the fame and adulation ever went to his head. A fuss simply distresses him, and any kind of a scene would just be unthinkable. Physically and emotionally he would be a wreck.

I knew the kind of mental turmoil Stan was going through when I reached Germany, and I was determined not to add to his strain. So right from the off I set about establishing my financial independence. My salary supported me, and although my rented apartment was modest it was comfortable enough. I made no claims upon Stan and did my best to ensure that I never added to his worries.

Of course I wanted him to join me, but if we were to share any future happiness I knew he would have to come to me because he wanted to, not because he felt he *had* to - that he was obligated in some way because I had left my home in Prague. That would have been the worse possible thing for both of us. He knew how I felt, but the decision had to be his - I could not make it for him, nor did I want to. All I could do was wait. And hope, of course - I seem to remember doing quite a lot of that.

Stan

I was thankful for one thing. That my children had grown up and left home. They were making their own way in the world, and whatever I did about Mila, although it might hurt them, would not disrupt their lives or damage their future. It was a comforting thought, and one I clung to during the next few weeks. Which left only Betty. She would be upset. But needlessly so, because our marriage was dead – that was obvious not only to us but to close friends like Charlie Chester and Doretta his wife. Neither Betty nor I was happy with the other – so why prolong a relationship which had so clearly broken down? The way I saw it, at least Betty had *a chance* of happiness without me, whereas with me she was almost guaranteed a life of misery. I had enough money for us both to be comfortable – so why not make the break as painlessly as possible? But deep down I knew that no matter how logical my argument, irrespective of what financial settlement I offered, and in face of all inducements, any suggestion of a divorce would be bitterly opposed. And it was the thought of all that bitterness which I found so upsetting.

Days passed – *weeks* passed – and still I did nothing. I must have been an impossible person to meet, let alone live with. I brooded endlessly. Charlie's advice weighed me down one day, and mother's encouragement lifted me the next. The arguments ran round and round inside my head. After all, I would ask myself, who was I going to make unhappy? Betty? She was unhappy anyway. And I was depressed enough to jump off Blackpool Pier. Then there were other things to think about. Like where would Mila and I live? England would be impossible – at least to begin with. The newspapers would crucify us. Mila would be painted as a scarlet woman and I would be branded as callous and unfeeling.

Then, one day, something snapped inside me. I just upped and left. There was nothing dramatic about it, no blazing row or anything like that, but I knew I risked everything if I stayed a moment longer – my health, even my sanity, and a chance of a *future* with Mila. I was fifty-three years old. How many years would be left to me? I decided that however many there were I couldn't spend them like this.

I never said anything – just packed a suitcase and threw some papers into a case. It was done too quickly to be given much thought. I crammed all sorts of stuff into that briefcase – share certificates, bank statements, contracts, sponsorship agreements – everything which came to hand during a mad half-hour of packing. Then I left home – for good.

Mila

Stanley flew into Frankfurt on 9 November 1968, and we have lived together ever since. And, thank goodness, we have been happy. Ecstatically so at times, despite the problems – and believe me we've had our share. But somehow we always see the funny side of a situation, and if that doesn't send us into hysterics at least it starts us chuckling – and worries become much more manageable when you laugh at them.

Like money worries, for example. When Stan arrived in Germany he hadn't the faintest idea how much money we would have to live on. Not that we cared to begin with. We were too busy floating on cloud nine to think about *money*. But after celebrating for a week it seemed prudent to enquire about the more mundane things in life, like how would we eat, where would we live, and did I have to hock my jewellery?

Stanley emptied his briefcase. Honestly I have seen neater waste-paper tubs. Everything was screwed up, creased, dog-eared or torn. I had to press half the papers with an iron before they were legible. But some of them impressed me. Like fifteen thousand one-pound shares in Rolls-Royce for example. That was Stan's largest single investment, and it seemed to me that owning shares in Rolls-Royce was even better than driving one. At least it did until they went bust – but who was to know that at the time?

Obviously Stan's wife was entitled to share in his assets, and Stan wrote to his solicitor instructing him to file for a divorce and to offer a very generous settlement. He did not mention me in the letter, so his solicitor had precious little to work on, but at least Stan had set the wheels in motion.

Meanwhile we started to think about *where* we could live. Stan was convinced that we would be hunted down like criminals once the Press got hold of the story of him leaving home. So we had to find somewhere quiet and off the beaten track, at least in the short term. We considered

Cyprus for a while, but then a man in my office mentioned Malta. He had been there at the end of the war and, according to him, it was beautiful. So we began to wonder what life would be like on a Mediterranean island?

Stan

It was like going into exile in a way – voluntary exile perhaps, but exile none the less. True, I had visited most countries in the world, but I had never *lived* abroad. The future would certainly be different from the past. For a start, for the first time in thirty-eight years, I wouldn't be getting all keyed up about the match on Saturday.

Oddly enough, thinking about where we would live made me think about England. I doubt I had ever thought of it before, not consciously. I was English, so I lived in England, that's all there was to it – at least it was until I asked myself what it *meant* to me. Then I realized it was a lot more important than that.

Playing for England, for a start. That was always a thrill, and an honour. I can remember the very first time. It was in 1934 and I was nineteen. I was in my father's barber's shop when a pal of his came in: 'Stan,' he said, 'you've been picked for England!' I couldn't believe it. I rushed down to the corner to buy a paper. There it was in black and white: 'Matthews chosen for England.' I tell you I was so proud I was speechless, even when I got back to father's shop – not from running but emotion. And father was proud too, even though he did his best to hide it.

The match was against Wales at Cardiff, and I was so nervous I could hardly think straight. I was sick of course, but even that failed to calm me down. I would have given anything *not* to play that day. Before the other players as much as took their shoes off I was fully changed and huddled into a corner of the dressing-room – wishing I was dead and trying to think of a way out of it. Then a man by the name of Roy Johns performed a miracle. Roy had been our goalkeeper at Stoke before being transferred to Preston, and he was playing for Wales that day. About half an hour before kick-off he came into the England dressing-room, looking for me. When he found me in the corner he wrapped a huge, gorilla-like arm over my shoulders and said, 'Don't be scared, Stan. These interntionals get better as they go on. You won't want to come off at the finish.'

Thank heavens for people like Roy Johns. I was still nervous but the feeling of panic lifted. Roy kept talking, about it just being another game and that kind of thing. He was so calm and so positive. Then he went back to the Welsh dressing-room to get changed.

In the event we took Wales apart. Freddie Tilson and Eric Brook were in great form. They got three goals between them, and a minute into the second half I crashed a fourth past Roy. Imagine that, I had scored in my first international! It was the stuff dreams are made of. I was too excited to spare a thought for Roy. He came into the dressing-room afterwards and grumbled: 'Next time I waste sympathy on the likes of you – shut me up will you!'

We swapped jerseys and shook hands, and even though Roy must have been nursing feelings of disappointment, he put on a great act of being disgruntled with me. I could never thank him properly, but I promised myself one thing: if the chance ever came my way to encourage a frightened kid I would take it, and I hoped I might do it with as much grace and kindness as Roy showed to me. And of course chances *did* come later and I told countless frightened young players about my first international, and the story of how *I* was helped also helped them. I was always nervous before a big game, but thanks to Roy I was never gripped by that terrible fear again.

But while sitting in Mila's apartment in Germany I remembered much more than just playing football. I remembered *England* – and all the kindnesses and the honours which had been showered upon me. Like getting my CBE and my Knighthood, for example.

Harold Macmillan was Prime Minister when I was awarded the CBE. That was an enormous honour – not just for me but for the game of football. It was the final accolade, or so I thought at the time. But there was more to come. In 1965 I was knighted. After the ceremony at Buckingham Palace I was taken to tea at the House of Commons by Dennis Howell, the Minister of Sport. He told me how it all came about.

'The Prime Minister sent for me,' he said (the Prime Minister being Harold Wilson, of course). '"Dennis," said the Prime Minister, "I've been thinking about Stanley Matthews. He goes all over the world playing football. He's a marvellous ambassador for the country. It's time he had a knighthood."'

Dennis Howell was taken aback: 'But Prime Minister, he's already got the CBE.'

'I know all about that,' Wilson said, 'But it's not enough.'

Howell was frankly doubtful about the awarding of further honours, and said so.

'Leave it to me,' said Wilson.

Some weeks later Dennis Howell was again summoned to Number Ten. 'That knighthood for Stanley Matthews,' said Wilson. 'The Honours Committee have approved it.' Then he grinned, 'But do you know what one of them said? "But Mr Prime Minister – Matthews was never *captain* of England."'

Both Harold Wilson and Dennis Howell thought that was very funny. I remember Dennis laughing when he told me, and some months later I was invited to Number Ten, where Harold Wilson told me the story himself: 'Never captain of England,' he said, 'I ask you – what do you think of that?'

So there I was – *Sir* Stanley Matthews, CBE. It was all a long way from a barber's shop in Hanley. It was sad that father never lived to see it, but I know what he would have said, 'That's very nice, Stanley, but no fuss now – remember that.' And I have, all my life.

After that, there were so many honours. I even had lunch at Buckingham Palace with the Queen and the Duke of Edinburgh. That was an amazing experience. What staggered me was how at ease I felt. I arrived, all knotted up with nerves, convinced I would use the wrong cutlery with the wrong dish, daft things like that, but within minutes I was chatting away as if I lunched there every day of my life. Both the Queen and the Duke of Edinburgh have an astonishing ability to draw people out. They are so natural themselves, and so interested in other people, that you forget to be nervous. You never quite forget who *they* are of course, but they are so completely without what the English call 'side' that you feel you've known them all your life. At least I did. They project so much warmth that even the most nervous people are reassured. Like the Queen's words when she knighted me: 'Still enjoying your football, Sir Stanley?' she asked. I doubt that anyone else heard her, she spoke so quietly, but there it was again – that friendliness which is so characteristic of her.

After lunch I thought the Duke was playing a gag on me. Well, maybe not a *gag*, but he seemed to be up to something. It was after the meal, when we were standing in the anti-room where coffee is served. I had just taken a sip when I heard a noise behind me. Half-way between a 'psst' and an 'ah-hem', if you know what I mean. Someone was trying to attract my attention – and when I swung round I saw the Duke. I was astonished. He was talking to some other guests a few yards away. He half turned away from me, but as he did I heard it again – 'psst!' I didn't know what to do. The Duke laughed and *seemed* to look in my direction, but he gave no sign of wanting me to join him. I decided I had imagined it and turned back to my coffee. 'Psst!' There it was again – unmistakable. Crikey, the Duke of Edinburgh wasn't supposed to say 'psst' was he? Then I felt a touch on my elbow. I swivelled round and a footman emerged from behind a pillar. He said, 'I'm not supposed to ask for autographs, but if you give me yours I'll give you a copy of the menu.' I almost choked with relief and agreed.

The footman whispered, 'Meet me in the car-park afterwards,' then he glided off and out of sight. But his touch on the elbow had been just in time. I was so agitated that within a second I would have been across the room to ask the Duke what he wanted. I met the footman afterwards. He turned out to be a Chelsea Supporter. I might have known a Chelsea supporter would nearly get me locked up in the Tower.

Mind you, he wouldn't be the first Palace official to get me into trouble. Another one did – this time at the Palace of Westminster. It was just before the World Cup in 1966 and a special sportsman's service was being held at Westminster Abbey. I was asked to act as flag bearer – another great honour and one that I could not possibly refuse.

Naturally the service was held on a Sunday and I motored down from Port Vale early in the morning with Jackie Mudie and Jimmy O'Neal, who played in goal for us at Port Vale. We arrived at the Abbey two hours before the service – partly because I am rarely late for anything, but mainly because I was anxious to find out what my duties were. An official met us at the Abbey and took us inside. Then he explained that I was to sit in the front row until the service ended, then I was to stand up, mount some steps, cross to a curtained niche behind the alter, collect the flag, turn about and carry the flag the length of the Abbey and out of the front doors. Outside I would hand the flag to another official and my ceremonial duties would be over. It sounded easy enough and the official was suitably reassuring: 'We'll go through it in detail later,' he said. 'Don't worry. I shall be sitting beside you, so I'll tell you when it's your turn.'

So, with nothing more to do, Jackie, Jimmy and I went for a stroll in the grounds until the service began. When it did the Abbey was packed. There were sports stars and personalities from every country in the world, and not just footballers – every sport imaginable was represented. Conrad Hunte, the West Indian cricketer, read the lesson, and very well he did it too. But what worried me was the absence of *my* official. The seat beside me remained empty.

I sat there in a mounting fever of anxiety. Surely the man would turn up soon? But the service progressed and the seat next to me remained conspicuously empty. I told myself he would return at any second – but he never did. In fact I never saw him again.

Then came a moment of silence. Nobody was doing anything. The sermon had been preached, the lesson read, the hymns sung. *It must be over?* It must be my turn! But still no official. I tell you, by this time I was beyond sweating – I was cold with fear.

I stood up and took a pace forward. My spine tingled as I imagined thousands of eyes watching my back. I climbed the steps. There was no sign of the flag! *No sign of it!* No official, no flag – just me stuck up in the front of Westminster Abbey, wishing the ground would open up and swallow me. But I was beyond the point of no return. I could hardly go back to my seat and pretend nothing had happened. I crossed to the curtained niche. Still no sign of the flag! Crikey. I took a deep breath and plunged my hands through a gap in the curtains. Whatever prayers I might have offered up during the service were nothing compared to the fervent prayer I offered then. I was ready to jump right through the curtains in the hope of escaping the back way. But then it happened – somebody thrust the flag into my hands. I never saw who was behind the curtain, but that didn't matter – I had the flag – that was all that mattered! I took a step backwards, swung the flag up, turned about and marched out of the Abbey. I was too relieved to be angry. I went *limp* with relief. I suppose I might have given that official a piece of my mind, but I never set eyes on him again. Goodness knows what became of him. Maybe staying out of my way was the best thing he could do. After all, the panic was over by then.

Anyway, there I was in Germany, sitting in Mila's apartment nursing thoughts of England. It wasn't that I regretted leaving – after all, I *wanted* to make a new life with Mila more than anything – it was just that England had been good to me and I didn't want people saying I had walked out without a word of thanks. I couldn't explain then, but I hoped I might be able to one day – and now that day is here.

Meanwhile various reporters had recognized me, so it seemed best to move on. When Mila described what she had learned about Malta – well, that seemed the place to go next.

Mila

We planned to slip into Malta like a couple of ghosts. The whole idea was to have a quiet look at the island, to see if we liked it and would enjoy living there. But the prime requisite was *no publicity*. Stan was having another fit of jitters about the Press and I must admit I was anxious to avoid being labelled Stan's mistress in the newspapers. So it was all very hush-hush and we almost tip-toed into the airport at Frankfurt. All went well until we embarked on the aircraft. Then Stan was recognized.

'Stanley! How are you?'

Stan shrivelled in his seat, but there was no escaping the man who bore down on us. He turned out to be an acquaintance called Monty, who was going to Malta on business. So I was introduced as 'a friend' and the three of us spent the journey together. Actually Monty was very helpful, and although Stan was evasive about a lot of things, he did admit that he might buy a house in Malta – if he and his 'friend' liked the place.

Monty said, 'You must meet George Magri. He knows *everyone*. And he will be happy to show you around.'

Well, there was no avoiding it, and when we landed at Luqa Airport we were duly introduced to George Magri who was there to meet Monty.

We liked George from the start. 'Where are you staying?' he asked.

When we told him he shook his head: 'You'll hate it there. It's on the wrong side of the island. You'll be much better off at the Sheraton.'

Which is where we decided to stay – *eventually*. But first we caught a cab to our original hotel. It seemed miles away. We bumped down one dusty lane after another. The landscape looked more and more desolate. It was like the back of beyond. Suddenly Stan said, 'Stop the cab,' and the driver dug so hard on the brakes that we nearly went through the roof. 'Head for the Sheraton,' Stan told him. That caused some excitement because turning in that little cart track was far from easy, but we survived the journey, and the Sheraton was excellent. And the best thing of all was that *nobody knew we were there!*

Stan hugged himself with glee. 'Peace, perfect peace. Even if those German reporters pick up our trail, the travel agent will say he booked us into that other hotel, and when they check we won't be there. We will have *vanished!*'

Then the telephone rang and a voice said, 'Hello Stan. It's Lewis Portelli. I'm down in the lobby, waiting to welcome you to Malta.'

Stan

.

I must admit I had forgotten all about Lewis Portelli. Well, after all I had never met the man, and what with everything else on my mind I hadn't given him a thought when we decided to visit Malta.

'How on earth did you know I was here?' I asked down the telephone.

'Friends,' he said, 'friends in high places.'

Lewis is a sports reporter. He had written to me years ago and once broadcast a telephone interview with me on his radio programme. But how on earth had he found me? That was my first experience of the Maltese bush-telegraph. The place is like a village. Everyone knows everyone else. They all have a cousin working here, a brother there, an uncle who knows so and so, or an aunt who can help. It's part of the charm of the island - once you get used to it. In fact Lewis had been tipped off by a friend at the airport. After that he simply telephoned the hotels. The Sheraton was third on his list and - lo and behold - he had found me. I had been on the island less than an hour! But if that was bad, there was worse to come.

'Stanley,' he said, 'my television show is tonight. I'd like you to be on it.'

'On television? Me?' I froze, 'You mean actually *appear*?'

'Just for ten minutes.'

I unfroze and almost dropped the telephone. When I thought of how careful we had been! All the secret arrangements . . . and now this - now he wanted me on *television*. I told Mila not to move, then I dashed down to see Lewis.

'Lewis,' I said, 'I can't appear on television for ten minutes.'

'Have *more* than ten minutes. Have the whole show. I'm sure my producer will agree - '

'No, you misunderstand. I can't appear *at all*!'

Lewis might have looked more hurt if I had kicked him - but I doubt it. I took him by the elbow and led him to the quietest corner I could find. 'Nobody is supposed to know where I am,' I told him. 'It's a *secret* visit.'

He looked at me as if I was mad. Then he explained about the Maltese bush telegraph. 'Your visit isn't secret,' he said. 'The morning papers will report your arrival. The whole island will know by tomorrow.'

I groaned and we talked some more before I went back up to Mila. 'Did you fix it?' she asked.

'We did a deal.'

'Oh, what a relief. For a moment I thought – '

'That I'd be on television. Well, you were right. I'm on in half an hour.'

On the way back from the studio to the Sheraton, I confided in Lewis about 'my friend' who was still locked in her room. He was very understanding and promised to help in every way possible. I gambled on his discretion – and it paid off, because Lewis never let me down and, together with George Magri, was largely responsible for easing Mila and me into life in Malta.

We liked the island from the start – and the people. Wherever we went the Maltese were unfailingly helpful and courteous. They went out of their way to make us feel at home. Not only that but the weather was marvellous and very soon Mila and I made up our minds to live there.

About a week after we arrived, Lewis was back again. Apparently a big football match was to be played at the Stadium the following week. Lewis wondered if I would play in a curtain raiser. 'Just a friendly game,' he said apologetically. 'The crowd will be small by your standards, but – '

A game of football! What more could I ask? Of course I agreed to play.

The big day duly arrived and Lewis took me to the Stadium. I was changing into my gear in the dressing-room when a priest came in. Now the Maltese take their football very seriously, but even so I was a bit surprised to see a priest in the dressing-room. Still, I had seen the other team by then and I thought we would need all the help we could get – if a prayer helped I was all for it. But then another priest came in, and another – and soon you couldn't *move* for priests. They all said hello and shook my hand. Then they introduced themselves. They were my team-mates. I was playing for *a team of priests*!

I took Lewis aside and asked him about it. He said, 'They are more like teachers than priests. They teach at my old school. St Michael's College.'

'But what do I call them?'

'By their names. Brother Charles, Brother David, Brother Ralph. . . .'

And so the Brothers and I went out to play football. Calling for the ball was a bit of a mouthful. 'Brother Ralph – pass it to Brother David!' 'Quick, Brother Charles – inside to Brother Henry.' 'Good shot, Brother William!' And once, when I was exasperated, I shouted, '*Oh Brother!*' and they all came running. But they knew a thing or two about football and we had a really good game.

After the match Lewis Portelli had arranged a little reception at his villa, and I was invited, with instructions to bring 'my friend'. By then Mila had met Lewis, so at least that wouldn't present a problem, but we were a bit worried about meeting all the Brothers in a social gathering. But our anxiety was needless. We got on like a house on fire and the Brothers became our firmest friends.

Mila

The Brothers almost adopted us after that first meeting. They invited us to lunch at the college the following week, and from then on we were always in their company. Within the month Stan became a regular member of their five-a-side team and the Brothers became part of our lives. Nothing was said about my relationship with Stan, not to begin with anyway, although when we knew them better we explained some of the problems surrounding Stan's divorce and how these things can drag out in England. They were very understanding, and in fact Brother Charles, the College Principal, made a marvellous suggestion. He said, 'If you don't want people to know where you are, please feel free to use this address. We will be happy to act as a post-box for you.' So from then on whenever Stan wrote to England his address was simply 'The St Michael's College of Christian Brotherhood, MALTA.' Not only that, but our other friends like Lewis and George co-operated too, so that anyone who arrived on the island looking for Stan was directed towards the Brothers. It seemed such a simple solution at the time, but it was to have some unexpected consequences.

By then we had firmly decided to settle in Malta, so we took a short lease on a flat in Mosta while we searched for a place to buy. The Brothers came up most nights and we played cards – or at least we did until Stanley caught them cheating! The Brothers thought it was uproariously funny, but Stan was outraged. 'You – Priests, and you *cheat* at cards!' he stormed. But the more indignant he got the funnier it seemed to everyone else. Imagine six priests falling about, clutching their middles while tears ran down their cheeks – and Stan looking on in horrified amazement. What made it worse was that I thought it funny too. Stan got over it in the end, but it took us the rest of the evening to persuade him to speak to us.

December arrived and we spent our first Christmas together, and on New Year's Eve we insisted upon taking the Brothers out to dinner. We went to the Hilton and had a marvellous evening – until we had finished the meal. Then the head waiter held a whispered conversation with Stan. Stan's face creased in a worried frown as the head waiter threw anxious glances at the Brothers, who all looked very distinguished in smart lounge suits worn over their black vests and dog-collars. When Stan finished his conference with the head waiter, he checked his watch and then announced, 'I've ordered coffee in the lounge. I think we'll be more comfortable in there.'

The head waiter fairly sighed with relief, but I said, 'I'm comfortable here. Besides it's such a dead atmosphere in the lounge.'

Just then it was announced that the cabaret would start in ten minutes. Now if there is one thing I enjoy, it is cabaret, so I settled very firmly in my chair and encouraged the others to do the same. But the head waiter hopped up and down with nervous agitation and Stan insisted that we move to the lounge. 'It will be much too noisy in here,' he said.

'But it's New Year's Eve,' I complained. 'Stan, you said it would be a party.'

By now the head waiter was actually trying to take my chair from under me. I swear he would have carried me out of the dining-room, chair and all, had I not stood up. He kept muttering about our coffee getting cold, while all the time glancing nervously at the Brothers and then at his wrist watch. Meanwhile Stan was ushering the Brothers towards the door. Then he came round to give the head waiter a hand with me. 'It's the cabaret,' he hissed. 'There will be girls – *you know* – with very few clothes on. They might embarrass the Brothers.'

But the Brothers heard him. They stopped dead in their tracks, like a squad of soldiers. Then they turned about with military precision and dashed back to their chairs, grinning from ear to ear and with eyes like saucers. The poor head waiter nearly had a heart attack, and later watched in horror as the scantily clad chorus line draped themselves all over the Brothers. We all agreed afterwards that it was a great way to greet 1969.

In fact the New Year opened with some perfect news. A letter came from my father saying he had succeeded in getting an exit visa for a holiday for mother and himself – and they would be able to come to Malta for two weeks!

We spent a wonderfully happy fortnight together. They stayed with us at the Mosta flat and I could not have been more content. I had my entire family around me and they all liked each other. 1969 promised to be the happiest year of my life.

Stan

Mosta is in the centre of the island and famous for its huge church, the vast domed roof of which is apparently the largest in the world, except for St Peter's in Rome. Brother David told me that during the war a German bomb crashed through the roof at a time when the place was crammed tight with people. The bomb landed on the altar, rolled the whole length of the church, went through the open doors, and bounced down the steps outside. Even when it smashed into a cart in the road, it failed to explode. 'The power of faith,' Brother David said knowingly. I was a bit sceptical at first – after all, a man who cheats at cards will tell you almost anything – but I found out later that it was quite true.

Getting out and about in Malta was sometimes a difficult business. Our friends protected us as much as they could, but by now the Press were on to the story. Most British newspapers have correspondents in Malta and these freelance reporters hounded us continuously. Many times Mila and I walked down opposite sides of Republic Street, doing our shopping as we went, before returning to the car from different directions. We both tried to see the funny side of it, but, believe me, it can be a wearing business at times.

And then there were the official invitations. Mila was always excluded, because most people on the island were still pretending she didn't exist. I would have avoided many invitations with a polite excuse, but Mila insisted that Malta was going to be our home, and that life wouldn't always be like this. 'One day we *will* be married,' she said with all the confidence in the world. 'But you can't live like a hermit until then. You *must* go. They will accept me in time.' But she always added, with a little grin, 'I hope.'

One such invitation came from the British High Commission – to attend a reception at the High Commissioner's Residence in Valletta.

Mila and I discussed it and decided it would seem discourteous to refuse, so I accepted. But on the day of the reception, we were both very depressed. We had received a letter from my solicitor: the divorce, he warned, would be a very protracted business indeed, and he confirmed that it might be years before we could marry. It was the first time it had been spelled out, in black and white, and we were appalled at the prospect of this cloak and dagger existence continuing for such a long time. We were numb with disappointment and gloomy all morning, but finally Mila produced a scratch lunch and decided it was time we snapped out of it. So she set out to cheer me up – and to *smarten* me up. She brushed the one good suit I had brought with me, ironed a shirt and polished my shoes until they gleamed, while all the time muttering the Czech equivalent of 'a smart soldier is a happy soldier', or at least something like that. And once my clothes were ready, she started on me: 'Come on,' she ordered, 'into the bathroom. I'm going to give you a shampoo.'

I tell you, these Czechs can be bossy at times! Anyway I submitted, as much to humour her as anything else. If she was determined to look on the bright side, I could at least do the same. So I sat on a stool at the sink and let her fuss to her heart's content, prattling on in her chatterbox way about *this* shampoo and *that* friction, and that maybe she would tint some 'natural' colour back into my hair when she finished. I was face down in the sink while this was going on, so I responded with a series of encouraging grunts and let her get on with it. Alternate bowls of hot and cold water were poured over my head, and she pummelled my scalp with lathers and frictions until I tingled all over. *It was great!* After twenty minutes of that I felt much better. No matter who else might be at the reception that night, nobody would be cleaner or smarter than me. My very own Czech geisha girl was seeing to that.

Finally she finished and I sat upright while she towelled me dry. Then she took the towel away. Even with suds in my ears I could hear the horror in her voice: 'Oh, my God! Oh, God – '

'What's the matter?'

'Oh goodness! Oh Stan – '

I thought she was ill! Her face was as white as paper and her hands trembled as I took the towel from her. 'Mila, are you all right? Sit down – come over here – '

'Oh Stan – your hair!'

I turned to the mirror. Then I said it: '*Oh, my God!*' My hair was yellow! *Bright yellow!* What with my beaky nose I looked like a goldfinch. Even my throat and the back of my neck was yellow. I tell you, really *bright yellow!* The colour of a ripe grapefruit. Canary yellow!

'Oh Stan, it will come off. It *must* come off! Darling, I don't know – '

'*You* don't know?'

I looked like a freak. Something out of the circus. And I was due at the British High Commissioner's place in a few hours.

'What the heck have you done?' I demanded. 'You and your fancy shampoos. Get it off – whatever you do – get it off!'

I nearly drowned that afternoon. Mila tried everything – but nothing would shift it. Every time I turned my dripping face to the mirror I prayed for a few grey hairs. And every time my hair remained as yellow as ever. Not blond, or anything like that, but a really bold, brassy kind of *yellow!* I had a bath. I took a shower: a hot shower, a cold shower, a tepid shower. But whatever I looked into the mirror this yellow-haired freak stared back at me.

I was in despair, 'My daughter thinks I'm having a nervous break-down, my best friends think I've gone religious, and now this British Commissioner will throw me off the island.'

'Stan, stay calm – '

'*Stay calm!*' I stormed into the bedroom. It was four o'clock. The reception was at seven. *Three hours!* Maybe it would be less noticeable when I was fully dressed? Shirt and tie, trousers, socks and shoes. I slid a sly look at the bedroom mirror. My God – *I looked worse!*

I was at the front door by the time Mila said, 'Where are you going?'

'Out! Get some fresh air. I need to think – '

'Like *that*? You are going *out*?'

Back to the bedroom for a hat and coat. The only overcoat I had was the black leather one bought in South Africa. And a black leather hat to match. I crammed the trilby down over my ears, turned the coat collar up to my chin, but even then a patch of yellow showed at my throat. It took five minutes to find a scarf, and all the time Mila watched mute and wide-eyed from the open door. I rarely lose my temper, but I boiled over that day. It was the final straw somehow. I had been worrying about money, there was that letter from the solicitor, a reception to face later – *and now this!* I slammed out of the flat without a word, stamped down the stairs and out into the street. *That was a big mistake!* It was like a furnace outside. Honestly, it was like walking straight into an oven. At least ninety degrees! You could have fried eggs on the pavement. Everyone was dressed in the lightest clothes possible, and there was me kitted out for the Arctic. Even standing still brought sweat running into my eyes.

'Stanley,' somebody shouted.

I jumped like a scalded cat. Being seen like this was as bad as running naked through the streets. Worse! Now people would be *convinced* I was mad.

'Stanley,' came the shout again, and when I looked round I saw Lewis Portelli, as cool as a cucumber in an open-neck shirt, shorts and sandals on his bare feet. He said, 'I thought it was you. I'd recognize that walk anywhere.'

'Stay away,' I growled through the scarf.

He might have been pole-axed. He stopped a yard from me and peered in astonishment. 'Are you *all right* Stan?' Then his eyes widened. 'My God,' he said in tones of utter disbelief, 'That's not a *leather* coat you are wearing, is it?'

I had an inspired moment. 'I've got a cold,' I said. 'Sweating it out. It's an old footballers' trick.' I coughed for effect and hoisted the scarf up my nose.

'Really?' His concern vanished and his face lit up with interest. Lewis is a football buff. Very knowledgeable. I groaned at the thought of this latest scrap of information being added to his card index system. Next he would use it on his television show and half Valletta would be walking around in black leather coats. People would die of asphyxiation and I would be blamed.

'Got to go,' I muttered, and was about to turn back to the entrance to the flat, when I realized something. Lewis had just seen me *come out*! To go straight back in would be even further evidence of insanity. I made up my mind. I swivelled past him and began to stride down the road. Lewis caught me up: 'Where to, Stan? Can I give you a lift?'

I nearly shook my head but my hat threatened to fall off. 'No,' I said, 'I'll just take a brisk walk round the block to build up a really good sweat.'

'Ah,' Lewis nodded his understanding. Then he fell into step beside me.

It must have been a mile and a half round that block! Lewis, good friend that he is, kept me company for most of the way, but the last hundred yards finished him. When he waved goodbye he was sweating like a frightened racehorse. *He* was sweating! It was like a turkish bath inside that leather. Steam was coming out of my ears. Then I saw my car parked on the other side of the road, and that gave me an idea.

Frank! Frank was the hairdresser at the Hilton. Frank always cut my hair. Perhaps he could help?

It took me ten minutes to drive across to St Juliens, and another five to find a place in the Hilton car-park. It had turned half past four. Would Frank be there? I examined my reflection in the rear view mirror, checked that no hair was visible, then I set off for the Hilton entrance as if the devil himself was after me. Holidaymakers were everywhere. I passed a flock of bikinis and sun tans, beach wraps and bathing caps on their way to the swimming pool. The commissionaire's jaw dropped when he saw me and an unexpectedly frightened expression slid over his face as he opened the door. Not that I took much notice. I was too busy with my own problems, tugging my trilby down with one hand and keeping my collar up with the other. Crossing the lobby I remembered that the hairdressing salon has those little wooden swing doors, like they use for Western saloons in the movies. You can peer over the top to see who is inside. I planned to do just that. If the salon was empty I would go in, if it was full I would turn on my heel and get out as fast as I could.

It was *empty*! Frank had his back to me, washing his hands in one of the basins. I let out the most enormous sigh of relief and dived through the swing doors.

Frank threw himself up against the wall: 'Jesus Christ! *Mafia!*'

Suddenly the commissionaire's scared look made sense. I peeped back into the corridor. Nobody was about. I removed my hat. 'Frank,' I hissed, 'it's me.'

He lowered his hands slowly and stared hard, the look of terror melting from his face. Then his eyes boggled: 'Sir Stan? Is that *really* you?'

'Frank, you've got to help me,' I said. Then I told him about the problem about the reception at seven and all the rest of it.

To his ever-lasting credit, Frank never even smiled. But there was still a problem. Excellent hairdresser though he was, he knew nothing about hair dyes. So he had to call in the experts from the Ladies Salon next door. He was back within a minute with Pauline, the girl who did Mila's hair. She guessed what had happened immediately. Frank got my head in a bowl, and Pauline flitted in and out with bottles and creams and goodness knows what. And half an hour later my grey hair was back. It was a miracle! They even removed most of the yellow stain from my neck. I couldn't stop looking at myself – full face, left profile, right profile, back and on top with the aid of a mirror. It really was a miracle. It wasn't quite *my* grey of course, but it was good enough. A damn sight better than yellow at any rate. I thanked them both – swearing them to secrecy – put my hat and coat over my arm and hurried across the lobby. Half-way to the door I got to feeling guilty about Mila. How badly I had treated her. After all, she had only been trying to cheer me up. So I bought the largest box of chocolates in the Hilton shop, and raced back to Mosta.

Mila was laughing and crying at the same time when I told her about it. I suppose we'd had our first row. We kissed and made up, but when she ran her fingers through my hair I backed away: 'Oh no – never again – don't you dare touch my hair.'

The reception at the British High Commissioner's passed off successfully, and who should I bump into on the way out, but Lewis Portelli.

'Stan,' he said, 'I've been watching you all evening. You're *amazing*! Three hours ago you had a heavy cold – now look at you!'

'To tell the truth, Lewis,' I said, 'it's a secret remedy. One day I'll tell you about it.'

But I never did.

Mila

Stan's hair turned back to yellow the following morning. Off he went to
see Frank again, grumbling furiously as he left. And after that he called
on Frank almost every day. It took months for Stan's hair to return to
normal – he has forgiven me now, but it took a very long time.

Meanwhile, we found our dream house. A bungalow actually, overlooking Marsaxlokk, which is a fantastically beautiful fishing village.
The bungalow was only half built when we found it, so the builders
agreed to incorporate our ideas into the finished project. Stan wanted a
tennis court *and* a swimming pool, while I wanted as much garden as
possible, and we spent hours on the site, pacing out this and that and
growing more excited by the minute. The view from the terrace and the
sitting-room is magnificent. But it would take months to complete the
bungalow, so we extended our lease on the flat in Mosta and waited it
out there, contenting ourselves with regular visits to the site to supervise
progress.

However, news on other fronts was not so good, with lots of gloomy
letters from Stan's solicitor about the divorce. But the correspondence
with England did have its lighter moments. Stan was still giving as his
address: 'The St Michael's College of Christian Brotherhood', and this
led some people in England to believe that Stan was taking up Holy
Orders. Various people, including members of Stan's own family, decided that he had retreated to a monastery. In fact this assumption
created a funny incident almost immediately. Mind you, it wasn't so
hilarious at the time, but it's amusing now to look back on. Stan received
a letter from his daughter Jean, saying she and her family were coming
over for a short holiday and that naturally she would like to see her
father while she was in Malta.

Stan was in an immediate panic. To his mind, Jean's visit could only
mean one thing. She was coming to spy out the land for Betty. Amazingly

perhaps, I had been kept completely out of the picture. Apart from Stan's mother and brother Arthur, and Charlie Chester, nobody in England knew *why* Stan wanted a divorce. But Jean's visit would put an end to that – or so Stan suspected.

Jean had rented a holiday villa, and so I obtained the keys from the agent and went out there to stock up the larder before she arrived. Then, the next morning, I stayed at our flat while Stan went to meet his daughter and her young family.

Stan

I went to meet Jean's plane at Luqa Airport and, of course, the flight was delayed. So I stewed in the lounge for an hour. What would I *say* to her? What would she say to *me*? I read her letter again: 'A week's holiday ... before Bob goes to South Africa ... just us and the children ... have rented a villa at St Paul's Bay.' No mention of Betty. But that was no guarantee that Betty wouldn't be with them. But Jean wouldn't do that to me. Jean was too straightforward for that. I sipped my coffee and watched the man at the next table puff cigarette smoke into the air. He looked so relaxed. Perhaps I should smoke? They say it's good for the nerves. I wondered what Bob was making of it all? I remember him saying, 'It's handy, having a famous father-in-law.' He will have changed his mind now. It's not so handy when they run away.

When the flight was announced I went up to the observation platform, to watch the passengers disembark on to the apron. I saw Bob first. Then Jean, with the children. But there was no sign of Betty. Even so, I stayed where I was until the last passenger climbed down the steps. Then the cabin staff came down, and the cleaning people went up, and I breathed a sigh of relief. At least I wouldn't have to face Betty. *Just* my daughter, *and* my son-in-law.

I braced myself and then went downstairs to the reception area outside the customs hall. There was the usual hustle and bustle, friends and relatives greeting each other, porters running trolleys into people's shins, taxi drivers touting for business. Then Bob came through, looking hot and sticky, clutching Matthew with one hand and a suitcase with the other. And Jean, harrassed and worried, with one eye on young Samantha, and the other on the porter with the rest of their luggage. Then Matthew caught sight of me and waved furiously. 'Poppa, Poppa!' he called – meaning me, because that is what he always calls me. I took a deep breath and went over to meet them.

It was just like old times, greeting them. Or maybe we pretended it was. The kids were a distraction of course, so I made a big fuss of them, and it helped to break the ice. Jean kissed me and Bob shook hands, and a few minutes later we were humping their luggage into my car.

That was a mistake. Using my car. I should have hired a taxi. You are at a disadvantage when you are driving. Your passengers can stare at you and there's nothing you can do about it. I tried to keep the conversation neutral – Wasn't it hot? What sort of flight had they had? Was it raining in Manchester? But they answered in monosyllables, and Bob stared at me in nervous fascination – as if I was an escaped lunatic – while Jean's eyes bored holes in the back of my neck. By the time we reached St Paul's Bay I was a nervous wreck.

Their villa was balanced on the rocks at the foot of the hill: a pink stone building with yellow shutters and a wide verandah overlooking the beach. I drove down the narrow track to the front door and switched off the engine. I told myself that all I had to do now was settle them in, then I would flee back to Mosta. I produced the keys, the cases were off-loaded and we went inside. The kids 'oohed' and 'aahed' at the sea view, Bob prodded the beds, and Jean inspected the kitchen.

She eyed the mountain of groceries Mila had stacked in the larder: 'Daddy, you shouldn't have gone to so much trouble. And you – *shopping*? I can't believe it. You've never been shopping in your life.'

'Ah, well – ' I fidgeted, already hopelessly confused about the best way to handle the situation, 'I – er – I did have some help. From – from a friend.'

Bob appeared as if by magic. He glanced from the larder to Jean, then eyed me with frank curiosity. 'That was kind of you, Stan, and ... um ... very good of your friend.'

It was even worse than I imagined. Why had I said *friend* like that? And why had Bob echoed it? Jean was checking the contents of the fridge like an auditor doing a stock-take – and Bob was watching me with the open suspicion of a store detective. Once or twice he seemed about to add something, but when I looked at him he just blinked and stared at me like an amiable owl.

I said, 'Well, there should be enough there to start you off – '

'There's enough here to *finish* us off,' Jean said firmly. 'Sauerkraut, red peppers, frozen pizzas, pickled herrings – Daddy, we just don't *eat* those kind of things.'

'Leave it,' I said hastily, 'leave *them*. Lot's of other stuff – salad and milk and – '

Suddenly Jean smiled: 'You're right.' She closed the fridge door. 'There are lots of other things, and I didn't mean to sound ungrateful.' She looked at Bob: 'Why don't you take Daddy out to the verandah for a chat? I'll sort the children out and then get some lunch.'

'*No!*' I jumped with alarm at her mention of a chat. That was the last thing I wanted. 'I can't stop – really. Now you're settled – '

'But you'll stay for lunch?'

'I can't. I promised to meet – ' I struggled for a name, *any* name, 'I promised to meet Brother Charles.'

Bob frowned: 'Is he a monk?'

'No – not a *monk* exactly – '

'But a priest?' Jean said helpfully.

'Well, sort of – '

'Not like a Jehovah's Witness?' sniffed Bob.

'No, not like that. He's a teacher – they are *all* teachers.'

'Gurus?' Bob ventured tentatively.

'No, of course – '

'But when *will* we see you?' Jean pleaded.

'Soon. I'll be around. Make sure you're all right – '

'Come to dinner.'

'No, it's your first night – and besides – '

'Brother Charles again?' Bob asked drily. He watched me closely.

'Lunch,' Jean said desperately. 'Lunch *tomorrow*.'

'Tomorrow?' I echoed. 'Yes – yes – tomorrow is fine.'

I would have agreed to anything by then, just to escape. I needed time to *think*! I said goodbye to the children, hugged Jean and tried to avoid her eye, then I went out to the car. Just as I was about to get in, Bob put an arm across my shoulders. He sniffed hard and said, 'It's sure good to see you again.'

'And you. See you tomorrow, Bob – and I hope your cold gets better.'

I looked in the rear view mirror as I drove away. Bob stood at the end of the track, staring after me with a puzzled expression on his face. I could almost *see* the questions in his eyes. And tomorrow he would find a way of asking them.

Back at the flat I told Mila about it: 'It was awful. Even worse than I imagined – and now I've got to go to lunch tomorrow.'

'You'll *have* to tell them.'

'How can I tell them?'

'We told my *parents*.'

'Your parents weren't going back to face Betty. And if Betty finds out she will tell the Press. And if the Press find out – I mean, *really find out* – they will make our life unbearable. You'll be branded as my mistress, and – '

Mila shuddered and we spent the rest of the day worrying. But of course I had no choice. I *had* to get through it, like it or not. And I didn't. 'It's not nice, telling lies. Especially telling lies to my own daughter.'

'You will be able to tell her *one* day,' Mila encouraged, 'and if she is the girl you say she is, she'll understand.'

I hoped so.

The next day dawned bright and beautiful. I was up at six as usual and padding round Mosta's narrow streets to get my exercise. Normally that blows my worries away, because I feel so much better for it. But today wasn't normal. Today was the day of the *inquisition.* I showered and changed, and moped around the flat all morning, but at noon Mila kissed me and pushed me through the door. 'Good luck, Darling,' she said. I felt like a soldier going to war, not a father visiting his daughter and her family.

Bob sniffed me like a friendly dog when I arrived, then led me into the villa. Jean had set lunch on the verandah overlooking the sea, and the two children bounced over to tell me what they had been doing since yesterday. I was more delighted than ever to see them. Talking to them and playing with them helped stave off the questions. But Bob was not to be denied for long. He sat down opposite with a purposeful look in his eye. 'Well then, Stan,' he said, 'had a busy morning at the monastery?'

'It's not a monastery, Bob – it's a school.'

Matthew's head jerked round: 'Do you live in a *school*, Poppa?'

'Not exactly *in* a school – the Brothers have separate accommodation – '

Bob groaned: 'I've seen it on TV. Very spartan. No electric light and a bunk two feet wide. Tiny little cells – '

'Like a prison?' Matthew tugged at my sleeve. 'Have you been sent to prison, Poppa?'

'*Matthew!*' Jean took his hand and hurried him away. 'Now you go and play with Sammy – but stay where I can see you, understand?'

'But I wanted to ask Poppa – '

'After *lunch*. You can ask him after lunch. Now keep an eye on Sammy for me and don't get into mischief.'

'Kids,' Bob grinned. He moved across to the dining table and invited me to join him. As I sat down he passed behind my chair and sniffed deeply.

'Still got your cold, Bob?'

'Me? No – no, I haven't got a cold.' He sat down with a little flurry of embarrassment and looked around the table. 'I'd open the wine if I could find the bottle opener. Jean, have you seen – '

'It's right there, on the table in front of you.' Jean turned to me with a smile, 'I gave the children their lunch earlier. I thought it best, gives us a chance to talk.'

I groaned inwardly, while returning her smile, and I was just trying to think of a nice safe subject to talk about when the corkscrew slipped in Bob's hand.

'*Jesus Christ!*' he yelped.

'*Bob!*' Jean squeaked, with a look at me.

Bob sucked his thumb and jigged up and down the verandah. Then he stared at Jean and a slow look of understanding crept into his eyes. 'Oh yeah – sorry Stan – the bloody thing slipped.'

'*Bob!*' Jean protested.

'Bloody *must* be all right,' Bob shot back indignantly, 'I mean, bloody's not *blasphemous*. I bet even monks swear at times – '

'Go and run cold water over that thumb while Daddy opens the wine.'

We both did as we were told and in Bob's absence I made a desperate attempt to shift the conversation by asking about the children. But Bob returned before I could develop the theme.

'Great job of shopping that, Stan,' he said appreciatively. 'Even thought of sticking plasters.' He held his thumb up for inspection. 'Not many men would have remembered something like that.'

Jean's eye lit with a speculative gleam, but Bob distracted her again. He was dipping into the salad bowl with wooden serving spoons, transferring huge quantities of lettuce and cucumber to his plate.

'Hmmmm.' Jean cleared her throat noisily.

Bob looked up, shifted his glance from her to me, then gave a little grin: 'Sorry, Stan – help yourself.'

'*Hmmmm.*' Jean went pink and aimed a ferocious glance across the table. Bob froze with the salad servers in mid air and large question marks in his eyes. Half a tomato fell back into the bowl with a faint plop. 'Aaah!' said Bob.

His air of embarrassment gave way to a conspirator's smile. Then to my utter astonishment, he replaced the serving spoons, folded his hands in his lap, and stared down at the floor. When I looked at Jean she was doing exactly the same thing. I thought they had dropped something, so I raised the edge of the cloth and peered under the table.

Bob droned: 'For what we are about to receive, may the Lord make us truly thankful.'

'Amen,' said Jean demurely.

'Are you having school lunch?' Matthew asked, appearing on the verandah. 'They're awful. I'm glad – '

'Matthew!' Jean snapped, 'I told you. Go and *play* – '

'But why is Dad saying – '

'*Go and play!*' roared Bob.

Matthew retreated hurriedly, and I hissed: 'Will you two *stop* this!'

'Stop what?' Jean asked in apparent bewilderment. 'We always say grace – '

'You do not!'

Bob said: 'We do since you went into that bloody convent!'

Jean flashed him another venomous look while I tried to explain: 'Look – just because I'm staying with the Brothers, it doesn't mean I've gone all religious – '

'No?' Bob cocked his head.

'No.'

'But *why* are you staying with them?' Jean wanted to know.

'It's not – it's not a *permanent* thing,' I floundered, 'it's just while I sort things out. They're helping me, that's all.'

'How do you mean?' Bob's head cocked to a fresh angle. 'With meditation, and things like that?'

'No! *Not* with meditation and things like that!' I snapped with exasperation. 'Look, I don't want to talk about it. Not yet – '

'Very well, Daddy,' Jean said primly, 'we understand – a man's faith is a private thing – '

'It's not a *matter* of faith!'

Bob scratched his head: 'You mean you haven't turned into a religious nut?'

'No I haven't – '

'Thank Christ for that!' He fell back in his chair and wheezed with relief. 'That's the best news I've had since we got here.'

'*Bob!*' Jean looked wildly around the table, 'I've left the mayonnaise in the kitchen. Would you fetch it, please?'

'There's some salad cream here,' Bob pointed to the bottle.

'I *prefer* mayonnaise,' Jean said icily.

'But we always have salad cream at home,' Bob protested. He held her look for a moment, then the colour rose up his neck. He pushed his chair back. 'Mayonnaise,' he said half under his breath, 'comes of saying grace.' Then he sniffed deeply behind my chair on his way to the kitchen.

Jean smiled nervously: 'Excuse me Daddy – he'll never find it, I'd better go myself. You start, don't wait for us.'

A moment later she hissed in the kitchen: 'Will you please *stop* swearing!'

'I'm nervous, that's all,' Bob hissed back. 'Anyway, swearing's all right, you heard – '

'That's not the point! And for heaven's sake stop *sniffing* over him, as if – as if he's a bitch on heat or something!'

'We agreed on the plane – if it's not religion, it's drugs.'

'So why *sniff?*'

'You can smell pot a mile off! It's got a sweet, sickly smell – '

'How would *you* know?'

'I asked the boys at the office.'

'At the *National Westminster Bank!* Ye Gods and little fishes! You let the *Bank* think that my *father* – '

'Of course not – '

'Oh – oh, *go* and sit down. Don't swear and don't sniff and for heaven's sake act *normal.*'

I had lost my appetite by the time Bob returned. I sat staring at the sea, munching a lettuce leaf while asking myself miserable questions. What was I *doing?* Was I so selfish, so inconsiderate, so – so *besotted* with Mila that everything had to be sacrificed? Jean, Bob, *their* children?

'Couldn't find the mayonnaise,' Bob said cheerfully. 'Have to make do with salad cream.'

Jean returned a moment or two later, slightly flushed and looking nervous. The meal dragged on, as awkward as a funeral supper. They were both determined to avoid asking further questions, and I was desperately racking my brains for an uncontroversial subject – and in the process the conversation dried up completely. Finally it was time to go. The children were called back from the beach and the family escorted me to my car. And I was within inches of making my escape when Bob asked brightly: 'What about a night out before we go back? Dinner somewhere, and you can show us the night spots.'

'But the children?' I parried. It was my ace card, but one look at Jean's face told me it was about to be trumped.

'I spoke to the maid this morning,' Jean smiled happily. 'She'll baby-sit for us, whenever we want.'

Bob grinned: 'What do you say, Stan? Saturday night, how about it?'

'Well – '

'And bring your friend,' Jean said. 'I really must thank *her* for all that shopping.'

Our eyes met and suddenly I knew that *she knew*. Or at least, she guessed. But it would be easier with Mila along – there would be the two of us to the two of them. We'd stand a better chance of bluffing it out.

'All right,' I said as I got into the car, 'I'll ask her if she can make it.'

'I'm sure she'll *try*,' Jean smiled, 'if you ask her nicely.'

Mila

Dinner with Bob and Jean wasn't quite the ordeal Stan had led me to expect – but it was far from easy. I was nervous, of course. After all, Jean was Stan's only daughter and quite obviously the apple of his eye. I *wanted* to tell her about the relationship I had with her father, and that we hoped to marry soon, but Stan was insistent that we say nothing for the time being, so we played it his way.

As soon as I met Jean I knew that she knew – and she knew I knew she knew – but we politely ignored what was in each other's mind and got on with playing charades. Thank heavens I liked her! That was the most important thing. One day I hoped to be able to tell her all about it. She had a nice sense of humour and I felt sure she would see the funny side of it. Meanwhile we had to get through that first evening together.

Dinner passed off quite uneventfully. My work at the embassy in Prague had taught me enough of the verbal thrusts and parries used by diplomats for me to use them on my own account. So I survived dinner. Then Stan asked me to dance. Really he wanted to discuss the evening with me, ask how I thought it was going. That was why he took me on to the dance floor. But Bob's eyebrows were in his hairline when we got back.

'Been dancing long, Stan?' he asked.

'Ever since I met Mila,' Stan answered happily.

'Oh – not long then.' Bob turned to me: 'You must be a very good teacher.'

Jean was still recovering from seeing her father on the dance floor: 'I never would have believed it. Daddy dancing. Did you teach him here – in Malta?'

I said 'yes' at exactly the moment Stan said 'no'.

'And Prague,' he added.

'That's right,' I said quickly. 'And Prague.'

'And then here.' Stan's confusion mounted. 'Here mostly perhaps. I suppose *mainly* here – when you think about it.'

Bob and Jean exchanged knowing looks. I squirmed. Stan's blow by blow account of lunch at the villa rang in my ears. I could see the rest of the evening collapsing into the same pattern. So I dragged Stan back to the dance floor and kept him there for the rest of the evening. It became like one of those marathon dance contests they hold in the States. My feet were aching by the end of it, but at least we escaped the need to answer further questions. Stan was exhausted. He said it was harder than playing at Wembley and not half as much fun – which shows how flattering he can be at times. When it was over we said our good-nights. 'I hope we meet again,' I said to Jean.

She smiled: 'I'm sure we shall.'

Stan took them to Luqa Airport the following morning and saw them off, while I stayed at the Mosta flat – *bathing my feet.*

We went to England a month after that. Stan had to meet his solicitor to discuss the divorce, and I was taken home to meet his mother and brothers. They were marvellous and almost made me forget the perse-cution complex I was beginning to get as a result of the British divorce laws. Of course it has all changed now, but *then* – well, after a few months of it you feel like a criminal. I was kept out of sight for most of the time because Stan was determined to avoid me being tagged as 'the other woman'. So it was a bit like our trip to Canada, all over again. I spent most of my time with his mother and his brother Arthur, and some of the time with his other brothers, Jack and Ronny, together with their families. They were all wonderfully kind to me, but I think they were simply so delighted to see Stan so obviously happy that they would have forgiven me anything. Jack in particular was forever saying, 'Don't worry, Mila – it will sort itself out. One day you *will* be married to Stan.'

But that day was a long way off – as Stan's solicitors warned him. Stan was offering a tremendously generous settlement – more than he could really afford – but it seemed to make no difference. It was going to be a very long time indeed before we could get married.

We returned to Malta in a gloomy mood, but our new friends soon took us in hand. Besides Malta is such a happy place, so full of sunshine, that it is impossible to be down for long.

Our bungalow was progressing and looked certain to be finished by Christmas. We named it 'Idle Hours', which seemed appropriate at the time, but in truth it has never been that.

Stan's presence on the island was by now a well-known fact, so we spent an increasing amount of time dodging reporters. Then, happily, Stan received an invitation to play an exhibition game in Austria, so – after making sure that 'Idle Hours' would be completed by November – we went to Austria, first for Stan to play in his match, and then for an extended holiday.

Stan

I can never remember that first holiday in Austria without thinking of Mila and pressure points. It all came about because of my injury. Playing on the hard grounds in Malta had aggravated my knee problem. I ought to explain that there is only one turf pitch in Malta – all the others are hard surfaces consisting mainly of concrete with a covering of sand. Anyway, by the time we left for our holiday in Austria my knee was so stiff and swollen that I could hardly bend it. Then Mila set to work.

Pressure points incorporate the same principles as acupuncture, and Mila was an expert. By manipulating various pressure points in my feet she was able to bring some relief to my knee – so successfully, in fact, that after a few days of the treatment the swelling subsided completely and the knee was as good as new. In fact Mila's expertise extended beyond that, and subsequently, in South Africa and elsewhere, Mila brought relief to many of our friends who suffered from back and neck troubles – simply by manipulating the pressure points in their feet. I won't delay the story now by going into the ins and outs of pressure points, but all I can say is I wish Mila had been in the dressing-room at Stoke when I was still playing first-class football at the age of fifty. Knee trouble was one of my main reasons for retiring, and had Mila been there with her healing hands I would have gone on for years.

Isn't it amazing, all those years in professional football and I had never even *heard* of pressure points. These days Mila has taught me some of the 'tricks of the trade', so I can manipulate feet for other people. I'm not in her class, but I get by. In fact I was at Wembley in 1979, just before an international match, when Kevin Keegan was having back trouble. Poor Kevin could hardly touch his toes, but he felt much better after a session with me working on his feet.

Kevin has an enquiring mind and was interested to learn, but some- times I think that professional sportsmen could do so much more for themselves if they took the trouble to find out more about this business of fitness. Of course it is understandable that a young man of twenty or so is so busy mastering his craft that he takes fitness for granted. Perhaps I was the same, at least until I was about thirty-two. Most players start thinking about retirement at that age, but I resisted it. I loved the game as much as ever and wanted to continue as long as possible, but none-the-less I could *feel* my strength fading and I began to worry about it. So one day I took some advice which changed the rest of my life.

I used to go to an osteopath in those days – a Mr Arthur Millwood at Bury. (Of course osteopaths use pressure points too, but I don't remember Mr Millwood using that expression to me.) Mr Millwood was a marvel. He too worked miracles on my knee, but it wasn't just his expertise as an osteopath which impressed me. What struck me was that he always looked so fit. So I asked him about it and discovered he was a vegetarian. Then he introduced me to the world of natural health clinics and dietary control.

He gave me the address of a clinic in Bristol, and I went there every six weeks after that. I left home on a Sunday morning and motored down to arrive in the afternoon. The routine never varied: no food at all on the Monday, no food on the Tuesday, a very light salad on the Wednesday, and on the Thursday I travelled back to Blackpool feeling very refreshed. Of course it wasn't *just* the diet. There would be steam baths and enemas, exercises and long walks along the beach at Weston-super-Mare.

Gradually I evolved my own system, so, although I continued to go to Bristol every six weeks, even at home I controlled my diet and exercise habits. The object was always the same, to reach peak fitness in time for the big game on Saturday. Even a fit body can be that little bit fitter on different days. Fridays and Sundays were no good for me: the *peak* had to be reached on the Saturday. So, for example, I developed the habit of not eating at all on Mondays, and on other days I went in for a lot of salads – cheese salads, egg salads, nut salads, all sorts. And as you know, I drank a lot of carrot juice.

Fasting can be good for you, but there was one occasion when I thought I had gone too far. I was forty-two and had been picked to play for England against Scotland at Wembley. As usual the match was at the very end of the season and the annual England–Scotland game was considered the show-piece of British soccer. Scotland had announced their side and had selected a young full-back by the name of Harry Haddock. In fact after the Scottish team was announced I couldn't open a newspaper without reading about Harry Haddock. I had never played against him, but according to the Press he was very fast. In fact some of the papers came out and said it: Harry Haddock would be much *too* fast for an old man of forty-two. I thought, 'Crikey, I shall have to be on my best behaviour for this game.'

Blackpool played their last match of the season on the Saturday before the international, but our manager, Joe Smith, gave me permission to miss the game in order to prepare myself for the international. So that was it – training started in earnest. If Harry Haddock was as fast as the Press said, I would have to be *super-fit* for the big match. So I had no food at all on the Friday, no food on the Saturday, and no food on the Sunday. A three day fast, broken only by an occasional drink of warm water. On the Monday I was due to report at the Hendon Hall Hotel in North London with the rest of the England squad, so I caught the train from Blackpool and treated myself to tea and toast in the dining car and I ate my first proper meal for four days in the hotel that night – a really marvellous salad, full of grated carrots and cheese and tomatoes and lettuce. Then I went to bed.

The following day we went to Stamford Bridge for a training session. My goodness, I felt weak! Terribly weak. There was no power in my shots and little strength in my legs. I got into an awful state about it. I was sure I had overdone it and that, come Saturday, Harry Haddock would run me into the ground. We returned to the hotel and I ate my salad and went to bed in a gloomy mood.

But I felt a little better when we trained at Highbury on the Wednesday. Not really a hundred per cent, but certainly a lot stronger. And at White Hart Lane on the Thursday it all came right for me. I felt sharp and quick and full of running. So much so that I asked Walter Winterbottom, the England manager, to excuse me from the full training session. Instead I spent some time skipping with the rope and sprinting in my running spikes, but I did no work at all with the ball.

Then I awoke on the Friday morning. We were training at Charlton that day, but even before leaving Hendon I knew I was as fit as I had ever been in my life. I felt tremendous. We reached the ground and I sprinted and turned and sprinted again. Fantastic! Then I panicked – I had peaked a day early! By tomorrow I would be over the top. Again I asked Winterbottom to leave me out of the team practice, and again he agreed, so I spent the rest of the session just walking up and down – afraid really to let go in case I pulled a muscle.

Then Saturday dawned. My mind was clear, my body felt good. I drank a cup of tea for breakfast, then went for a walk. I used my training shoes, which were an ordinary pair of shoes with weights screwed into the soles and heels. The Hendon Hall Hotel is near the Great North Road, and I remember walking to Mill Hill and back. My goodness, I felt fit – as sharp as a razor. I decided that was it – no more exercise, just back to the hotel to rest until we went to the Stadium.

And so to Wembley. I tell you, I have never been fitter than when I walked out on to the turf that day. Forty-two years old or not, it would have taken a greyhound to catch me. At full speed down the touchline I could have run right through the gates and out of the stadium. At least that's what it felt like. As soon as I got the ball I pushed it past Harry and ran. I always did that when I was playing someone new – pushed the ball past him to test his speed. It's speed over the first ten yards that counts – rarely more than that. And thanks to my preparations I had the beating of Harry that day. People afterwards said I was taking two yards from him, and believe me, two yards is more than enough. So I thoroughly enjoyed myself that afternoon – but I doubt if I would have even been *playing*, had it not been for Arthur Millwood's advice ten years earlier.

Mila

Austria was a tonic. We stayed at an hotel in Villach and had a marvellous time, made even more enjoyable by the people we met, some of whom became firm friends. Foremost among them was a man called Urs. Urs was a Swiss businessman in the rag trade. He was very prosperous and surrounded himself with all the trappings of a wealthy man – a magnificent home in Zurich, a custom-built Porsche, and a very good-looking wife. Urs was witty, urbane, widely travelled and well read. Urs was a sports enthusiast with season tickets for the Zurich Football Club and access to every sporting function in Switzerland. And Urs was a dwarf.

We met him on our first day there. He recognized Stan and quietly introduced himself. We took to him immediately and spent a lot of time in his company after that initial meeting. It's funny how nature compensates: poor Urs was little more than three feet tall, and his deformed body must have caused him untold heartbreak at different times in his life, but once Urs was seated at table amidst company you forgot all about his size. His personality fairly sparkled and his conversation was spiked with enough wit to have kept Oscar Wilde happy. Stan agrees that Urs was one of the most fascinating people we ever met.

I remember one day in particular. We were at the side of the swimming pool and I was manipulating the pressure points in Stan's feet as continuing treatment for his sore knee. Urs joined us and wanted to know what I was doing. So I told him all about pressure points. He was fascinated: more than that, he felt that such a subject should have a wider audience. So within minutes I found myself giving a lecture to everyone there. And of course, after the lecture came the demonstration – first on Stan, then Urs, then on another friend. Then they had to try manipulating for themselves, so that within half an hour everyone at the poolside was doing it. Legs waved in the air as couples tried it for

themselves, one partner manipulating pressure points while the other
cried out with a series of 'oohs' and 'aahs' and 'that's marvellous, do it
again!' Some new people booking into the hotel took one look and
retreated down the drive, thinking they were interrupting some kind of
freak-out. Little Urs ran after them, but that just made things worse.
They leapt into their cars and roared off into the sunset.

So it was a glorious holiday, and after promising to meet Urs and his
wife there again next year, we returned to Malta and a pleasant surprise.

Stan had been invited to South Africa, on a three-month coaching
trip. It was an exciting and unexpected development. I had never been
to South Africa, but Stan was full of praise for it, so naturally he wrote
back accepting the invitation.

Meanwhile 'Idle Hours' had been completed and we were able to
move in. It was everything I had hoped for – our first home together,
and believe me, no couple could have had a more idyllic location in
which to start married life. That's all we needed – to start *married* life.
But the solicitors were as depressing as ever about that, so we tried not
to think about it and got to work in the garden at 'Idle Hours', determined to cram every inch of the thin soil with flowers and shrubs.

The months passed. We were busy and happy. Then it was time to go
to South Africa. Stan was over the moon about showing me the country.
I think that, deep down, it is his favourite place: he has so many friends
there that at times you would swear he is a native born South African.
He loves the country, and the people, but I must admit that I had a few
reservations about making that first trip.

His friends worried me. Stan thought so much of them that he overlooked what an ordeal it would be for me to meet them. After all, many of
them knew Stan's wife and for Stan to spring me on them would be a bit
of a shock. I wondered how they would react? I still hated this tag of
'mistress', and Stan and I both flinched at imagined newspaper headlines.
So I was feeling more than a little nervous by the time our plane touched
down at Johannesburg – especially when I learned that Stan's oldest
friend in South Africa, Lubbe Snoyman, was at the airport to meet us.

How wrong I was to worry! Lubbe and other friends like Viv Grainger
couldn't have been kinder, or done more to put me at ease. Within days
I felt I had known them for months, and now it seems I've known them
a lifetime. We were friends from the first meeting.

Lubbe and Stan go back a long way together – to 1953 in fact. Lubbe
was one of South Africa's leading footballers in those days – in fact he
kept goal for Johannesburg Rangers, the oldest club in South Africa.

Then, in 1953, Johannesburg Rangers were making a tour of the British Isles, and Lubbe had heard so much about Stan that he was determined to see him play. His chance came when England were playing The Rest of the World at Wembley. Lubbe was up in Inverness at the time, but that didn't stop him: undeterred by the long journey he travelled down to London for the game.

Lubbe says he has never been so disappointed in his life. He had heard and read so much about Stan that he was on the edge of his seat with anticipation. But England were losing at half-time and Lubbe was convinced that it had been a waste of time and money to drag all the way down to Wembley. In the first half Stan had barely kicked the ball and had been marked out of the game by two defenders. Lubbe was so fed up that he was in two minds about staying for the second half. The rest of the story is Lubbe's.

Long after everyone had left the ground I remained in my seat near the Royal Box, wondering whether I had dreamed it. It was incredible. Matthews in the second half had laid on a one-man show. He pulled England right back into the game and very nearly won it for them. The Rest of the World side was mesmerized by his performance – and so was everyone watching. England were well down at half-time but, thanks to Matthews, they were a different proposition after the interval. They narrowed the gap to 4–3, and with ninety seconds to go Matthews was through again, side-stepping and jinking his way to the goal-line. Then he was pulled down. You couldn't even blame the defender – there was just no other way of stopping Matthews. Despite the protests from The Rest of the World side it was a clear penalty – and Ramsey made no mistake from the spot. 4–4! There was barely time to re-start play, but start they did and Matthews was away again. Only the final whistle saved The Rest of the World from defeat, because by then they were totally demoralized. To my mind, and in the opinion of everyone around me, that game should have been re-titled 'The Rest of the World v Stanley Matthews' – because that's what it amounted to. I had never seen anything like it. There and then I knew I had seen a unique player, the like of which I would never see again in my lifetime.

Lubbe sat in a daze as the stadium emptied, but he was convinced of one thing, that he had to get Stan out to South Africa – *so that the soccer-crazed people there could see him.* And he started work on the project the very next day, by telephoning Bill Perry, an ex-South African team-mate of his who then played in the Blackpool side with Stan. Lubbe's idea was to persuade Stan to go to South Africa as a one-man band, an unheard-of thing for a player to do in those days. None-the-less Bill

Perry sounded Stan out and a day or two later he returned Lubbe's call, saying that Stan was interested in the idea.

Lubbe was delighted, and he returned to South Africa determined to sell the idea. He had some support, because Freddie Fell, the President of the South African FA had been to Wembley for the Rest of the World game and he was as enthusiastic as Lubbe. But the Southern Transvaal FA in Johannesburg refused to believe that *any* single player would draw a large enough crowd to make the venture economically viable. Lubbe pleaded, but the FA Committee remained resolute. So Lubbe leaked the prospect of Stan playing in South Africa to the local Press. They clamoured their support for the idea, but the FA Committee still refused to consider the proposal. Then, just as Lubbe was pulling his hair out in desperation, somebody stole his idea.

Football officials in Natal quietly contacted Stan and offered him a contract to play one game in Durban. Stan accepted. When the news reached Lubbe he rushed round to the Transvaal FA breathing fire and brimstone: 'You see! See what's happened now! At least some people know a good idea when they hear one!' There were a few red faces on the Committee by the time Lubbe finished with them, but at least he forced a decision – they would stage a game in Johannesburg if Lubbe could persuade Stanley to play.

Lubbe drove the four hundred miles down to Durban with a friend of his, Eric Litchfield, who was the sports editor of the *Rand Daily Mail*. When they arrived they went straight to Stan's hotel.

Stan was staying at The Edward, Durban's best hotel, right on the front of the beach. It was a five-star hotel and they were treating Stan like royalty. That was the first time I met him. Frankly, it was a bit like the first time I saw him play – disappointing to begin with. He was damned awkward about granting Eric and me an interview, and even when we met he greeted us with a good deal of reserve. Come to think of it, he seemed downright suspicious. But we South Africans can be thick-skinned when it suits us, so Eric and I stuck it out. I explained who I was and that I had been at least partly instrumental in him being invited to South Africa. Then I made my pitch about him playing in Johánnesburg, after which I stated that in my opinion he could earn a small fortune in South Africa as a one-man entertainer. He heard us out and accepted the invitation to play at the Rand Stadium the following week, but I can't say we were too taken with his personality. And the following morning he was even more morose. He hardly spoke to me and was downright rude to poor old Eric. Then I realized what he was doing. He was motivating himself for the big game that afternoon. Later – when Stan and I became friends – he told me he needed three days to get himself into the right state of mind for a big match. He had to think about the conditions of the pitch, and study his opponents and their tactics, so he withdrew into his shell like a tortoise. He would have been surprised and embarrassed about the effect his behaviour had on other people – and very upset to think he had been rude – because it was completely unintentional. It was just that his mind was on other things – the big match and all it meant to him.

It was interesting to listen to Lubbe talk about Stan at the height of his playing career. Naturally I had seen Stan play in several exhibition games by then, so I can vouch for Lubbe's impressions. Stan *does* go all broody and introspective before a big game. But it's quite understandable. After all, a concert pianist, a professional singer, and indeed almost anyone who sets out to entertain the public gets nervous before a performance. And it seems to me that the biggest stars get the most nervous of all.

To return to Lubbe's account of Stan's first visit to South Africa, the game at the Kingsmead Stadium in Durban apparently went well for Stan, and with the match over he relaxed and settled down to enjoy himself. He travelled up to Jo'burg with Lubbe and Eric Litchfield, and the three of them had a high old time of it from what I can make out. But by the time they reached 'The City of Gold' Stan's thoughts were turning back to football and his game on the forthcoming Saturday. A very strong Southern Transvaal side had been selected to play against Stan's team, which was comprised of former professional footballers who had played in Britain. This is how Lubbe recalls those few days.

Transvaal were pinning their faith on a left-back called Morrie Jacobson. And Jacobson was good, very good. To give you an idea of just how good, Tom Whittaker, the Arsenal manager, described Morrie as the greatest amateur full-back ever to play on an English soccer field. And don't be fooled by the fact that he was an amateur – all players in South Africa were amateurs in those days. Morrie had offers by the score to turn professional, but accepting them meant playing abroad and he wanted to remain in South Africa. And Morrie had a particular reason for wanting to play against Stan. It stemmed from the Springbok tour of England the year before. We were in Newcastle and it was after I had made the trip down from Scotland to see Matthews play at Wembley. I was discussing Matthews with Joe Harvey, the Newcastle Manager.

'He's a menace,' Joe said bluntly. 'I've nothing against the man personally, but the sooner he's out of the game the happier I'll be.'

I was astounded. Naturally I protested, but Joe would have none of it. 'It's like this,' he said. 'Matthews has ruined more promising full-backs than I've had hot dinners. They're never the same after he's manhandled them. It's a crying shame to see them destroyed. The man is merciless. He humiliates them.'

Morrie Jacobson was in the hotel, so I asked Joe to repeat what he had said to me in front of Morrie. Morrie was a short, tough chap – everything you imagine when you think of the ideal full-back. He listened to Joe Harvey, then turned on his heel. 'Bull,' he said – and that was that. It wasn't that Morrie was conceited, though he had some reason to be because he was a very fine player – it was just that he could never envisage anyone humiliating him. And he said so.

So it promised to be quite a duel between Morrie and Stan that day. I must confess I was looking forward to it. And so as to be scrupulously fair, just as I answered Stan's questions about Morrie, so I answered Morrie's questions about Stan. Not that there were many. Morrie was obsessed with Stan's age. Stan was thirty-eight then and Morrie was convinced that 'An old man like that won't last the pace.' I shrugged and said Matthews had lasted the pace in Durban all right.

Anyway, the day of the match dawned bright and beautiful. It was May then, which is our winter, but even so the temperature would be higher than Stan was accustomed to. Then there was the altitude to contend with. Johannesburg is a long way above sea level. Even young athletes have trouble with their breathing until they become acclimatized to the thin air. I've seen young tennis champions, men in the prime of physical fitness aged about twenty-six or so, really suffer and break down in a game because of Johannesburg's altitude. So Stan was up against it – what with Morrie, the temperature and the altitude – not to mention that the players on his side had never played together before.

I called in to see Stan before the game, just to make sure everything was to his satisfaction. I got my head bitten off for my trouble, but I was used to it by then so it was water off a duck's back. Then I went to my seat and settled down to enjoy myself. The Rand Stadium was packed – thirty-six thousand people, which was a capacity gate. Everyone was looking forward to the tussle between Jacobson and Matthews. The morning newspapers had devoted acres of space to the match, and the general opinion was that Morrie would run Stan into the ground. They kicked off – and during the opening minutes Morrie did just that. Whenever Matthews had the ball, Jacobson took it away from him. Not once, but time after time. The crowd went wild. Tom Whittaker's assessment of Morrie Jacobson's play rang in my ears. Was Morrie going to humiliate Matthews? I remembered Joe Harvey's words, and thought of the full-backs who had been 'destroyed' by Matthews. Joe would have loved what was happening in the Rand Stadium. Morrie won every tackle. The crowd erupted – cheers for Morrie and whistles of derision for Stan. I squirmed in my seat. I was virtually the only man there who had seen Stan play before. It was my big mouth that had campaigned long and hard to bring Stan to Jo'burg. I had staked my football reputation on the man.

Transvaal scored, then again, and again after that. 3–0 in the first half-hour. It looked like a walkover.

Then – with fifteen minutes of the first half left – it happened. Stan went around Morrie as if the tough little full-back wasn't there. I swear Morrie didn't even see him. And after that the comedy began. There can be no other word for it. Stan was like a matador teasing a bull. The crowd fell silent at first. Thirty-six thousand people sat in a trance. Then there was a buzz of excitement as they realized what was happening. Then roars of excitement as Stan swept down the right wing time and time again. I breathed the most monumental sigh of relief at half-time. Stan's side was 4–1 down, but I had no doubt it would come right in the end.

And of course it did. Stan's display in the second half was magical. If anything he played even better than he had against The Rest of the World at Wembley. Poor Jacobson! Stan pushed the ball through his legs and ran round him, turning him one way, then the other, all but turning him inside out. Morrie was screaming and shouting to his colleagues for support, waving outstretched arms for more men to cover Matthews. More men were sent. It made no difference. In fact the climax of the afternoon came when Stan dribbled past FIVE defenders on the goal-line and then squared the ball back for his team to score the winning goal. It was an unforgettable display. Everyone who saw it talks about it to this day. I know I shall never forget it, and it confirmed what I already knew – that Stanley Matthews was the greatest footballer the world has ever seen.

Two things happened after the game – one bad and one good. The bad was that Morrie Jacobson was never the same player. Joe Harvey's assessment was terribly accurate. I was the manager of Johannesburg Rangers by then, and Morrie's subsequent form was so poor that I nearly dropped him from the side. He came out of it, he was too good a player to collapse completely, but the flair and attack which are the hallmarks of a truly exceptional full-back never returned, and I think I'm right in saying that he was never capped for the Springboks or even Southern Transvaal after that.

The good news was that everyone in South Africa wanted to see Stan play. Invitations came from far and wide. For instance I remember Eric Litchfield driving Stan to the neighbouring Portuguese colony of Mozambique. Stan played one game, and when he and Eric returned to Jo'burg the boot of their car was stuffed with escudos. Wherever Stan played he delighted the crowds, and he earned a small fortune in the process. And more than that: he and I became firm friends from that day to this.

Stan

Lubbe was right: I *did* earn a lot of money on that first trip to South Africa. Properly invested it would have earned a fortune by now. But I'm forever making the wrong decision when it comes to business – and that first trip was no exception. For example, just before I set off on the return journey to England, I met a solicitor at some social gathering. I think Lubbe introduced him. Anyway he and I got on well together and at the end of the evening he said, 'Stan, I'll give you a tip about the money you've made here. Leave it in South Africa. I'll help invest it. Take my advice and buy some land at a place called Margate. That place will boom over the next few years.'

He meant Margate in South Africa of course, not the seaside resort on the Kent coast. But I turned him down. Well, I figured it this way: it was a long way from Blackpool to South Africa (at least twenty-four hours' flying time in those days), and although I enjoyed that trip I had no plans to return. So it seemed silly to invest money there. But return I did, the very next year, *and* the year after that, *and* the one after that – and so on and so on. In fact I went to South Africa almost every summer for ten consecutive years. I even went to Margate. The solicitor was still there. He showed me the sites my money would have bought. By the time I returned with Mila in 1971 that land was worth more than a million pounds! But that's life, and I don't regret it. Had I taken his advice I would have an ulcer by now, just worrying about all that money – and believe me, health is worth more than money any day of the week.

But to return to my arrival in Johannesburg with Mila. Lubbe and my other friends accepted her immediately, so we felt safe while we were with them – but Mila kept in the background on all other occasions. For instance she never accompanied me on any public appearances, and if I met anyone in the hotel – visiting entertainers from England, for example – Mila always slipped quietly away. The cat and mouse game with the

Press continued. It was a dreary business, but far preferable to the kind of headlines which kept us awake at nights.

Apart from that, the trip was great. In our free time we went on safari and did the sights generally – all of which was made more enjoyable by my many friends in South Africa who were as generous and kind as ever. And the time spent coaching was fun, not work.

For a start, black African kids have so much natural talent. Their ball control is fantastic. They run with the ball, they dribble, they attack, and their enthusiasm for the game has to be seen to be believed. Football is *their* game. They live and dream for it. Every kid in the street is kicking a tennis ball – and of course they idolize Pele.

I travelled all over the country – to proper stadiums, schools, rough bumpy pitches, some without a blade of grass – everywhere and any-where – coaching and talking about the game. Generally the sessions ended with me organizing a match – even if only a five-a-side game – but sometimes, if the facilities were lacking, I would just talk about football, and answer questions of course.

I remember one day in particular. We were a hundred and fifty miles out in the bush. (By *we* I mean Harry and me. Harry was my assistant. He drove me everywhere, made the introductions, did all the arranging and so forth.) Well that day had been long and tiring. We had made six appearances, which included three matches and three lectures on the game generally, so understandably we were a little fatigued. Even worse than that, by late afternoon, my throat was beginning to seize up. In fact it felt so sore that I could hardly talk. But we still had one call to make, so I said to Harry, 'Tell you what: this last one will only be a lecture. Why don't you do it? You pretend to be me.'

He and I were about the same build, and by then we were so deep in the bush that the kids wouldn't have seen a newspaper photograph of me anyway – so they had no way of knowing. It seemed a safe bet, so once he got over his surprise, Harry agreed to swap places.

When we arrived at the village we were greeted by the Chief. I introduced Harry as Sir Stanley Matthews, we all shook hands, and the Chief introduced the twenty or so boys who had turned up to listen to me. This will be great, I thought. I can sit with my feet up while Harry gives the lecture. So I sat at the back and Harry got stuck into my talk. He had heard it more than a dozen times by then, so he knew it nearly as well as I did. And he gave it very well. But then came the questions.

They were straightforward enough to begin with: 'If a goalkeeper punches the ball and it hits the bar before going into the net, is it still a goal?' That kind of thing. Harry dealt with them easily and gave what a theatre critic might call an unruffled performance. But there was one boy who knew a thing or two about the game. Gradually his questions became more testing. Harry dealt with them carefully and accurately, but he sensed this lad was a bit out of the ordinary. Then the boy asked: 'Please, Sir Stan –' I resisted the urge to stand up. 'Please, Sir Stan,' the boy said, 'is there only one way to score from a penalty? I mean, can you only shoot direct?'

Harry hesitated. The boy had trapped him. Harry knew it – the boy sensed it – and I was *sure* of it. Here was a question to which Harry had no answer. 'How do you mean?' he asked, playing for time.

The boy savoured his moment of victory: 'Must a penalty be a direct shot at goal?' he asked.

Harry dried up. He opened his mouth twice – but no words came out. I could see my reputation as a football expert dying a terrible death on the dusty floor of that hut. Then Harry had a moment of inspiration. Suddenly he smiled. 'Why that's *easy*,' he said. 'In fact that's *so easy* I bet even my driver could answer that one.'

So I jumped up and croaked out a reply: 'Yes, Sir Stan,' I said, 'I *do* know that one. There are two ways to score from a penalty. Direct from the spot, or indirect. For instance, I could push the ball two yards, you could run round me and shoot – and the goal would count if the ball went in.'

Harry stifled a great sigh of relief and threw a triumphant look at the boy. 'There's your answer,' he said happily. The boy looked crestfallen, but recovered his spirits later when Harry awarded him a prize. So we all parted as friends. It was a masterly piece of quick thinking on Harry's part and we laughed about it all the way home, but it really does demonstrate the tremendous interest the blacks have in the game, because many an English soccer fan would be caught out by that one.

So the three-month coaching tour passed all too quickly. Wherever we went, the enthusiasm for soccer was tremendous. I remember going to one village and when we arrived the space around the football pitch was packed tight with hundreds of people. They lined the touchlines – in fact *they were* the touchlines, because no lines had been marked on the ground. So we played and I remember thinking something was wrong. The pitch was atrocious – all stubble instead of grass, which made ball control very difficult – but I was used to that by then, so it wasn't that which nagged away at the back of my mind. But *something* did. We turned round at half-time and all through the second half I tried to work out what was wrong. But it defeated me, and by the end of the game I was no wiser.

The following day we were due to play in the same village and on the same pitch, and I was determined to fathom out what was wrong. So I arrived at the ground early – before the crowd turned up. Even then it took me a while to figure it out. Then I paced the pitch. It was *two hundred yards long*! I paced the width. It was a *hundred and fifty yards wide*. I measured the goals. They were two yards wider *and* one foot higher than they should have been! I tell you, that pitch had been laid out for a team of giants. When the officials turned up I pointed out the problem. Not that much could be done about it. The goal posts were cemented into the ground. So we played again on the same pitch and, as far as I know, it is still played on today. The boys don't care – just so long as they can play football.

I must have travelled all over South Africa on that trip, but Johannesburg was our base. This suited me fine because we had a lot of friends there and were to make a lot more. Bobby Locke was one of them. I bumped into him one Tuesday morning and we went off to have coffee together. I first met Bobby way back in 1948 when he was playing in the British Open at Lytham St Annes. We became pals then, but I hadn't seen him in years, so we had a lot of catching up to do.

Apart from being a truly great golfer, Bobby is one of the world's best story-tellers. I can listen to him for hours. Golf stories by the hundred of course, but more than that: stories about his life, his travels, his experiences – and a lot about his father. 'My dear old dad,' he would say, 'I remember one day . . .' and off he would go again. His father had played a big part in his life and we had both survived strict upbringings, so we had a lot in common. 'I remember one day,' he said, 'I was about eight at the time and had been playing golf a couple of years. Long enough to pick up bad habits, because I mis-hit a ball and threw my club down in anger – the way I saw a man do it the day before. My dear old dad was furious. He shouted: "If you let your temper get the better of you, then you don't deserve to be on the golf course." He gave me a real dressing down, but it was the last time I ever lost my temper on the golf course.'

So Bobby and I both learned a thing or two from our fathers, and after that reunion we met every Tuesday morning for coffee. It was just the two of us at first, then Lubbe became a regular, and gradually Tuesday morning coffee became something of an institution. Not just among our resident Jo'burg friends either – word got round and visiting celebrities dropped in whenever they were in town. I remember people like Dickie Henderson, Brian Rix, Terry Scott, Alex Forbes, Andrew Cruikshank and many others – too many to mention – who at various times would turn up at our Tuesday morning coffee club. There were no rules, no membership fees – people just dropped in, stayed an hour, had a chat and went on their way. The hard core membership grew to about eighteen in the end and there were always three or four visitors to add news of the outside world.

It put me in mind of earlier days, in Blackpool just after the war. Some of my Blackpool team-mates and I used to meet Charlie Chester once a week for coffee. Charlie had his gang then, five or six other comedians who had teamed up with Charlie in an act called 'Charlie Chester and his Gang'. They did radio shows and toured very successfully all over the country. Anyway Charlie and his Gang met us once a week for coffee – in the cafeteria in Littlewoods. They were riotous times, but I think we were banned in the end because of one of Charlie's gags. He and the boys pretended they were store designers from Littlewood's head office. Charlie had shop assistants holding opposite ends of a piece of string while he measured counters and display units. More and more assistants were co-opted into this work until the store ground to a halt in a maze of strings stretching all over the place. It was hilarious to watch, but Littlewoods decided that they were better off without our custom. Coffee mornings in Johannesburg were sedate affairs compared to that.

So, what with one thing and another, the three months in South Africa passed very quickly and Mila and I were just preparing to return to Malta when I had a pleasant surprise. *The Sunday Times* of Johannesburg asked me to go out the following year to do some more coaching – but this time would I stay for a whole year? Mila and I discussed it and decided to accept. Apart from the fact that we both liked South Africa so much, it seemed an ideal place to be while the details of my divorce were thrashed out in England.

Mila

A few other things happened before we left Johannesburg, however. Perhaps the most important was that we met Stan's daughter Jean again. Her husband Bob had emigrated to South Africa almost immediately after his visit to Malta. Initially Bob had stayed with Lubbe until he found his feet, then he sent for Jean and the children, and by the time we arrived the family had settled happily into a delightful bungalow at Bryanston, a suburb of Johannesburg. Naturally Stan was anxious to see them again.

Poor Jean and Bob – poor *anyone* in that situation – they were in the middle. Quite understandably Jean wanted happiness for *both* of her parents, and she would have been less than human not to have dubbed me 'the other woman'. My status was still undefined. The solicitors locked in battle in England were only vaguely aware of my existence, and miraculously the Press had still not linked Stan's name with mine. But, especially after the pantomime in Malta, Stan felt he had to offer Jean an explanation, and I heartily agreed.

Luckily both Jean and Bob were full of sympathetic understanding when we went to see them, and of course their children were excited to see their 'Poppa'. So began my friendship with Stan's daughter and his son-in-law, and with their delightful children – which I am glad to say is stronger than ever today.

But no account of our first visit to South Africa would be complete without telling the story of Stan's comb. Poor Stan was very embarrassed because it was one of those rare occasions when he volunteered a story about himself – and it backfired.

I first heard the comb story in Malta, but it has been told and re-told for years – ever since 1948, in fact, when England played Italy in Turin.

Now you might expect Italians and Englishmen to be the most excited people around when it comes to a match between England and Italy.

You might expect that – but you would be wrong. The people who get the *most* excited are the Maltese. They go wild. The reason is simple. Every Maltese is a soccer fanatic, but half the population are fervent admirers of the Italian game, while the other half are passionately pro-English. So when the two countries play each other, Malta comes to a standstill. People sit glued to radios and television sets until the final whistle – then the Island fairly erupts. The supporters of the victorious team take to the streets. Processions are formed, fireworks scream into the sky, motor horns blare and sirens sound on the boats in Valletta harbour. There is tremendous excitement. It is all enormous fun, and Stan says that Maltese soccer supporters are among the keenest and most knowledgeable in the world.

The story of Stan's comb started, as far as I was concerned, after we had been in Malta for almost a year. Thanks to the Brothers and other friends like Lewis Portelli and George Magri, I was fairly well accepted by then, and able to accompany Stan to parties and functions without causing too many eyebrows to be raised. At one such party Stan was surrounded by a group of admirers who were anxious to praise his past triumphs. This is usually my cue to talk about the weather, or whatever else comes to mind, in order to save Stan embarrassment. But on that occasion a man prominent in the Island's affairs was doing most of the talking, and I was having difficulty in getting a word in edgeways. Almost ecstatically he recalled taking a group of Maltese football fans over to Turin for the 1948 game in which England beat Italy by four goals to nil.

'But the most magical moment of the whole game,' he said to his circle of listeners, 'was when Sir Stan took out his comb and combed his hair.'

Stan looked at him in blank astonishment.

'Imagine the scene,' said the man, closing his eyes to picture it better. 'The stadium is packed with eighty thousand screaming Italians. The ball is pushed out to the wing. Matthews collects it on the half-way line. He beats one man, then two, then a third. He takes the ball to the Italian goal line. Then he stops. He just stands there, with one foot on the ball. Contemptuously he surveys the Italian defence. And then ... *then* he withdraws a comb from his pocket – and combs his hair.'

There was a collection of 'oohs' and 'aahs' from the admiring audience, but the biggest gasp of all came from Stan. He blushed scarlet and had difficulty with his speech for a moment. Then he said, 'Mr Minister – with respect, I think you must be mistaken – '

'I was there!' the Minister insisted, 'I *saw* it. The whole crowd saw it.'

Stanley struggled to overcome his embarrassment: 'But Mr Minister, I've *never* carried a comb on to a football pitch in my life – '

The Minister ignored him. 'The crowd went wild,' he said, turning back to the rest of the party. 'Then Sir Stan slid the comb back into his pocket and took off for the Italian goal.'

Stan was making desperate signals to me for help, but what could *I* do? What could *Stan* do, come to that? Of course he denied the story as tactfully and diplomatically as he could, but nobody believed him.

On the way home he said, 'I remember that game. It was a boiling hot day. Quite probably I brushed sweat out of my eyes – but a *comb*....'

A few days later Stan was stopped in the street by another Maltese who had seen the big game in Turin in 1948. 'That was great,' he said, 'the way you humiliated the Italians with that comb.'

'No, no, no,' Stan protested.

A month later, Lewis Portelli telephoned: 'Stan, there's a friend of mine here from Italy. I promised I would introduce you. Could we meet for a coffee in the morning?'

They met, and the Italian too had seen the game in Turin. He said, 'We might have won, until you did that trick with the comb. That destroyed our confidence.'

'But it's not *true*,' Stanley told him.

Poor Stan! Deny it as much as he could – nobody would believe him. I remember a group of people once asking to *see* the magical comb. Afterwards Stan grumbled, 'That was more than twenty years ago. The comb wouldn't have a tooth left by now.'

But still the story persisted. I heard it so many dozens of times, from Maltese and Italians who visited Stan, that eventually even *I* began to believe it.

Then we went to South Africa. One evening Stan and I were guests of some friends who took us to dinner at the local golf club. The facilities were magnificent, and after being given a guided tour of the club house we adjourned to the dining-room where a buffet was being served. Food was heaped on to our plates, and at the end of the line we reached the chef who was supervising the proceedings. Our host introduced us: 'Gino is Italian,' he said. 'He still supports Italy, even though he has lived here for ten years.'

Gino shook hands with Stan. 'I saw you play,' he said proudly, 'in 1948 when England beat Italy in Turin.'

'Really,' said Stan.

Gino slapped a beefy hand to his forehead: '*Mama Mia!* What a game!

Magnifico! But that business with the comb. *O vache de morta!* So cruel, so tormenting!'

So once more poor Stan got hot around the collar. Naturally our host wanted to know the story too, so Stan suffered agonies of embarrassment while Gino the Chef recounted what he thought – what he was *convinced* he had seen in Turin that day. Stan denied every word of it, but again nobody believed him – they thought he was just being modest.

He was pulling his hair out afterwards: 'Crikey, that story will *not* go away. First Malta, and now here. I deny it until I'm red in the face but people won't believe me.'

I calmed him down, and a few minutes later he had his idea: 'I know what I'll do,' he announced. 'I'll accept the wretched thing. In future I'll just agree – it's got to be less embarrassing than going through this performance every time.'

And so we come to the incident in Cape Town. We were there two weeks while Stan coached the local side. On the last night our hosts took us to a very smart Italian restaurant. The food is out of this world, they told us, and so it was. About twenty of us went and we had a marvellous evening.

At the end of the meal the Italian owner came to our table to ask if we had enjoyed the food. Then he recognized Stan. 'Stanley Matthews! How wonderful to meet you. I saw you play – in Turin, when England beat us 4–0.'

Stanley flinched, then he took fresh heart, remembering his idea. He looked round the table and waited until he had everyone's attention. Then he said, 'So you saw me take out my comb and comb my hair?'

The Italian blinked. 'No,' he said, 'I never saw that.'

Stan

And so my first trip to South Africa with Mila came to an end. It had
been enjoyable for both of us and we looked forward to returning the
following season. But prior to leaving Johannesburg I was hospitalized
for a minor operation. It was nothing to get excited about and I was not
worried at all until I was wheeled into the operating theatre. Then two
nurses appeared and asked for my autograph. I had received a sleep
inducing injection by then and was too muzzy to hold a pen, let alone
sign my name – so I suggested I sign their autograph books afterwards.
They swapped nervous glances. 'We'd much rather you sign *now*,' they
chorused, '*before* the operation.'

I wondered if they knew something I didn't? Things like that can have
an oddly disturbing effect. I survived all right – though it put me in mind
of some of the experiences I have undergone with doctors in my time.
One of the strangest happened during a tour with Blackpool almost
thirty-five years ago. First we went to the United States, then to Australia,
and we took in Hong Kong on the way home. The round trip took six
weeks, and it was an ambitious project for a club in those days.

I remember us arriving in Hong Kong on a Wednesday after the Australian tour. We were booked to play two matches – one on the Friday,
and a second on the following Tuesday. We liked Hong Kong and I
think Hong Kong liked us because both games were a sell-out well in
advance of our arrival. In fact tickets were so hard to come by that
tailors were offering to make us a suit in exchange for two tickets. So
naturally we accepted the offer and Blackpool were the best dressed
team in the First Division for a year or two after that.

They had a beautiful stadium and a capacity crowd of thirty thousand
watched us win the first game 3-1. But the second promised to be
altogether different. Hong Kong were putting up their 'national' team
and every paper on the island tipped them to win. So I desperately

wanted to play, but unfortunately I suffered a groin injury in the opening match, and from past experience of such injuries I knew I was doubtful. In fact the following morning I told Eric Haywood as much: 'You'll have to leave me out, Eric. This will take at least a fortnight to mend.'

Eric was our Assistant Manager at Blackpool and in charge on that trip. He heard me out, then suggested I let a local doctor look at the injury. I turned the idea down flat – until one of the officials of the Hong Kong FA personally vouched for a man they used themselves. I was as convinced as ever that the big match was out as far as I was concerned, but after some persuasion I agreed that nothing would be lost by a consultation.

The doctor arrived at eight o'clock the next morning, to be followed into my hotel room by a young boy carrying an attaché case. 'This is my Number One Son,' said the doctor. I groaned aloud. Not only did this doctor *look* like Charlie Chan, but he even *spoke* like him. The two Chinese, father and son, stood in the doorway, bowing up and down like ducks bobbing on the water. I gritted my teeth and told them to get on with it.

The attaché case contained an infra-red lamp. Number One Son plugged it in while father inspected my bruised groin. Then a tin containing a black ointment was produced and Charlie Chan massaged the stuff into my thigh. It was revolting stuff that looked like axle grease and smelled like curdled yak's milk. Anyway it all went on – the whole tin – as Charlie Chan kneaded my flesh furiously, like a baker making dough. Then the lamp was applied and I had heat treatment for half an hour. After which they went away, with the promise – or the threat – that they would return at four o'clock that afternoon.

Sure enough, father and son were back at tea-time with another tin of black axle grease, which they proceeded to smother all over my thigh. Then I spent a further half-hour under the heat lamp. It was all a waste of time as far as I was concerned, but Eric Haywood was anxious not to offend the Hong Kong FA – who were only trying to help, after all – so I suffered in silence.

The next day was a Sunday, and the whole performance was repeated over again. The treatment was relatively painless so I suffered it, but when I turned in that night I was as convinced as ever that the match on Tuesday would be played without me.

Yet, when I awoke in the morning I had to admit that much of the stiffness had gone out of my injury. It certainly felt much easier – at least it did until Charlie Chan and Number One Son arrived to slap another

With Charlie Chester (*right*) and 'King Rat' Tommy Trinder, Stan becomes a Companion of the Order of Water Rats.

'Sir Stanley Matthews, CBE, *This is Your Life!*' Stan greets his brothers, (*left to right*) Jack, Arthur and Ronnie.

Right: At the Sportsman's Service at Westminster Abbey, Stan carries the FIFA flag – with pride and considerable relief, after an administrative error!

Below: Another unforgettable day, as it's now Sir Stanley Matthews who chats with Minister of Sport Dennis Howells at the House of Commons after receiving his knighthood from the Queen at Buckingham Palace.

Far right: Stan and Mila.

Below right: Celebrities have a habit of dropping in on the Matthews in Malta. Stan talks football with Michael Caine.

The trouble with coaching these lads ... is that pretty soon they are beating you at your own game! Stan gives a few tips to a three-year-old Ghanaian in Accra in 1957 (*right*), and gets his come-uppance in Nairobi (*below*).

re long Stan had his own team. 'Sir Stan's Men' on the road to Rio.

kfast with golfer Bobby Locke and (*left*) Lubbe Snoyman, who helped to run 'Sir Stan's Men'.

Stan and Mila at 'Idle Hours', their home in the beautiful fishing village of Marsaxlokk, on Malta. The name turned out to be inappropriate.

Never idle for long: coaching in 1979 ...

... and playing in 1981. On 19 April 1981, sixteen years after his farewell to first-class soccer, Stan turns out in a charity match at Grangemouth ... and is still beating his man.

can of grease all over me. Then the heat treatment, then they went away again – until four that afternoon. On his way out Charlie Chan said, 'Our medicine is velly good. You will be okay for big game.'

Even then I disbelieved him. Well, I had been in football long enough to know how my body responds to various injuries. Groin injuries took a fortnight, they always had and – as far as I was concerned – they always would.

But I felt fine the next morning. There was *some* soreness, it was true, but never enough to stop me playing. I exercised and did some light training, all without ill effect.

'Great,' said Eric Haywood, 'you can play in the big game.'

'Perhaps,' I conceded, 'but only for twenty minutes or so. Then you will have to pull me off.'

So we settled for that. The twelfth man was duly warned to be ready to come on after the first twenty minutes, and we left for the Stadium.

The crowd gave us a good reception, but naturally enough the biggest cheer was reserved for the home side. I watched their players warm up, and sure enough, some of them looked very good indeed. It promised to be quite a battle.

We had Jimmy Hagan on our side. Jimmy was with Sheffield United then but had joined our tour as a guest – which was bad luck for Hong Kong, because Jimmy's form was electric that day. He scored almost before the sound of the opening whistle had died away, and we were 2-0 up within ten minutes. After that it was a rout. We won 10-1 and the crowd and the Press went into raptures about our performance. I felt sorry for the home side because they really didn't deserve such a hiding. But when we went four up they felt they had 'lost face', which to the Chinese of course is a fate worse than death. So they lost confidence after that and it became an exhibition match for us.

But the most astonishing thing was that I played for the entire match. My groin never gave me a single twinge. Even at half-time, when Eric was prepared to substitute the twelfth man, I felt as fit as a fiddle.

'Eric,' I said, 'I feel great. I'll last the full ninety minutes with no problems.' And I did.

I never saw Charlie Chan again, but I have often thought about him. Just imagine, with Mila doing my pressure points and a can of Charlie Chan's ointment in my kit – crikey, I could still be playing League Football today!

Mila

So we left South Africa and returned to Malta – just in time to receive an urgent summons from Stan's solicitors in Stoke. Apparently the divorce proceedings had bogged down completely and the solicitors wanted Stan in England for consultations. Poor Stan – despite all the fun he had worked hard in South Africa, and was looking forward to putting his feet up at 'Idle Hours'. But the divorce dominated our lives, so of course he had to go. Thus within a day or two of arriving at Luqa Airport we were back again, this time to put Stan on an aircraft to Manchester.

While he was away I worked on the garden and planned our holiday. We were returning to Villach in Austria for a fortnight and were delighted to receive a letter from Urs, our Swiss friend, saying he and his wife would be there at the same time. And from Villach we planned to go to the Black Sea and spend a further two weeks holidaying with my parents. After which we would fly to Rome and thence back to Malta. So it promised to be a month of fun, sunshine and good company, and we were both looking forward to it.

But Stan returned from his meeting at Stoke in a gloomy mood. His divorce, and hence our marriage, looked further away than ever. I hid my disappointment as best I could and concentrated on cheering him up. After all, we were still together and that mattered more than anything. At least it did to me – and it did to Stan too, but his attitude was odd somehow for a couple of days. I felt sure something had happened in Stoke which he was keeping from me. It hurt to think of him being secretive. It was so unlike him, so unlike either of us, because we shared everything. But I said nothing in the hope that he would feel able to tell me about it – eventually.

And of course he did. On his third day back at 'Idle Hours' he gave me a sheepish grin and said, 'Oh by the way – I heard a rumour about you in Stoke.'

At once I knew this was it: this was the *secret*. But how could there be a rumour about me in Stoke? I said, 'The only people I know there are your mother and brothers.'

He shook his head: 'I didn't hear it from them, I heard it from ...' and he mentioned the names of a couple of very old friends. I had never met them but I knew they were friends of long standing as far as Stan and his wife were concerned.

'What can those people say about me?' I said. 'They've never met me.'

'All very silly,' Stan said, looking more and more embarrassed. 'I wasn't really going to tell you. No, perhaps I won't – I mean perhaps it's best if I don't – '

'Stanley!'

'Well, it's so stupid – '

'So tell me.'

'It's a bit of a joke really,' he said, trying to grin.

I was mystified, then alarmed. Why was he so embarrassed? 'Please,' I said.

'It's a laugh – '

'So share it.'

'Well,' he said, taking a deep breath, 'the rumour is that you're a spy. That you're a communist spy.'

'A *spy?*'

He nodded: 'And that you go under three different names, and that British Special Branch want to see you.'

Perhaps I should have laughed? How would you react to something like that? But I couldn't laugh, because the truth was I didn't find it funny – and despite Stan's pretence, neither did he. My surprise turned to shock, and the shock turned to anger. And, as well as that, I suppose I was just a little bit afraid. Utterly preposterous though it was – suppose someone believed it? Suppose *Stan* believed it? But a look at his face reassured me at least about that.

He knew I was upset, and for once it was his turn to calm me. We joked about it in our usual way, and after that we tried to put it out of our minds.

Luckily, perhaps, the next few days were busy. As we would be in South Africa for such a long time, we decided to let 'Idle Hours' on a short lease. The decision meant I had to pack some of our more precious possessions away and list everything else on an inventory. Of course

Stan gave me a hand but, as any woman will confirm, even well inten-
tioned *husbands* are more nuisance than help on such occasions, so most
of the work fell on Katie and me. Katie, the daughter of a local fisherman,
was our maid, our friend, our protector, and our *confidante*. In fact no
account of our life in Malta would be complete without mention of
Katie. When we moved into 'Idle Hours' Stan decided I should have
some help around the house. He mentioned the matter to a friend and,
as is always the case in Malta, his friend knew someone who might fit
the bill. The following day, more out of curiosity than anything, Katie
came to see the *Englisez* who lived in the bungalow on the hillside. She
later told me that she was prepared not to like us and expected to leave
after a couple of days. Thankfully, however, we all got on from the
moment we met.

Katie has many good qualities, but I will mention only one here – her
discretion. If Katie decides to keep something quiet, not even the KGB
could make her talk. Naturally, with her being at 'Idle Hours' so much,
we had to tell her some of our problems, and in particular our anxiety
to avoid the Press. We did so with some trepidation, but our reservations were quite unnecessary, because Katie turned into our staunchest
ally.

We owe so much to our friends in Malta. We could never have kept
our story quiet without their help. Indeed, looking back, it is almost
possible to feel sorry for the curious reporters who arrived on the island
in search of Stan. We were protected behind a bewildering smokescreen.
First, the reporter would have to deal with the Brothers, then Lewis
Portelli, then George Magri. They were our first line of defence. Occasionally, however, an especially persistent reporter would slip past even
them and succeed in tracing our address. But long before he reached our
doorstep we would have been alerted by the Maltese bush telegraph.
The reporter would arrive to find our gates closed and blinds drawn at
every window in the bungalow. Then he would retrace his frustrated
steps down to Marsaxlokk, to make enquiries there. A helpful Maltese
would direct him to Katie's house. Katie would shrug: 'Sir Stan is away
from the island and won't be back for months.' And that would be the
end of another scandalous headline!

So Katie helped me pack, and a week or two later Stan and I left for
Austria and a reunion with Urs at Villach. Urs was as much fun as ever
and the fortnight flew by, as did our time on the Black Sea with my
parents. Then we returned briefly to Malta to conclude arrangements
with the people who were taking 'Idle Hours', before boarding an

aircraft again, this time to Johannesburg for our first really long stay in South Africa.

Disappointment awaited our arrival. Stan's wife was in town – staying with Jean and Bob at their home in Bryanston. Both Stan and I had looked forward to a reunion with Jean and Bob and their children, but clearly a visit was out of the question for the time being. So we comforted ourselves with thoughts of our other friends – and met with another shock.

Lubbe was his usual warm self towards Stan, and so was Viv Grainger, but I detected a slight coolness as far as I was concerned. I dismissed it at first, as imagination on my part, until a day or two later. Then Lubbe took us home and Dawn, his wife, practically refused to speak to me. Her attitude amazed me. We had become such firm friends on our previous trip, but she was now making me feel an unwelcome guest in her home. Stan and I cut our visit short and went back to our hotel to think about it.

'I've known Dawn twenty years,' Stan said. 'She's a wonderful person. Why should she be so rude?'

It was a week or so before we found out. Dawn thought I was a communist spy. *She really did!* Of course it didn't take us long to realize that the 'rumour' could only have come from one source, but the problem was what could we do about it? We rushed round to Lubbe's home and confronted Dawn. Eventually we convinced her of the truth, but it was an embarrassing incident and makes me uncomfortable even to think about it. Crikey (as Stan would say) what was I supposed to be spying on for heaven's sake? Junior football in South Africa? Stan's Post Office football team in Malta? But logic is not always to the forefront of these things and mud has a nasty habit of sticking. Thankfully, however, although it took some time, Dawn and I became the firmest of friends again. Stan loved her and so did I because she was a truly generous person whose warm personality lit the lives of everyone around her.

Eventually Stan's wife returned to England and we were able to visit Jean and Bob again. It was at a tennis party at their home one day that Stan ran into a very old friend – David Tomlinson the actor. Stan and David have been pals for years, so they had plenty to talk about. And then David asked where we were staying. When we told him, he shook his head: 'You should be at the Mariston Hotel – it's where we all stay when we're in Jo'burg.'

And so David introduced us to the Mariston and another chapter of our story began.

Stan

We liked the Mariston from the moment we moved in. It was part hotel, part apartment block – so long-stay guests like us took an apartment with its own kitchen and all the amenities of home, while retaining access to the main facilities of the hotel. It was the best of both worlds and we soon made ourselves comfortable.

And David Tomlinson was right about the steady stream of show business personalities passing through. Many were old friends, like Dickie Henderson, Terry Scott and dear old Sandy Powell. I invited all and sundry to our Tuesday coffee mornings, so attendance increased by leaps and bounds.

Meanwhile the coaching flourished to such an extent that after a few months Ray Cotterill, the dynamic promotions manager of *The Sunday Times*, came up with a new idea.

'What we should do, Stan,' he said one day, 'is form our own team. Suppose we put a squad of about sixteen boys together? Then you could coach them consistently and play them in matches all over the country!'

It seemed a wonderful idea, because I love coaching kids. To help a boy develop his talent is for me the most satisfying experience. The frustrating aspect of my work in South Africa was that I was unable to spend time with the same lads on a regular basis – so I never saw how they progressed after a few lessons. On the other hand Ray's idea was a perfect solution, and a few weeks later he enlarged even on that. Coca-Cola were joining in as co-sponsors of the project. The team would be known as 'Sir Stan's Men' and their football shirts would bear the name Coca-Cola on one side and *The Sunday Times* on the other.

It was proposed that I tour the schools in the Soweto township to recruit my boys, and if the idea paid off I would have a career for the rest of my life, as manager/coach of 'Sir Stan's Men'. Mila and I were thrilled with the prospect and accepted immediately.

So the plan was put into practice and I began a tour of the schools. As I said earlier, the natural talent possessed by some of those black boys is enormous, so the difficulty was often more to decide who to leave out than who to include. But eventually I assembled a squad of sixteen boys aged from fourteen to sixteen and appointed one of them, Gilbert, as Captain.

Gilbert, and another fellow called Sammy, were to become my two right-hand 'men'. They were both characters in their own right. Gilbert was an intelligent, likeable boy from Soweto with the happiest smile you've ever seen. He greeted the news of his appointment as skipper with a beaming ear-to-ear grin which stayed on his face for weeks. In fact just the mention of football would win a smile from Gilbert. His enthusiasm was unbounded and he proved a model of dedication for the rest of the boys. I tell you, I grew so fond of Gilbert that given half a chance I would have adopted him. Gilbert was fabulous.

Sammy, on the other hand, was smart. He was a young man of about thirty who was appointed my assistant. Sammy's job was to drive the team to our games in a mini-bus, and to help me arrange the matches, help look after the boys and their kit, and to generally make himself useful. All of which Sammy did, though at times his idea of being useful was far different from mine. And that's when Sammy played dumb. When I pointed out his wrongdoings an expression of pained concentration would appear on his face. His head would be cocked to one side and a hand would be placed behind one ear, as if he was hard of hearing. 'Huh?' he would say, 'What's dat, Sir Stan?' I would repeat myself. 'Huh?' Sammy would say. This would go on for about ten minutes, with me continually re-arranging my words in an effort to make myself clear. But I was wasting my time: not only did Sammy understand, but by then he had worked out my reaction to what he had *really* been doing. But the performance would continue: 'Huh? What's dat you say, Sir Stan?'

So my little squad and I went into training. Sammy did a tour of the schools every day except Monday, and collected the members of the team in the mini-bus. Then he would take them to Soweto where I would be waiting.

Those kids were great little footballers, but they weren't a football *team*. That was my biggest problem. Take defence, for example. None of them wanted to know about defending. To defend was somehow *unmanly* in their book. Black teams did not defend, black teams attacked. My boys were magnificent in attack, they could run with the ball, dribble, swerve, shoot – they had every trick imaginable when it came to attack – but nobody wanted to know about defence. I experimented with different formations: 4–4–2, 4–4–3, everything I could think of. It made no difference: once they took the field all they thought about was attack.

The problem showed itself in other ways. Set pieces, for example. We would practice set pieces – corner kicks, free kicks from just outside the box, long throw-ins – and they worked out fine in practice. But in a match the boys got so excited that they forgot every word about it.

The easy way out would have been to drill the boys in the same way that some squads are coached today in Europe. But it would have broken my heart to do that. They had so much natural flair that a regimented approach would shackle their skills and abilities – it might even stifle their enthusiasm for the game – and I knew I would never forgive myself if I did that. Somehow I had to blend my knowledge of tactical play to their native flair. If only I could do that, I told myself, I would have a team of world beaters.

So – for what remained of the season – I coached during the afternoon and pondered on the problem at night. I scraped my brains for some small snippet of past experience which would help solve the problem. I remembered this game, that coach, this manager and that club captain. All of which reminded me of one of the shrewdest, craftiest men in football – Joe Smith.

I've played under quite a few managers in my time – people like Tom Mather, Bob McGory, Tony Waddington, Walter Winterbottom – but the biggest character of all was undoubtedly Joe Smith at Blackpool. Joe was a legend in his day. He had the same caustic wit as Bill Shankly and was just as ruthless in striking a bargain. Like when he bought me from Stoke in 1947.

Stoke were managed by Bob McGory then. Bob was a dour Scot with the thickest accent you've ever heard. When he telephoned me I used to say, 'Look Bob, put it in writing and I'll know what you're talking about.' Anyway, Bob and I were having our differences in 1947, and what with one thing and another, I felt ready for a move. The club I fancied was Blackpool. My war years had been spent there, I had bought a small hotel in the town, and altogether I reached the conclusion that Blackpool would suit me fine. So after thinking it over carefully I asked for a meeting with the Stoke directors, and when it was granted I requested a transfer.

The directors refused at first, but I persevered, pointing out that looking after my hotel meant I had to live in Blackpool, which in turn involved me in so much travelling that even home games for Stoke were away fixtures as far as I was concerned. Finally the directors relented and granted my request for a move to Blackpool, but I was sworn to secrecy while the negotiations went on. Well, I kept quiet but the story got out somehow, and within days the papers were full of it. I ducked and parried questions from reporters and kept out of the way as much as I could, but Stoke can be a small town at times, so I was glad to go up to Scotland the following week – to play for Great Britain at Hampden Park.

The match, against The Rest of Europe, promised to be a good one, but that was not the reason why so many football club managers were there. They were on business. The war years had created a lot of restlessness and several players on the park that day were known to be looking for a change of club. So the scheming and manœuvring behind the scenes promised to be every bit as hectic as those on the pitch.

As for the match, well the score makes it sound one-sided. We won 6–1, but that was mainly due to the way chances were snapped up by our forwards. And what a forward line it was – one of the best I ever played in. Billy Liddell, the Liverpool and Scotland player, was on the other wing, with another Scot, Billy Steel, inside him. Tommy Lawton was centre-forward, Wilf Mannion inside right, and then me. Wilf put us ahead early on, then they equalized, and a moment later Wilf scored again, this time with a penalty. Then Billy Steel hit an absolute rocket of a shot from thirty yards out which wrong-footed every player on the park – a tremendous goal. In the second half Tommy scored two typical Lawton goals and rattled their centre-half so badly that he scored the sixth for us by turning the ball into his own net.

Meanwhile the wheeling and dealing had started in the back rooms, as the managers wielded their cheque books. Billy Steel played for Morton then, and half a dozen clubs were after him, with Liverpool and Middlesbrough as favourites. However Billy's spectacular goal in the match must have added a couple of thousand to the bidding because Derby County came up with an offer of £15,500 and that clinched it – Billy was a Derby player by the end of the day.

In another room, Bob McGory and Joe Smith were getting nowhere with their talks about me. Bob was sticking for a top price, while Joe was playing his violin about what an old man I was. 'We'll get a couple of seasons out of him,' Joe insisted, 'that's all. Then he'll be put out to grass.' I might have been a race-horse, to listen to him.

Finally, when agreement seemed impossible, Joe had an idea. He got out the whisky, a drink for which Bob was known to have a true Scot's fondness. The two of them sat emptying glass after glass, and at last a price was agreed: £11,500 and I was a Blackpool player. They both nursed man-sized hangovers the next morning, but Joe was jubilant: 'The cheapest bottles of whisky I ever bought,' he said. 'Saved me at least a thousand on the transfer fee.'

And so began my association with Joe Smith. The story of how he bought me was typical. He wasn't exactly mean, but by crikey he was canny when it came to paying for anything. I remember an argument we had about complimentary tickets. In those days a player was allowed one stand ticket for every home match – for his wife or his father. Well, I had a wife and two children by then, so it was hardly enough. One day I caught Joe in a good mood and scrounged two paddock tickets from him as extras, and a month later I went back again – this time for four.

'Four?' Joe was horrified. 'You mean four tickets? All for the same match?'

Blackpool was a top side then and we were getting good gates – but that cut no ice with Joe. He was like the Beadle in Oliver Twist. 'More?' Joe would cry in horror.

I tried a soft approach: 'You remember when you gave me two paddocks last month? We won then. It must be a lucky omen.'

'That was two – not four.'

'I know but – '

'Four tickets! Good heavens, you'll want your own bloody turnstile next!'

That was Joe all over. He was the same about the football boots. Boots were provided by the club – or if you bought your own you were paid a boot allowance of two pounds ten shillings. But Joe knew I got mine free, so he refused to pay me a penny. It came about when I went to South America with the England side in 1950. I bought myself a pair of lightweight boots. They were fantastic – so supple you could bend them in half like a pair of bedroom slippers. So when I returned to England I took them to the CWS at Manchester and asked if they could make me a similar pair. They agreed, and from then on they made my boots for me, without charge in exchange for advertising. The boots were so light and the soles so thin that I used about four pairs a season, and whenever I took delivery of a new pair I sent the boys at the factory some cigarettes to show my appreciation. But meanwhile Joe had stopped my boot allowance, so I was forever out of pocket on the deal.

One day I made up my mind to tackle him about it. It was the start of a new season. We were away to Spurs in the first match. We beat them 4-2. Our next match was at home against Burnley, and just before the game I went to see Joe and asked for two pounds ten for a new pair of boots.

He looked astonished. 'You get them for nowt,' he said.

'I know that, Joe – but I have to send the boys cigarettes, so it works out costing me money.'

He shook his head: 'I'm not paying for their cigarettes.'

I pleaded, but Joe was adamant. 'I know you,' he said. 'If I give in once you'll be at it forever. Like that business with the tickets. Anyway, fancy lightweight boots, four pairs a season – I don't hold with it. A pair of boots lasted me two years when I played.'

So I explained all over again: how, the lighter the boots were, the faster I ran.

'Fine,' said Joe, 'you don't need boots at all. Play in bare feet – you'll be a sensation.'

I saw red then. 'Right!' I snapped, 'I'll do that. I mean it, Joe. No boot allowance – no boots. I *will* play in bare feet.'

Off I stormed to the dressing-room. Crikey, I was in a temper. I stripped off and changed into my kit – all except for my boots. Then I sat and seethed. Five minutes before we went down the tunnel, Joe called me back to his office. 'Here's your money,' he said with an old-fashioned look. 'But you were bluffing, weren't you? You wouldn't *really* have played in bare feet?'

That was the only time in all the years I knew him, that Joe ever backed down. And he grumbled about me for weeks afterwards. Telling everyone I had put one over him, when it was nothing of the kind: all I got was what I was entitled to, but Joe never saw it that way. To his mind it was the thin end of the wedge: a dangerous precedent might be created – and that would never do. Like the business of the taxi money, which was forever cropping up, especially when we played in London.

We had an established routine in those days. We travelled down by train on the Friday, booked into an hotel, had dinner early and went to a show – generally The Crazy Gang at the Victoria Palace. Anyway, one day Huddersfield were in the same hotel. Now Huddersfield were a Second Division club – not First Division like us – but despite that we discovered that they had perks which were denied to us. They had taxi money and were allowed to take a taxi to the theatre and back. So we went to see Joe.

He turned red in the face: 'Taxi money? What do you want that for?'

'It's a long way to the theatre – '

'Nonsense! The walk will do you good. You can do it in half an hour.'

'Joe, it takes longer than that. Last time it took forty minutes and we missed the start of the show.'

Joe pondered that. Then he said: 'Tell you what – I don't want to be unreasonable. I'll compromise. Walk half-way, then catch a bus.'

That was Joe's idea of a compromise. I tell you, he was a hard man. Mind you, we *did* get the better of him in the end. We got our taxi money for the *return* journey after the show. But the most we ever got for the journey there was our bus fare – from half-way.

Despite everything, we all liked Joe – because he always stuck up for us when it came to an argument with the board. If he sometimes treated players hard, he often treated the directors with contempt. A newspaper pal of mine told me a story once, about Joe and George Formby. George and his wife were great Blackpool supporters and followed us all over the country. One day, we were in an hotel somewhere or other before the match, and my newspaper pal collared Joe for an interview. George Formby was with Joe, and the three of them decided they would go for a walk and talk at the same time – but first Joe had to visit the Gents. They all went and were talking football when my reporter pal recounted that one of the Blackpool directors had held forth the night before on Blackpool's need for young players. According to him the side was getting too old.

Joe was washing his hands by this time: 'Silly old fool,' he said. 'The man doesn't know the first thing about the game.' Then he went on to say a good deal more, using much stronger language. Suddenly a toilet was flushed and a door opened in one of the cubicles – and who should come out but the director they had been talking about.

'Joe,' said George, as the man left the Gents, 'He must have heard what we were talking about.'

Joe shrugged: 'He shouldn't have been listening,' he said. Then he took the others off for their walk as if nothing had happened. But believe me, more than one football club manager of my knowledge would have swooned on the spot.

Another thing about Joe was that he never weighed you down with tactical discussions before a match. 'Just get two quick goals,' he would say, 'then I can enjoy my cigar at half-time.' And that was it. If you pushed him further, with questions about the other side for instance, he would look at you in astonishment. 'Why ask me?' he would say.

'Professional footballers, aren't you? International most of you – that's why you're in my team. Let the other side worry about *you*. Now don't forget, two goals before half-time, then I'll enjoy my cigar.'

So we worked tactics out among ourselves. We had a good skipper in Harry Johnson and Harry could always be relied upon to come up with an idea or two about the other side. In fact, Harry and I pulled a diabolical stroke on Sheffield Wednesday when we won the cup in 1953.

Sheffield were a very strong side in those days and we were unlucky enough to be drawn against them in the third round of the cup. Not only that but the match was at Hillsborough, so very few people gave us a chance. And to make matters even worse, at least so far as I was concerned, I was suffering from an injury which had kept me out of the side for two months. It was an odd sort of injury, not one that I'd ever had before. It wasn't a pulled muscle, but it had that kind of *feel* about it, and no matter what we did – hours with the physio, brine baths, heat lamp treatment – nothing would shift it. Eventually Joe Smith made an appointment for me to see a specialist at a hospital in Manchester.

'It's muscle adhesion,' pronounced the specialist. 'You'll have to come in for a couple of days.'

So I went into hospital on the Sunday before our third round cup-tie with Sheffield Wednesday. The specialist gave me a drug which put me out like a light, then he went to work. They had to break the adhesion down, which involves some fairly brutal manipulation of the muscle. When the adhesion is released the muscle cracks with a sound of a whip-lash – or so they told me. I never heard it because I was still fast asleep.

Anyway I exercised cautiously the following morning, and to my delight I felt very much better. So much so that I began to harbour hopes of playing in the cup-tie. In fact I telephoned Joe from the hospital.

'Joe, I think I'll be all right for Saturday.'

'You've not kicked a ball in two months.' he answered.

I said I knew all about that. The main thing was I would be fit. I still remembered how to kick a ball. Joe sounded unconvinced: 'We're leaving for Buxton on Thursday morning,' he told me. 'Telephone me there Thursday night and let me know how you feel.'

So I was released from hospital on the Tuesday and on my way to Manchester station I bumped into a newspaper chum of mine. 'Hello Stan,' he said, 'I hear you've got a pulled muscle.'

I said I had no such thing and explained all about muscle adhesion, then I went home to Blackpool. But the following day half a dozen newspapers ran a story saying I had pulled a muscle and was doubtful for Saturday's game. I ignored them and went out to do some light training on Blackpool beach.

I reported to the ground on the Thursday, but Joe had already left for Buxton with the rest of the team. So I trained in the gym, and in the evening I telephoned Joe. 'I'm fit,' I said excitedly, 'I'm a hundred per cent fit. I'm okay for Saturday's game.'

Joe was still cautious. I ought to explain that no substitutes were allowed in those days. If a player broke down in the middle of a match his team-mates had to carry him until the final whistle. Joe generally left the question of fitness to the player himself. After all, as he said, we were all experienced professionals. We knew full well what a burden we would be to the rest of the team if we failed to complete ninety minutes. None of us would risk letting the side down by electing to play for selfish reasons. Finally Joe said, 'Get Jack Duckworth to try you out in a five-a-side with the reserves tomorrow. Then phone me.'

So the next morning – Friday – the assistant manager, Jack Duckworth, played me in a five-a-side game with the reserves. I felt on top form. It was just so marvellous to be back in the game again. I could hardly wait to reach Joe on the telephone afterwards. 'Jack agrees,' I said, 'I'm a hundred per cent.'

Joe barely hesitated – and he even spent money for once. 'Okay,' he said, 'get a cab and join the rest of us here at Buxton.'

So Saturday dawned and I was in the team. It was my first match for two and a half months and every newspaper in the country told Joe he had made a mistake: 'Matthews has a suspected pulled muscle,' they said, 'and is doubtful to last the match.'

It made gloomy reading for the rest of the boys. We knew it would be a hard match anyway. Sheffield Wednesday were on top form and, what with the ground advantage as well, they were clear favourites to win. Besides they were a bogey side as far as I was concerned. A player called Curtis was in their side then, and whenever we played them Curtis followed me everywhere. He stuck to me like glue. Where I went, Curtis went, breathing down my neck for the whole ninety minutes. He never gave an inch, let alone a yard.

But the newspapers had set me thinking, and when Harry Johnson called for ideas on tactics before the game, I took him aside. 'Listen Harry,' I said, 'you know most of the Sheffield lads. Why not wander into their dressing-room before we go out? Say the newspaper stories are all true and that Joe Smith needs his brains testing. Tell them I've got a pulled muscle and won't last the game out.'

Harry looked surprised, but I pressed on before he could interrupt: 'Really lay it on thick,' I said. 'Say you and the rest of the boys are fed up with Matthews being big-headed enough to insist on playing – even when he's not fully fit.'

I must have been convincing because Harry asked: 'You haven't *really* pulled a muscle have you?'

'Harry, you know me better than that.'

So he grinned and went off to see the Sheffield team in their dressing-room. When he came back he said, 'Your name's mud, Stan – but I think they bought it.'

So out we went. More than sixty thousand fans crammed into Hillsborough that day and the noise was deafening. I watched Curtis carefully during the early minutes. He was laying deep, giving me as much as twenty yards! *Twenty yards!* Last time we played them I was lucky to get twenty inches!

I limped about for the first ten minutes, just to make Curtis that little bit more confident – then Harry Johnson gave the signal and we began to play. Sheffield were never really in the game after that, and to add insult to injury I was given so much room that I scored our first goal. Poor Curtis. Football can be as much of a psychological battle as a physical one. For instance, a team can lose 10-0, and in the dressing-room afterwards someone will say, 'Remember when they were only one up and we hit the cross-bar? If we had scored then what a difference it would have made.' So very true, because the morale of the side would have been lifted at a crucial moment. Confidence is everything, and at Hillsborough that afternoon we had the confidence because we knew our ruse had worked. By the time Sheffield realized what was happening we were well on top and on our way to Wembley. Mind you, I think Harry and I were first off the pitch at the end of the game and we never pulled that trick again. But I bet Joe Smith enjoyed his cigar that day.

Mila

So Stan pondered on how to get the best out of 'Sir Stan's Men'. It was almost the end of the season by the time the squad was assembled and in training, but I know Stan had high hopes of them for the following year. However our first 'tour of duty' in South Africa had come to an end and it was time to go – first to England, then for a holiday in Austria, and then on to Malta for a month or so before returning to Johannesburg.

Our stay in England was brief. Just long enough for Stan to get the bad news from the solicitors about the divorce. It was always bad news as far as I could see, and progress seemed painfully slow – if indeed there was any progress at all. We joked about being allowed to get married when in our seventies, and got on an aeroplane for Austria.

It was during that trip that we met one of the most extraordinary characters I have ever known. Dr Muller, an expert in extra-sensory perception, and a quite, quite remarkable human being. In fact he was so extraordinary that even Stan's scepticism about such matters was shaken rigid. Meeting Dr Muller – like so many things in our life – came about quite by chance.

We were delighted to be greeted at our hotel by Urs, our Swiss friend, and his beautiful wife. Their presence alone assured us of a good holiday, but we did have one problem. Stan had twisted a muscle in his back and was suffering a certain amount of pain. We hoped that the Spa waters would bring him some relief, helped by the rest he would have, plus me working on his pressure points, all supplemented by the healing hands of the masseur in the hotel. We figured out that if that lot didn't work, he really was in trouble. So we got to work.

In fact it was the masseur who told us about Dr Muller. Apparently the doctor had been one of Austria's leading bio-chemists until some years earlier. Then a very close friend of his died. His friend had been acknowledged as the greatest clairvoyant in Europe. For some time after his death no change took place in Dr Muller's life, and then – about three years later – he opened what in effect was a small clinic. He charged no fee for his services and, from all accounts conducted himself in a rather casual, almost eccentric way. According to the masseur, however, the doctor performed some quite astonishing acts. For instance, he was able to diagnose a person's ills merely by looking at him.

Well, Stan's back improved gradually, but he was still suffering some pain, so one day I suggested a visit to Dr Muller. Stanley was far from keen. In his opinion, extra-sensory perception was so much nonsense. He has great faith in doctors, but he likes his doctors properly qualified and to practice medicine in a traditional way. In short, Dr Muller had about as much appeal to Stan as an African witch doctor. Nothing venture, nothing gain, I reminded him – and one afternoon we went to see Dr Muller.

If you take the road out of Villach towards Vienna and travel for about thirty-five kilometres, you will come to a small village. That is where Dr Muller lives. There is no need to know more, since he is quite famous in the district and anyone will set you right once you are in the neighbourhood. Besides there are even street signs directing the way to his home.

When we reached it, we found his house was quite ordinary and unpretentious. It was set at the end of a country lane. Dogs barked around the back, and there were a number of beehives in the garden. The sort of small house that could be found in any Austrian village. Then we went in to meet Dr Muller. We had no appointment, since he doesn't make any, and he had no idea who we were or why we were there.

We found him in a small room at the front of the house. A middle-aged man dressed in shorts, who greeted us shyly. There was nothing remarkable about his appearance, nor about the room. A desk and a few chairs, simple furnishings, nothing ostentatious.

He never asked our names, so we never told him. He simply directed us to a pen and paper on the desk, then took himself off to a corner, where he sat down. He explained that he had to sit apart from us, so that our aura did not interfere with his. Then he asked why we had come and what it was that we wanted to know.

I explained that Stan had been suffering from back trouble.

Dr Muller turned away from us and stared into the corner. 'Your back will get better,' he said. 'It is nothing serious. You are very fit. You have low blood pressure and an enlarged heart. In fact there is nothing at all wrong with you – except that one vertebra is worn out.'

It was *all true*. Stan *does* have low blood pressure and an enlarged heart, and one vertebra is worn out!

Dr Muller and I were talking in German, and when I translated for Stan he was astonished. In fact he was so impressed that he risked another question. 'Ask him if I should take a course of pollen injections – I think they would be good for me.'

So I did. Mr Muller answered at once. 'Yes,' he said, 'pollen injections will do you no harm at all.' Then he threw me a glance over his shoulder. 'But not for you,' he said. 'Under no circumstances must you take pollen.'

It was my turn to be staggered. I love honey but it has disagreed with me since childhood. So clearly I could never take pollen injections. But how had Dr Muller known that? His diagnosis, however, was not yet finished. 'What you *should* take,' he told me, 'are the iron tablets which your doctor prescribed recently.'

Only weeks before, a doctor had given me iron tablets to take. I hadn't liked them very much so I had ignored the advice. Now I was completely bewildered, but I translated for Stan as quickly as I could, while Dr Muller watched me with an amused glint in his eyes. 'Take up that pen,' he said pointing to the desk, 'and draw an outline of the house where you live. Just an outline, nothing more.'

I did as I was told, then carried the paper across to him. He turned away and stared into the corner. After a moment he said: 'You live on an island. A small island, and your house is on a hillside. They discovered the remains of dwarf elephants there years ago.'

I translated, and Stanley and I stifled gasps of amazement. Malta *is* a small island. We *did* live on a hillside. The elephants meant nothing to me then, but later, when I recounted this story to some friends in Malta, they said, 'But *of course*, the skeletons of elephants were discovered in the caves at *Ghar Dalam* not far from "Idle Hours".'

I honestly cannot remember what else we asked Dr Muller that day. All sorts of things, and every one of his answers was astonishingly accurate. We were in a daze when we left. Dr Muller would accept no money for the consultation, and when we shook hands he said, 'Don't say goodbye, I will see you again.'

We told Urs the story over dinner that night. Usually he was as sceptical as Stan about things like extra-sensory perception, but with Stan there to vouch for my account of things he could hardly fail to be impressed. And he was – at least until I reached the end, when I mentioned Dr Muller's parting comment about seeing us again.

'And *will* you see him again?' Urs asked.

Stan shook his head: 'Of course not.'

But later in the evening Stan got to thinking. 'You know,' he said, 'a man with Dr Muller's ability could make a fortune. I wonder if he would help with my football pools?'

I thought it was a joke at first, but Stan was quite serious – unfortunately. Perhaps I should explain that we were worried about money at this time. Rolls-Royce had just gone into liquidation, so Stan's largest investment had gone down the drain – and if Rolls could go bust, well, it seemed anything could happen. None-the-less, I felt that to ask Dr Muller to fill in a pools coupon was somehow not on, and I was saying as much when another friend joined us. Her name was Brit and she was a Professor of Latin at a German University. She too was on holiday, and during the day she often partnered Stan at tennis. Anyway she became interested in our story about Dr Muller and offered to drive us out to see him again the next day.

When we arrived Dr Muller greeted us with shy courtesy. Then he looked sharply at Brit: 'Why don't you chew your food properly?' he asked. 'You know very well that your mother died from cancer of the stomach.'

Colour drained from Brit's face and she fled back to the car, where she waited until we finished.

It was hardly a happy start, but none-the-less, and against my better judgement, I put Stan's question about football pools to Dr Muller. He was very angry. 'I am not interested in money,' he said when he had calmed down, 'and I will not use my gifts for such purposes.'

Naturally I apologized, and to make amends I explained that it was understandable for Stan to be worried about money at that time. There was a strike in England and most of our funds were locked up in shares, and we were consequently a little anxious.

Dr Muller accepted my apology with a shrug: 'Your shares are all right. But you should have accepted the advice of your financial advisor and invested in beer.'

That meant nothing to us, and we left shortly afterwards. Brit was waiting in the car, still white-faced and still trembling. 'Ever since I was a child,' she said, 'I have been told to chew my food properly. And my mother *did* die of cancer of the stomach.'

So we drove back to our hotel in a sombre mood. Stan did his best to relieve Brit's anxieties. 'After all,' he said, 'Dr Muller certainly is not right about everything. I mean he said we should have taken advice about investing in beer. We've *never* had such advice, so he got that wrong for a start.'

Before dinner that night I wanted an evening bag which I had not yet unpacked. So I went to our suitcases in search of it. When I opened one case I discovered a number of unopened letters. Then I remembered! Some post had arrived for us just before we left for the airport to come to Austria. I had shoved it in the case, promising that I would read it later. I had forgotten all about it.

One of the letters was from Fred Martin in London. Fred is Stan's financial advisor and had written to suggest Stan buy some shares in a brewery which was being taken over by another company. Had Stan opened the letter and acted on the advice he would have made a handsome profit. Dr Muller had been right again.

The talk at dinner that night turned again to Dr Muller. Even Urs was impressed. 'Perhaps I should consult him about my business,' he said. But I remembered how angry Dr Muller had been about the football pools, so I persuaded him against the idea. So Urs thought again. Then he said: 'There is *one* problem he could help with. I've just advertised for a housekeeper for my mother. I've had replies from twenty-one applicants. Why don't I ask Dr Muller who to appoint?'

Urs's mother was very old and quite blind, so I felt it was the kind of human problem which might appeal to Dr Muller. So the next day we went back to Dr Muller for a third time, and on this occasion Urs came with us.

Stan asked Dr Muller two questions that day. The first was about a film. Some months earlier a Canadian film company had approached Stan to discuss making a film of his life. We had heard nothing for some time, so Stan wanted to know if anything would come of the idea.

Dr Muller stared into his corner. 'Yes,' he said eventually, 'there will be a film. You will not be in it, but you will make some money from it.'

Stan's second question was whether he should play in a football match. A local club was celebrating its twentieth anniversary and they had asked Stan to take part in a special game. His back was feeling a good deal easier and he was inclined to accept – besides Stan would have to be *really* sick not to want to play football.

Dr Muller considered the matter: 'Yes, you can play – but only for forty-five minutes.'

Stan was delighted. 'Will we win?' he asked.

I translated and Dr Muller smiled: 'Yes, your side will win.'

We waited in the car while Urs had his interview with Dr Muller. We heard what went on afterwards and there was no doubt that Urs, who had been so sceptical, was shaken and disturbed by the experience. Many years previously Urs had been operated upon for his disfigurement – it was hoped at the time that the operation would enable him to grow taller. As things turned out the operation was not only unsuccessful but it even worsened poor Urs's condition. The first thing Dr Muller said on meeting him was: 'That was a crime what they did to you in . . .', naming not only the town but the actual hospital itself. Urs was flabbergasted.

Dr Muller did choose a housekeeper for Urs's mother, and he also advised Urs on a number of matters relating to his business. Then, just before the end of the meeting, he said something else. 'You took out some life assurance recently, in favour of your wife. You are a rich man, take out some more. I am a great believer in life assurance.'

Urs was pleased with the advice and, as far as I know, he acted upon it.

Two days later Stan played in the special football match. The club's current side was to take on a team of former players, and Stan was to play for the old boys. When he went to the dressing-room he was dismayed to find a collection of overweight, middle-aged gentlemen, most of whom were smoking cigarettes even while they pulled on their football jerseys. So Stan took a quick look next door. The other squad was full of young twenty-year-olds, brimming with youth and vitality.

Just before kick-off Stan trotted over to where I was sitting. 'Dr Muller is wrong this time,' he whispered. 'This lot will hammer us.'

But Stan's side was 3–0 up at half-time and they went on to win the match comfortably. Dr Muller was right again.

And what happened to poor Urs? Less than a year later we had a letter from his wife. Urs had been killed in a motor accident. Financially his widow had been left very well off – because Urs had increased his life assurance following his last holiday in Austria.

So Doctor Muller was right about everything. He was even right about Stan's film – though it was some time before we found out.

After our holiday we returned to Malta and our beloved 'Idle Hours'. I love flowers, and the neglected state of the gardens appalled us when we returned. So as soon as we had unpacked, Stan and I threw ourselves into the task of converting our patch of barren hillside back to the mass of colour it had been when we left. It was hard work but I enjoyed it –

at least for most of the time. But some of the 'half-time' rests were fatal. My back ached and my arms felt loose in their sockets, and every muscle I owned twisted in agony. All I wanted was to drown myself in a really hot bath. But Stan would finish his tea and jump up saying: 'Right – let's get started – we'll never finish this way.' God, there are times when I positively *hate* his fitness. And to think he was the one who wanted to call the house 'Idle Hours'.

But the work progressed, we got the garden into shape, and settled back into the pattern of life in Malta. Which meant getting used to autograph hunters turning up at all hours. I had grown accustomed to it on our travels and took no notice, but somehow it was different when we were at home. Stan's presence on the island was now too widely known for even the Maltese bush telegraph to protect us, so we had to cope with a new situation which found more and more people beating a path to our door. We were always alert for pressmen of course, but these were mainly tourists who had found out where Stan lived and had come to 'pay their respects'. Most of them were very pleasant, but some were absolute pests. I remember working in the garden one day, when a large car nosed up the lane and into our entrance. Four men got out and started to photograph the house. I looked up from the flower bed, expecting them to say something, even if only 'Good afternoon'. But they ignored me. Two of them walked round the garden while the others clambered up by the swimming pool, their cameras clicking like crickets. I stood up. Perhaps they hadn't seen me? But they had seen me all right. In fact they looked right through me. And my temper boiled over when they started to peer through the windows.

'Can I help you?' I asked.

'Stan Matthew's house?'

'Yes.'

'Not in, is he? Wouldn't mind a picture of him.'

'No, he's not in,' I said, as frostily as it is possible to be when you're as warm as I was.

'Oh well, not to worry – so long as we've got the right place, like. Hate to waste film on the wrong house.'

There was no answer to that! At least none I could think of. I stood glowering while they took their pictures, and as they climbed back into the car one of them jerked his head at me. 'Must be the maid,' he hissed at the others.

'Bit snotty, ain't she? Fancies herself I s'pose, being Sir Stan's maid an' all that.'

'All the same, these Maltese. All this talk of independence – it's gone to their heads.'

Then they drove away. I looked down at my muddy jeans and soiled sweater and burst out laughing. But I laughed even more when they scraped their car against the stone wall in the lane. Then I went indoors for a long soak in the bath, and when Stan got home I was feeling a good deal more human. Naturally he saw the funny side of it, but *of course* he had to carry the joke a step further. For days afterwards he was clapping his hands and telling me to fetch this and that – as if I were not so much a maid as a trained labrador.

So 'Idle Hours' was proving to be a good deal busier than we imagined. A few days later another large car hauled itself up from Marsaxlokk, and again four men got out. One of them was Arthur Newman, brother to Paul Newman, the actor. He explained that they were shooting scenes for a film called *The Mackintosh Man* and had been all over the island looking for the perfect location. And now they had found it. It was 'Idle Hours'.

'Oh *no*,' said Stan at his firmest, 'we want peace and quiet. Not a film crew tramping over everything – breaking – '

'We'll pay for any damages,' Arthur cut in swiftly.

'You'll not get the chance,' Stan said, 'it's not on.'

'Only four days – three if the light's good.'

'No,' said Stan, 'positively, definitely, absolutely, *no!*'

So of course *The Mackintosh Man* was shot at 'Idle Hours'. Arthur was very persuasive and – well – Paul Newman *was* Paul Newman. John Huston was directing and Carl Foreman producing, and the crew were all English, cockneys most of them. They couldn't believe they were going to film at Stan's house, and when they arrived the film was forgotten. The house rang for days with: 'Stan, remember that game against Scotland?' and 'What about that Cup Final, Stan?' Poor John Huston had the devil of a job getting any work done.

They were with us for almost a week, mainly because the crew invented all sorts of excuses to delay this or prolong that, merely to talk football with Stan. And I didn't help. I remember watching one scene from the kitchen window. They had tried about nine takes and – *at last* – the tenth looked perfect. Even John Huston was smiling with relief. I was absorbed, and then – just as the scene ended – my elbow caught a potted plant and sent it crashing on to the stone floor. '*Cut!*' stormed Huston, glaring at the kitchen window. I fled.

But it was a lot of fun, and when the boys weren't talking football with Stan, or actually filming, they were betting. They gambled on everything. On the temperature in the pool, the number of potholes in the lane winding up from Marsaxlokk (hundreds!), how far it was to the hotel ... on everything! It was catching somehow, like a disease. It got so bad that one night, when Stan and I were sitting with our feet up at the end of the day, he said, 'I think they'll finish tomorrow.'

And I said, 'I don't. They'll be at least two more days.'

He grinned: 'I'll bet you five pounds.'

And we *never* bet.

But the most astonishing thing of all was that another of Dr Muller's predictions had come true! We *were* involved in a film, though not in the way Stan had expected.

The next day there was an incident with the star, Paul Newman. He and Stan got on famously. Unfortunately they share the same sense of humour. Anyway, Paul had to make a simple exit from the house, carrying a suitcase and – because he was 'The Mackintosh Man' – wearing a raincoat. The cameras were set up on the terrace outside and trained on the front door. Huston was in his chair, with Carl Foreman next to him. The light was perfect, the sea in the background was as calm as a mill-pond, and there wasn't a cloud in the sky. An expression of blissful relief settled over John Huston's face. He was two days over budget, but get this scene done and they could be away back to England. All was set. And then Paul realized that his dresser had left the raincoat back at the hotel!

All hell broke loose. Huston fired the unfortunate dresser on the spot, and Carl Foreman got into a long involved argument about how long it would take for somebody to fetch the raincoat. I served cool drinks all round in the hope of bringing the temperature down, and then Stan had an idea. 'I've got a raincoat,' he said, and set off to collect it from his wardrobe.

Stan's raincoat was a Gannex mac – the sort made famous by Harold Wilson. As a matter of fact Stan got it probably in the same way as Harold Wilson got his – he had it given to him. Stan was at a reception at Number Ten one day, and who should he meet but Lord Kagan, who, I think, was plain Mr Kagan at the time. Anyway, a week later when Stan got home to Blackpool, there was a Gannex mac, with the compliments of Mr Kagan.

The Gannex, of course, was slightly different from the mackintosh used in earlier scenes, but Huston decided that nobody would be the wiser if Paul carried it over his arm. That decision made, Huston returned to his seat on the terrace and the crew huddled over their cameras.

Paul, Stan and I were still in the house, and I was just about to take the glasses back to the kitchen, when Paul suggested to Stan: 'Tell you what. Make a new career for yourself. When they shout action *you* go through the door. Straight up,' he grinned, mimicking the cockney crew, 'you'll be a star – overnight sensation.'

I glanced nervously through the window. Huston was as restless as a bull in a stockade and getting just as angry. Carl Foreman was puffing furiously on his cigar. Even the crew looked anxious. Any further delays could cause a riot, but when I turned back to warn Stan it was too late. He had fallen for Paul's idea – hook, line and sinker. He was already wearing the Gannex and fumbling in a cupboard for a pipe which he occasionally smokes.

'Action!' came a shout from outside.

'Hang on,' Paul shouted back.

'For Christ's sake,' growled Huston.

Stan found his pipe and went to the front door.

'Ready,' Paul shouted.

Huston growled a reply, and a moment later someone shouted, 'Action!'

Stan opened the door, stuck the pipe in his mouth, and in his best Harold Wilson voice, said: 'Quite frankly, the pound in your pocket today is not worth a light.'

The crew fell about – but John Huston's roar of outrage must have been heard in Valletta, let alone Marsaxlokk. *'GODDAMMIT! CUT!'* he bellowed, then he stormed into the house: 'For Chrissakes, I'll murder that son of a bitch!' Now John Huston is a very big man and he was so boiling with temper that I feared for Paul's life. But he was bent over a chair, clutching his middle and crying with laughter.

It took us a while to calm John down – if a man simmering like a roasting chestnut can be said to be *calmed down*. It turned out that he and Paul were always playing that sort of trick on each other, and Paul was simply paying him back for something that had happened the day before. But how were Stan and I to know?

Huston fixed Stan with a baleful glare: '*Sir* Stanley,' he said with heavy patience, 'I'm sure you'll see this scene to better advantage on the terrace with the rest of us.'

Stanley agreed. But Huston wasn't taking any more chances. *I* was still in the house. 'Mila,' he smiled, offering me his arm with old world courtesy. 'We'd be honoured if you would join us too.' So meekly I took his arm and we left Paul wiping his tears.

Then of course Paul proved what a complete professional he is by doing the scene perfectly, and they got it on the very first take. All was forgiven – Huston was purring like a cat and Paul was grinning like a delighted schoolboy. Hugs of congratulations all round, and that was that – the filming was over.

But Huston had the last laugh, because the story has a sequel. Some months later when we were in South Africa, Lubbe invited us to his home one Saturday for a film show. The film that night was to be *The Mackintosh Man*. So of course Stan told them the story, and how they were about to see so much of 'Idle Hours' and where we live in Malta. We even told them about Stan's début as a film star, even though his efforts died on the cutting-room floor. But the finished film contained virtually nothing of 'Idle Hours'. I think there was one shot of Paul on the terrace, and the famous one of him leaving through the front door, but they could have been filmed *anywhere*. There was nothing at all of the house, or the background. '*But it's true*,' we protested to Lubbe and the others afterwards. But they never believed us.

Stan

So we returned to South Africa and the Mariston Hotel. I was looking forward to the challenge of 'Sir Stan's Men' and to running them for a full season. We arrived, booked into the hotel, and had barely finished unpacking when Gilbert arrived, eyes shining with excitement at the prospect of so many games of football ahead of us. Apparently the rest of the squad were waiting to greet me at the stadium. So what could I do but leave Mila to sort out the apartment while I went to Soweto with Gilbert.

The very name Soweto is enough to send some people into shock, but for three years I lived as a black man with a white face in Soweto. True, I travelled back to Johannesburg every evening, but during the day I was invited into so many homes and made so many black friends that the place became 'home' as far as I was concerned.

To some Soweto is awesome, while others find it fascinating. One thing is for sure – it is huge. Soweto's predominantly single-storey bungalows sprawl for miles, and right in the centre is the football stadium, which is where Gilbert and I went to work.

And work we did, so that as the weeks passed our team knitted together and began to play some very attractive football. Defence was always a problem, but one day I had an idea. 'Listen Gilbert,' I said, 'when we attack, we *all* attack – when we defend, we *all* defend.' They liked that. It appealed to them, so we tried it in a few matches and it worked. But the set pieces continued to be a headache. The boys developed the ideas beautifully in training, but the excitement of a game drove everything out of their heads. One day Gilbert took a knock and I pulled him off, to sit out the rest of the game with me on the bench. Then we were awarded a free kick right outside the box. Gilbert jumped up and down with excitement. 'The set piece,' he shouted, 'Sir Stan – the set piece! *Now* is the time to use it!' How right he was – but the boys on the field took not a blind bit of notice. They blasted the ball against the wall of defenders in their usual boisterous fashion. Gilbert was in despair. 'How many times must I tell those boys,' he moaned. Then he gave me an old-fashioned look, rolled his eyes, and burst out laughing.

Early on in their career 'Sir Stan's Men' played other teams in Soweto and adjacent townships, but soon their fame spread, helped of course by *The Sunday Times*. I wrote about our games regularly every week, and as more and more people read about my squad of schoolboys so the challenges flowed in. Soon we were travelling everywhere – Durban, Pretoria, Bloemfontein, and even outside South Africa to Botswana, Swaziland and Lesotho.

We had some marvellous trips. We took to the road at the weekends, with Gilbert riding in my car, while Sammy chugged along behind with the rest of the boys in the mini-bus. Invariably Mila accompanied us and the team adopted her as a sort of combined mascot and school matron and weekend 'mum'. Thanks to the generosity of Coca-Cola the boys never went thirsty, because we carried a few crates of Coke on board wherever we went. But *feeding* Sir Stan's Men was like painting the Forth Bridge – as soon as one meal finished it was time for another.

For instance, we might stop at a crossroads. Sammy would toot the horn behind. Gilbert would hop out to see what was the trouble. Then he would return, saying, 'Sir Stan – the boys are hungry.'

Those words are engraved on my heart. 'Sir Stan – the boys are hungry.' They would descend on the nearest café like a swarm of locusts. Startled restaurant staff would watch them consume an enormous meal, and then they would pile back into the mini-bus and away we would go. A mile or so later Sammy would toot his horn. 'Not again,' I cried in disbelief. Gilbert went back to check – to return, sure enough, with the cry, 'Sir Stan – the boys are hungry.'

I remember one tournament in particular. About a dozen teams were competing and we were waiting our turn, when Gilbert tugged at my arm. 'Sir Stan – the boys are hungry.'

'But you're on in about fifteen minutes. Gilbert, it's *bad* to eat before a game. You won't have time to digest your food.'

'But the boys are *hungry* Sir Stan.'

'Toast,' I said firmly. 'Come on, I'll get you tea and toast.'

'Hungrier than toast. Sir Stan, the boys are *starving*.'

So they had chicken. They had eaten an hour or so before, but they settled down at the tables like a flock of vultures. Then, just as the meal was served, an official rushed up to say we were on. Kick-off for our match was in five minutes' time. 'Leave it,' I said to the boys. 'Come on, there's no time now.'

But 'Sir Stan's Men' never walked away from food. They took it with them, like an army on the march. Then they changed into their kit and ran out on to the pitch, licking their fingers and chewing drumsticks as they went. I tell you, there were so many chicken bones about that the centre circle looked like a burial ground. But we won, 3-1, so what could I say?

In fact the team won so often that we began to run out of opponents – at least at schoolboy level. So we started to accept challenges from teams of men. One such challenge came from a team in Lesotho.

Lubbe came with us on that trip. The game was on a Sunday and we travelled on the Saturday. When we arrived, Sammy took the boys off to their youth hostel while Mila, Lubbe and I settled into an hotel. It was late afternoon by the time we booked in, and after a wash and brush up Mila and I met Lubbe in the lounge bar for an aperitif before dinner. Then Gilbert burst in, out of breath and in a heck of a state. 'Sir Stan,' he gasped, 'Sammy's in jail.'

'*In jail?*' we chorused.

Poor Gilbert was too agitated to provide any details. All he could do was clutch my hand and drag me after him to the jail. Lubbe followed hot on my heels, and we arrived to see Sammy's face peering out through the bars in the back room of the police station.

'What did he do?' I asked the black sergeant.

'Insulted a police officer.'

Lubbe and I groaned aloud. We both knew Sammy. Sammy could be a cheeky devil when the mood took him, but surely people aren't locked up for being cheeky?

There was worse to come. Sammy would have to stay in jail until Monday, when he would be taken before the local magistrates.

'But these are schoolchildren,' I protested. 'They must be back at school on Monday.'

The black sergeant said that wasn't his problem.

Gradually the story came out. Apparently Sammy had driven the wrong way down a one-way street. Another black policeman had waved him down – and then the 'incident' had occurred. I knew I would never get the full details from Sammy. Just imagining it was bad enough. 'Huh,' he would say, a hand behind one ear, 'what's dat, Sir Stan? What's dat you say?'

Bail was out of the question, and we were told that Sammy would be detained in Lesotho until he had appeared before the magistrates. Even that was no guarantee of his release, because all sorts of dire penalties awaited those who insulted a police officer.

'I want to see the officer in charge,' I said.

The sergeant said he was in charge.

'The *senior* officer,' I insisted, not to be put off.

The senior officer apparently was dining out that night, and wouldn't thank anyone for disturbing him. Lubbe and I exchanged uneasy glances. Meanwhile Sammy watched us through the bars with a look which said he expected a lynch mob at any minute.

Lubbe and I did a tour of the town, one restaurant after another, until we found the senior police officer. His sergeant was right – the senior police officer was *very* displeased. None-the-less we told our story and persuaded him to return to the police station with us, where Sammy's smile of welcome lit up the night sky for ten miles in every direction.

We got him out in the end, but by crikey it took some talking. Sammy was made to apologize and put on his best behaviour – and then he was released. Lubbe gave him a dressing down afterwards, but all he got in return was: 'What's dat, Mr Snoyman Sir – what's dat you say?'

It was ten o'clock by the time we had taken Sammy to his hostel and returned to our hotel. Rushing around all those restaurants had whetted my appetite and the same must have applied to Lubbe, because as I parked the car he said: 'Sir Stan – the boys are hungry!'

So we had a late supper and went to bed. The next morning dawned bright and beautiful and full of promise for our big match. I went for my morning run, showered and changed, and then hurried down to join Mila and Lubbe for breakfast. But just as I sat down, Gilbert appeared in the doorway.

'Oh no,' I groaned, 'what's Sammy done now?'

'But for once Sammy was blameless. It was the hostel: they hadn't served breakfast – or at least not a breakfast to satisfy the likes of 'Sir Stan's Men'.

'Sir Stan,' said Gilbert predictably, 'the boys are hungry.'

We had stayed at the hotel before and I knew that Morris, the head waiter, was a football enthusiast, so I called him over to our table and explained the problem. Then I asked how much he would charge for sixteen extra breakfasts? Morris worked out a price. Now I ought to explain that although both *The Sunday Times* and Coca-Cola were exceedingly generous in their dealings with me, I *did* have a budget, and I prided myself that the budget was never exceeded. But Morris's bill for breakfast would have knocked a hole right through my careful calculations.

So Mila put on her most appealing smile and asked: 'Surely Morris, you can do a *special* price for children?'

Morris eyed Gilbert doubtfully. I wondered if rumour of the fearsome appetites of 'Sir Stan's Men' had reached Lesotho.

Morris wavered with indecision, so I tried to think of a way to clinch the deal. Then I had an idea. 'I'll throw in a football,' I offered – and that did it. Morris gave us a reduced price which took account of one football, and Gilbert shot off to collect the rest of the squad.

They filed into the dining-room fifteen minutes later, with Gilbert at the head and Sammy ushering the stragglers in like a sheepdog. They had never been in an international hotel before, so they were understandably shy and nervous, casting looks from side to side like the visitors to a waxworks. The other hotel residents looked on curiously as the boys sat down quietly at adjoining tables, while Mila fairly purred at their good behaviour and angelic expressions. Then I realized that the boys were waiting to be served – and breakfast was a buffet meal at that hotel. So I took Gilbert aside and explained the procedure.

His eyes widened. 'Say it again, Sir Stan – we don't want to get it wrong.'

'You just help yourself to whatever you want. Fruit juice, grapefruit, cornflakes, bacon and eggs – have what you fancy.'

Gilbert still seemed doubtful, so I led him over to the counter and gave him a tray. 'Fruit juice?' I asked. He nodded. So I placed a glass of fruit juice on his tray. 'Cornflakes?' He nodded again. So I loaded him up and we were about to go back to the table when he said, 'And grapefruit please, Sir Stan.' Now perhaps I should have explained that one usually has one or the other, but it seemed an unnecessary complication when there were other things I wanted to tell him. 'Explain to the boys,' I said, 'that they finish their starters,' – I waved at the fruit juices and so forth along the counter – 'then they come back for a cooked breakfast.'

Gilbert blinked, and then a smile gradually started to slide over his face. But he seemed to have understood so I sighed with relief and returned to my table. Lubbe had embarked upon a long and funny story so, having dealt with 'Sir Stan's Men', I settled down to listen to Lubbe's tale and enjoy my breakfast.

Now Morris could probably explain what happened next better than I can – but Morris isn't speaking to me any more. All I know is that the

boys were very quiet and well behaved. Sure they went back and forth
to the counter, but there was no stampede or anything like that. Mila
and I were locked into Lubbe's story and we were conscious of *movement*
– chairs being pushed back, trays being carried past, a certain low
hubbub of conversation ... but nothing more than that. At least not
until we looked up.

The front section of the counter was totally bare. Earlier enough fruit
juices and grapefruits and cereal dishes had been stacked there to feed
an army. Now it was empty. Morris himself was at the side of the room,
making a display of those little pots of marmalade which hotels go in
for. But his mind wasn't on his job. In fact he wasn't even looking at
what he was doing – he was staring at 'Sir Stan's Men' with a look of
terrible fascination on his face. I followed his gaze. The other end of the
counter was virtually empty of food. A few of my boys were there,
heaping rashers of bacon and sausages and fried eggs on to their plates
– but they were having to scrape around in the bottom of the serving
dishes.

I let my gaze wander to the next table where Gilbert was leaning back
in his chair and patting his stomach. He gave me a look of undying
gratitude. 'That was some breakfast, Sir Stan,' he said happily. 'We
managed it okay, but I had to go back three times for mine.'

The boy next to him burped gently. 'I went *five* times,' he said proudly.

Morris left his table of marmalade pots and came over to see me, with
a horror-stricken expression on his face. He searched for the right words,
groping for a way to express his true feelings. Then he looked at Mila
and a fixed smile came to his face as he asked if a special price was her
idea of a joke.

Her smile in return was radiant: 'Morris, you ought to feel compli-
mented. You ought to be pleased that the boys enjoy your food.'

Lubbe chose that moment to get out. We had decided to spend the
rest of the morning at the hotel, having a gentle work-out on their lawn
as preparation for the game in the afternoon, so Lubbe decided it was
time to start work. He led 'Sir Stan's Men' out of the dining-room while
I settled the bill with Morris, who was only partly mollified by the size
of my tip. On the way out I passed the table which Morris had decorated
with his little pots of marmalade. Not one remained – the table was
empty. I quickened my pace but Morris's groan of pain reached me in
the corridor. I never looked back.

Outside Lubbe was busy coaching the boys. We knew we were in for
a tough game that day. The opposition were fielding a team of men

against our lads – so we were inferior in size and height, strength and stamina. Maybe that's why 'Sir Stan's Men' were so concerned to build themselves up, because every now and then a hand was raised to a mouth and a pink tongue licked into a pot of marmalade. I cast a few anxious looks back at the hotel and hoped that Morris was otherwise engaged.

Anyway we practised for an hour or so, had a chat about tactics, and then it was time to pack up. I wanted to get to the ground early because I thought the opposition might be training there and it would give me a chance to look them over. But as we gathered our things together, Gilbert came to see me: 'Sir Stan,' he said, 'the boys are hungry.'

I couldn't believe my ears. Lubbe's jaw dropped and Mila cast her eyes to the sky.

'You *can't* be hungry,' I told him. 'Not after that breakfast.'

But ten minutes later found me on my way to find Morris. He met me at the dining-room door, throwing anxious glances over my shoulder as he barred my way. Luncheon too, it transpired, was a buffet meal and nothing – repeat, nothing – would induce Morris to allow 'Sir Stan's Men' over the threshold.

I pleaded and cajoled and persuaded – then I sent for Mila. She and Morris entered into negotiations, and ten minutes later she emerged with a deal. Morris would serve chicken and chips on the lawn – at a special price which included two more footballs *and* a pair of football boots. It was a triumph of diplomacy for Mila, but another blow to my hard-pressed budget. So Morris posted guards around the dining-room and departed for the kitchen, to emerge some time later with a string of waiters bearing huge platters of fried chickens.

We lost that day 10-1. It was the biggest defeat we ever suffered.

Generally we had a team talk after a match, but not that day. Lubbe hustled the boys into the mini-van, had a quick word with Sammy, and then leaped behind the wheel of my car. 'Get in Mila, Stan – and be quick about it,' he ordered. Then he hurtled out of town at a breathless pace.

I looked over my shoulder and saw Sammy blazing along in the mini-bus behind us. 'What's up, Lubbe?' I asked. 'Have we fallen foul of the local law again?'

'Crikey no,' he said, 'I just want to get home before tea-time.'

Mila

It was about this time that Stanley met Livingstone in Darkest Africa. Not the story you learn at school – the one about the explorer – but *my* Stanley and Bill Livingstone. This is how they met in Johannesburg. It was on a Monday – Stan's day off from 'Sir Stan's Men'. We always did the same things on a Monday, which for me generally meant getting up late to a leisurely breakfast and a lazy morning. Then I would go shopping and meet Stan at the Carlton Hotel for lunch. Which is what happened on that particular Monday, except when I arrived at the Carlton Stan was in the lobby, being shown some blueprints by a grey-haired man I had never seen before.

'Mila, come and meet Mr Bill Livingstone. He's the inventor of the electric car.'

Well, Mr Livingstone was absolutely charming. I've known some pleasing men in my time, but without doubt Mr Livingstone was the most polished I have ever met. And so interesting. Apparently he was setting up a factory in South Africa to manufacture his electric car, and he was full of it – in a nice, enthusiastic way – so that he insisted on showing us his blueprints and plans. The oil sheiks had just plunged the world into crisis, so obviously a golden future awaited the electric car – and its inventor. Well Mr Livingstone chatted away, absolutely bubbling over with enthusiasm, then he said: 'Why not join me for dinner tonight? I'd like you to do some public relations work for my company.'

He meant Stan of course, not me, and naturally Stan said he didn't know the first thing about electric cars. But Mr Livingstone brushed that aside: 'You know the newspaper boys here, don't you? You arrange the Press Conferences, and *I* will tell them all about the electric car.'

So we agreed to meet him for dinner. It turned out to be a sumptuous meal at the best restaurant in Johannesburg. There were six of us. Mr and Mrs Bill Livingstone, his factory manager and his wife, and Stan and me. During the evening Bill Livingstone was as ebullient as ever. He talked non-stop of building a factory outside Pretoria, and of his forthcoming contracts with the South African government, and of an industrial empire to rival Henry Ford's. None of it was boastful, he wasn't bragging or anything like that – it was just that he was so excited that he wanted to share his dreams with us. And he did. In fact his enthusiasm was so infectious that we sat with stars in our eyes, contemplating a breathtaking vision of the future. I tell you, it was like having dinner with Howard Hughes.

At one point in the evening, he said to Stan: 'You must come and see the site for the factory. Please come, and I'll give you the surprise of your life.'

Well who could resist an invitation like that? So we accepted, and the evening ended with everyone feeling on the crest of a wave. Bill Livingstone signed the bill with a flourish, and we all went home.

About a week later we went to Pretoria with him to see the acreage which the government had set aside to build his factory. It was a vast area and very impressive. Then Bill drove us to a beautiful spot about three miles away. 'And this,' he announced, 'is the site for your house.'

'*Our* house?'

'But of course. You are going to do important PR work for me, so you must live in a grand house. I shall build it here for you.'

We couldn't believe it. Anyone else and I would have said he was a nut. But Bill Livingstone was impressive. For instance, I was having trouble renewing my visa to stay in South Africa. 'Nonsense,' said Bill. 'Leave it to me.' And he drove into Pretoria to the government offices. I waited in the car but Stan went with him. Doors opened as if by magic. Everyone seemed to know him. 'Good afternoon, Mr Livingstone.' 'Nice to see you again, Mr Livingstone.' 'Can we be of help, Mr Livingstone?' Stan followed through the corridors of power and everyone fell over themselves to please Mr Livingstone. So much so that they were back to the car within half an hour, with my visa updated and everything in order. It would have taken me, or anyone else, weeks and weeks – but Bill Livingstone accomplished it in minutes.

On another day he took Stan to the Toyota car factory – one of the biggest in South Africa. They were greeted like visiting royalty. 'Yes,' Bill Livingstone assured the General Manager, 'yes, I *can* fit my electric engines into your cars. A modification here and there – but it *can* be done.' The General Manager's sigh of relief could be heard in Tokyo. Blueprints were studied while the Toyota engineers nodded acceptance to this and agreement to that – and the meeting was over. Mr Livingstone was on his way again, with Stan on his heels.

It was the way he operated – rushing from one meeting to the next, never standing still for a moment – and leaving a breathless, awestruck audience in his wake. And he was forever taking photographs, or asking me to take pictures of him and Stan together. Nothing concrete had been decided upon in respect of the PR work, but meanwhile we certainly all got on well together.

Then he and his wife moved into the Mariston. They had been staying at another hotel but decided, what with us living there, that the Mariston would be much more convenient. So we saw even more of them, in fact they came to dinner once a week. It was still the custom then for the better off folk in Jo'burg to hire films and screen them in their own homes, so whenever Bill came to dinner at our place he brought a new film. We protested, saying it was an unnecessary expense, but Bill would have none of it. 'As a matter of fact,' he said, 'I get them for nothing. Stan, you must come with me next week and I'll get you fixed up.'

Sure enough, the following week, Stan went with him to the company that hired out the films. 'This is my pal Sir Stanley Matthews,' said Bill. 'You'll look after him, won't you?'

'Of course, Mr Livingstone.'

So after that we had our own films, whenever we wanted them. In fact Stan got to know the young chap in the film office so well that they became good friends.

Meanwhile, 'Mrs' Livingstone was being a bit of a pest. She was a poor cook and a hopeless housekeeper, and as if that wasn't bad enough, she was usually stoned by lunchtime. It turned out that she and Bill were not married at all. She had changed her name to Livingstone by deed poll and come out from England to live with him. Their relationship was turning sour. Bill was forever dashing here and there on business, and she hadn't the resourcefulness to amuse herself. So after a few months she upped and left to return to England.

Poor Bill – we felt very sorry for him. Consequently his appearances at our dinner table grew more frequent and we did our best to make sure that not all of his time was spent moping in his apartment. But in truth he only seemed mildly upset about his 'wife' leaving him – and as often as not he was too full of his plans for his magical electric car to think about anything else. Stan and I were pleased that his business activities were at least keeping his mind from his domestic worries.

By this time work had started on Bill's factory. The shell of one factory block had been built and a prototype electric car was ready for demonstration. Stan and I were invited to see it. I actually *drove* it – round and round this huge barn of an empty factory. Other prototypes lay half unpacked in big containers. Bill swept an arm, explaining where the production lines would be and things like that, and growing more excited by the minute. In fact he seemed every bit as ready to conquer the world as on the day we met him.

Then he disappeared. Just moved out of the Mariston and vanished. We never saw him go and heard not a word from him. Stan grew so worried that he telephoned the manager at the factory – only to be told that Bill was away on a business trip. It seemed odd that he hadn't said goodbye, and that he had not as much as mentioned it to us, but that was the way he was. Something had cropped up which had to be dealt with there and then – whether it was in Jo'burg, London, or Paris. As I said, just like Howard Hughes.

Stan

Meanwhile, my little squad of black schoolboys was getting better and better. 'Sir Stan's Men' were taking on all comers and achieving some very creditable results. For instance, we went back to Lesotho for another game against the men who had humiliated us 10-1. Lesotho fielded the same team as before: giants who were stronger, taller, more experienced, possessed more stamina, and who seemed set fair to dominate our team of schoolboys just as they had on the first occasion. But this time was different. It would be nice to say we won, but that is the stuff of story-books. We did make a draw, however, 1-1, and that is as near to a story-book ending as you'll get in real life. 'Sir Stan's Men' played like champions, and I cannot tell you how proud I was.

It was the same in their other matches. Their skills on the ball, their intelligent running, their sense of attack – all were a joy to watch. Of course defence still gave me a few headaches, and they never properly mastered the use of set pieces during the course of a match, but overall I was very pleased with them.

So too were *The Sunday Times* and Coca-Cola, because they came up with a bonus. It was suggested that I take 'Sir Stan's Men' to England at the end of the season, so that the boys could see soccer played in some of the great stadiums there.

Well, it was a wonderful opportunity for the boys – but what about me? News of my divorce negotiations had leaked out in England. None of the details were known – Mila's name had been kept out of it – but what would happen if Mila and I returned, with a team of little black boys?

It put me in a terrible fix. It could be the trip of a lifetime for my lads from Soweto. None of them had ever been on an aeroplane, none of them had even been out of South Africa – except for their trips across the borders with 'Sir Stan's Men'. Whatever I did, I knew I would never forgive myself if I deprived the boys of such a chance.

Then I had an idea. The boys still clung to this idea that to defend was a 'sissy' thing to do. Their idols – Pele, Eusebio, and others – were all attacking players, and 'Sir Stan's Men' continued to insist that black players never defended. So why not take them somewhere where they could see black teams in action? Why not take them to South America? Let them see for themselves that to defend was an integral part of the game.

So I put my suggestion to *The Sunday Times* and Coca-Cola and, to my enormous relief, they liked the idea. I was elated. The boys would get their trip, and because they would see black players in action they would obtain the greatest possible benefit – and I would avoid those dreadful headlines. Everyone was delighted.

The Sunday Times and Coca-Cola got down to planning the details of the trip, and I announced it to 'Sir Stan's Men'. Can you imagine the reaction of a little black boy from Soweto, when he learns he is to fly half-way round the world? Not only that, but our sponsors had decided to provide the team with a uniform: a very smart blazer with 'Sir Stan's Men' on the breast pocket, with matching trousers, white shirts, ties, everything. *And* pocket money to spend in Rio. I tell you, our squad looked smarter than an Olympic team from any country you care to name – they looked tremendous! And proud? So proud that their eyes shone and the grins on their faces seemed as permanent as their hair or their arms and legs. 'Sir Stan's Men' were walking on air.

It showed in their football. With each game they became that little bit more confident. They stroked the ball with an extra sureness. When they passed they did so with the certainty that the pass would be accurate, and that the recipient would have positioned and balanced himself just right to accept it. They got better and better and better – then they went over the top!

It happened about a month before we were due to leave for Rio de Janeiro. I had gone to the stadium at Soweto as usual, for a training session in the afternoon. Sammy had done the round of the schools in the mini-bus to collect the members of the squad, and the boys had disappeared into a dressing-room to get changed. I waited out on the pitch ... and waited and waited ... but nothing happened. The boys remained in the dressing-room, so I went in to chase them out.

They met me in silence. Generally the dressing-room rang with the sound of their excited shrieks. Usually they couldn't get changed fast enough. As a rule they were in and out on to the pitch within five minutes. But not that day.

They sat on the benches, with their arms folded and their eyes cast down to the floor. Nobody moved when I went in, and not one of them said a word.

'What's up?' I asked. 'Come on – I've been waiting out there for fifteen minutes.'

'We're on strike,' piped a voice from a corner.

'You're *what*?'

One of the bigger boys cleared his throat: 'That's right, Sir Stan – we've gone on strike.'

I don't know what I said then. I think I was too stunned to say anything. It took me a minute or two to catch my breath. Then I sat down and looked round the room. 'What about?' I asked eventually. 'Crikey, what the heck are you on strike *about*?'

There was a general shuffling as the boys looked round for a spokesman. Gilbert wasn't going to speak for them – that was obvious. Gilbert sat opposite me nursing himself as if he was suffering from stomach ache. I caught Sammy's eye. 'Sammy,' I said, 'what's this strike *about*?'

A hand shot behind his ear and he crooked his head to me. 'What's dat, Sir Stan? What's dat you say?'

I was too bewildered to be angry, or even amused. After all, the average age of this little band of desperados was fifteen. And they were *going on strike*?

Then one of the boys said: 'Strike's for the same as any other strike. We want more money.'

'Oh?' I said, and waited.

'This trip to Rio,' the boy said. 'It could make you famous.'

'Oh, could it?'

He nodded: 'We do all the work, we play all the matches – but all the newspapers keep on about is "Sir Stan's Men". You get all the credit and we don't even get enough pocket money.'

Now if ever a squad had been blessed with generous sponsors it was us, with *The Sunday Times* and Coca-Cola. They had been open-handed to a remarkable degree.

'We want *twice* as much pocket money,' the boy continued, 'or we're not going anywhere. The Rio trip's off as far as we're concerned.'

I blinked around the room in astonishment. The build-up and the publicity had gone to their heads – either that or someone had put them up to this.

'We've already made you famous in South Africa,' the boy summed up. 'Why should we make you famous in Rio as well?'

I found my voice then, but only enough to ask: 'So you don't want to go on this trip?'

'Not without more money,' he said defiantly.

I unlaced my boots and crossed the room to collect my shoes from my locker. Then I walked to the door.

'Where are you going, Sir Stan?' someone asked.

'To *The Sunday Times*. To tell them to cancel the trip.'

'Don't you want to go?'

'I've been to Rio before.'

'Don't you want to go *again*?'

'I can go another time.'

'Don't you want to go with *us*?' persisted the spokesman. 'You'll be famous if you come with us.'

I opened the door and went out into the corridor. Then I walked through the swing doors and out into the sunlight. I had the strangest feeling crossing that pitch, with the empty stadium looming on all sides. I had left clubs before – Stoke, Blackpool, Stoke for the second time when I retired. Even Port Vale. You leave *some* friends behind you whenever you move on. But this was different. This was in a special category all of its own. Then I thought crikey, don't be so ridiculous. It's not even a *proper* club! Just a bunch of kids, that's all. Why get *upset* over a bunch of kids?

So I was giving myself a right talking to by the time I reached my car. I unlocked the doors and lowered the windows to let some air inside. Then I slung my boots on the back seat and started the engine. As usual I had parked right inside the stadium itself, and I was just about to drive out when a mighty shout rang out from the direction of the dressing-rooms.

'Sir Stan! *Wait!* Sir Stan – wait for us!'

And the boys came streaming across the turf, running in a diagonal line to cut me off from the exit.

Gilbert reached me first. 'Sir Stan,' he panted, catching his breath, 'Sir Stan, wait a minute please.'

Then it all poured out, with everyone talking at once. How it was all a big mistake – how sorry they were – and how much they all wanted to go to Rio.

I climbed out of my car and looked at the boy who had been spokesman. 'So the strike is off?' I asked.

Gilbert and Sammy closed up on either side so quickly that he was sandwiched between them. 'That's right, Sir Stan,' he said. He hesitated a moment, then smiled in a shame-faced way, 'And I want to say sorry, Sir Stan. *Really* sorry. I was wrong.'

It takes courage to say you are wrong. I've known grown men lack that kind of courage, let alone a fifteen-year-old boy. So I cuffed him gently round the head to let him know I bore him no hard feelings.

'And what about you Sammy?' I asked. 'Don't you want to go on strike?'

His eyes popped: 'What's dat you say, Sir Stan? *Strike?* What's dat you say? There ain't no strike round here.'

The others joined in. 'No strike round here, Sir Stan. No *sir* – no strike at all.'

Sixteen very anxious pairs of eyes focused on my face, waiting for my next move. I glanced at my watch. 'Well, you could have fooled me,' I said slowly. 'Seems to me this is a funny kind of training session. With players standing around talking. Seems to me that *real* players would be working out by now, running round the track....'

It was as far as I got. They raced away with delighted squeals of excitement – and a moment later they were flooding past me around the track.

I sat down and changed back into my football boots. For a moment I just watched them, sixteen black boys running around the track in an empty stadium in Soweto. African schoolboys, under a blue African sky. By crikey, it was a bit different from when I'd been working-out as a fifteen-year-old at the Victoria Ground in Stoke. Odds were it had been raining so hard that being thrown in the bath after would have made me no wetter. Strike! I tried to imagine Mr Mather's face if I'd said I was going on strike. My word, how times have changed!

I never mentioned the strike to *The Sunday Times* or Coca-Cola. Well, I figured it this way: what would the world be coming to if men couldn't have an honest difference of opinion now and then? 'Sir Stan's Men' were growing up, that's all it amounted to. And meanwhile they were back in training, and loving their football as much as ever. That's all that mattered to me.

Mila

Then Bill Livingstone turned up again – and he came back in style. In fact we saw him almost every day for about a week, and every time he called on us he was wearing a different five hundred pound suit. (In cost, I mean, not weight!) I tell you, I have never seen a smarter or a more elegant man – and when he returned he exuded affluence on an even grander scale than before.

He arrived in a huge, air-conditioned American car, and came back the next day driving an even bigger one. 'Come and see my new house,' he said – so we did. Now there are some fabulous houses in Johannesburg. I've been to Hollywood and seen the houses there, but believe me the houses in Jo'burg are bigger and better. Bill Livingstone had such a house, overlooking the Vaal Dam. The view across the Dam was breathtakingly beautiful, especially when seen from the terraced gardens or the huge kidney shaped swimming pool.

Bill had made it! He chattered away excitedly about his contracts to build electric cars, and talked in telephone numbers when it came to money. We were delighted for him. Whatever the problem had been – indeed, if there had been a problem *at all* – quite obviously Bill had overcome it and was clean through to the other side.

So the three of us started to go out together again, and it was just like old times. But there was something wrong. The party needed a fourth, so I suggested that my friend Ruth join us. Now Ruth was a strikingly beautiful woman in her mid-forties. Sadly she had been widowed for some years and although there had been plenty of offers she had not remarried – mainly I suspect, because of her money. For Ruth was rich. Her husband had been rich, her husband's family were rich and indeed, Ruth's own family were rich as well. So Ruth was a bit cautious when it came to men. But I figured that introducing her to Bill was like introducing Barbara Hutton to Onassis – they were both loaded, so what could it matter?

Well, they mixed like gin and tonic. Ruth arrived for that first date, swathed in mink and dripping diamonds. She looked like a million dollars, and she probably was. Bill was enchanted. He got so excited that he forgot to talk about his electric cars, and I had never known that happen before. The following day he sent her flowers, and the courtship started in earnest. Like everything else Bill did, there were no half measures. He did not just *send* her flowers, he *bombarded* her with flowers. Half the florists in Johannesburg ran out of stock trying to keep up with him.

Bill set about courting Ruth the way generals lay siege to a town. It was a blitz. For his shells Bill used red roses and expensive gifts, but they were shells for all that – the object was the same: unconditional surrender. So it hardly came as a surprise when, three months later, we were invited to their engagement party.

It was like a scene from an opera. Not a crowd scene, more like the inside of the princess's palace on the day her prince arrives. It was held at the famous Tower restaurant, and about twenty guests attended. Bill and Ruth exchanged rings and the assembled company toasted the happy couple in champagne, and then more champagne, and even more champagne. I was delighted. After all, *I* had brought them together – as Bill acknowledged with a special toast to me half-way through the evening. So it was a super party and after Bill had signed the bill with his usual flourish, everyone left walking on air.

Ruth had a beautiful home of her own of course, so there was some discussion as to where they would live when they married. But that was a mere detail, because after the engagement party Bill seemed to spend more time at Ruth's apartment than he did at his house. In fact he as good as moved in with her.

I couldn't have been more pleased. Two of my best friends had fallen in love, and I had introduced them. It deserved an award, or at least recognition – Mila Winter, the best match-maker in Johannesburg. Perhaps I could do it professionally.

Anyway the pace of events quickened after the engagement party. First came the announcement that Bill and Ruth were taking a trip to Europe – Switzerland first, and then on to London. It reminded me of Stan taking me to Canada and I thought it was marvellously romantic.

Then, almost the day before the happy couple left for their trip, Stan came home looking puzzled: 'I met Wolf in the lobby. He was asking about Bill.'

Wolf was the manager of the Mariston.

Stan added: 'Wolf says Bill hasn't paid for his apartment here.'

I shrugged: 'Bill must have forgotten. You know how busy he's been. Does Wolf want us to remind him?'

Stan shook his head: 'It's more than that. Bill didn't pay the Fourways Hotel when he stayed there. They threw him in jail.'

'Jail!'

Stan nodded: 'The Head Waiter bailed him out.'

I thought he was joking at first. Even when he insisted that Wolf had been serious, even *then* I refused to believe it. Bill Livingstone being thrown into jail, and being bailed out by a head waiter. *For debt?* It was ridiculous. Of course it was a mistake. Wolf had got it all wrong. We talked it over and agreed – it was so preposterous that it was absurd. Then Stan went off to collect a film from the rental shop while I prepared dinner. When he came back he said: 'Guess what – the young man in the rental shop is looking for Bill too. He lent him five hundred rand the other week.'

'Bill lent him five hundred rand?'

'No, the other way round. That young fellow lent *Bill* the money.'

'Bill *borrowed money*? From the man in the rental shop?'

Stan nodded: 'Not only that. Bill took another thousand from him to invest in the electric car business.'

I went cold all over. Suddenly I was gripped by the most terrible premonition. What had I done? Introducing Bill Livingstone to Ruth? What in heaven had I been responsible for?

And I was still trying to express feelings of terrible doubt when the telephone rang. It was a lawyer, asking for Bill. He wouldn't say what it was about, but a horrible suspicion was forming at the back of my mind – some voice deep inside of me was *telling* me what it was about! We told the lawyer that Bill wasn't with us, and then hung up.

After that we spent the rest of the evening worrying. Or at least *I* did. Stan did his best to reassure me by saying that there was some rational explanation, but my feminine intuition was working overtime by then and nothing Stan said would comfort me.

We went to bed and I awoke the following morning feverish with worry. I was at Ruth's apartment by eight o'clock. She was still in bed but I insisted that the maid fetch her at once. And when Ruth came into the drawing-room I said, 'You can't marry Bill. You *mustn't* marry Bill!'

Well this complete turnabout on my part took some explaining. I did my best, but when I finished she was far from convinced.

'My former husband was a businessman,' she said. 'They live like that
– up one day and down the next. I couldn't possibly refuse to marry Bill
because of something like that.'

'But you mustn't – it's all my fault – you *can't* marry him!'

'Mila, be sensible. He overlooked a couple of bills. That's all it
amounts to – stop getting in a state – '

'No,' I said, 'it's more than that. I just *know* it is.'

'But you were so *for* him. So full of his electric car business – '

'I know. That's what makes it worse. But I was wrong. . . .'

We talked, we argued, we had a scene, tears, everything. How do you
explain a hunch to someone? Especially a hunch about the man with
whom she is in love. I persisted, and Ruth argued back. She flashed her
engagement ring at me and took me on a tour of the apartment. 'Look
at all these gifts,' she cried as we went from room to room. 'That silver
vase, this gilt mirror – '

'I don't care. Ruth, I don't care about the presents. I only care about
you and this marriage. Something is wrong – honestly. . . .'

Eventually she agreed to prolong the engagement. She and Bill were
leaving for Europe the next day anyway, so the wedding could not take
place until they returned. I settled for that – her promise not to surprise
everyone with a wedding in Europe. So, sighing with relief I returned to
the Mariston – but on the way I bumped into a friend of ours by the
name of Mrs Virginia Wolf. Suddenly I remembered that Bill had stayed
with them – with Mr and Mrs Wolf – some time previously. Odd to
have remembered that little snippet of information then, but as soon as
it came into my mind the thought sparked other questions. Like *why*
had Bill stayed with them? Why? Was it because he had been thrown
out of the Fourways Hotel? Was *that* the reason?

Gripped by panic I dragged Mrs Wolf off for a coffee in the Mariston's
restaurant.

'Such a delightful man,' she sighed when I mentioned Bill.

I felt like little Miss Marples in an Agatha Christie novel – but I
probed away quite shamelessly.

'You know he is marrying Ruth?' I said, trying to draw her out.

'I know,' Mrs Wolf said wistfully. 'Such a shame, such a very great
shame.'

'A shame?'

She sat opposite me, winding her handkerchief around one finger and
giving me coy little looks from under her eyelashes. She hesitated, as if
wondering whether to confide in me, then in a whisper she said, 'You

know, Mila, well the truth is my dear that – ' she giggled, 'well the truth is I've fallen in love with him myself.'

Mrs Wolf was at least eighty years old, and hitherto I had always thought of her as happily married. But I stifled my surprise as she continued: 'He's such a popular man, and so clever with money – not a bit like poor Arthur.'

Poor Arthur was her husband – a good man and true who had kept her in comfort if not in luxury from the day he married her. Poor Arthur was a very distinguished man in his own profession. Poor Arthur might not be a business genius, but he was nobody's fool. So I was even less prepared for what followed.

'Mrs Wolf,' I said when I got my breath back, 'how do you *know* Bill is so clever with money?'

She glanced over her shoulder and around the restaurant, her manner becoming more secretive by the minute. And she spoke in a whisper. In fact I had to strain to catch her words. 'I really ought not to tell you,' she said, 'but – well, we are old friends. Bill let us in on the ground floor – that's one of his expressions you know – "in on the ground floor".'

Mrs Wolf never winked in her life – but she came close to winking then.

'How do you mean?' I asked. I had a nasty suspicion about what she meant, but Miss Marples had taken over completely by then.

Mrs Wolf fairly quivered with excitement. 'It's terribly exciting,' she whispered, 'Bill has allowed us to invest in his electric car business. We are going to be *rich* Mila – very rich indeed.'

My worst fears were being confirmed. I stared across the table as Mrs Wolf bounced up and down with the thrill of it all. And there was no doubt in my mind that she was just as thrilled by Mr Bill Livingstone as the prospect of being rich – even very rich *indeed*. I let her swoon all over me until I judged the moment to ask how much Bill had *allowed* them to invest.

'Ten thousand pounds,' came the starry-eyed answer.

I didn't know what to do. Bill Livingstone had been kindness itself to Stan and me. And there was his promise of the PR job, with the prospect of the big house which went with it. But the hunch grew stronger and stronger, so after saying goodbye to little Mrs Wolf I telephoned Ruth.

Ruth took the news in her stride: 'But Mila, everyone in town is investing in Bill's business. He's setting up some kind of franchise operation. Why even my dentist invested two thousand rand – he told me so himself.'

'That makes it *worse*, not better.'

But Ruth thought otherwise, and the tone of her voice said I was interfering in matters which were none of my concern. Perhaps she was right – but I felt so *responsible* for bringing her and Bill together. And my feminine intuition was working overtime.

By the time Stan came home I had worked myself up into a terrible state. Not that Stan was much help.

'But I *like* Bill,' he said. 'He's one of the nicest people we've met in a long time.'

'I like him too,' I wailed, 'but I think he's a crook.'

Stan refused to listen. He reminded me of our visit to the government offices, where everyone had done handstands for Bill. Not only that, but the government was building his factory for him. And what about Toyota? They were breaking an arm and a leg to do business with him. All of those people could not be wrong about Bill – *could they?*

I spent another sleepless night, and by the morning I was determined to have another meeting with Ruth. I would do anything in my power to break her from Bill. So I dressed and hurried round to her apartment. But I was too late – the happy couple had already departed for Switzerland.

The next few days passed without incident. In fact nothing happened for about a week. Then the dam burst. Our telephone was red hot with calls about Bill. Had we seen him? Where was he? Could we help contact him? Call after call after call. The Mariston switchboard was virtually jammed with people telephoning our apartment to find out about Bill.

Bill had borrowed money from everyone. Even Ruth's maid had lent him ten rand! His manager at the electric car factory had invested *fifty thousand* rand! But that was just the tip of the iceberg. Hundreds of people had lent him money or invested in his business. An army of people selling Red Cross flags could not have raised as much money as Bill had raised in Johannesburg. Now they all wanted to know what was happening to their money and I spent hours on the telephone saying, 'Bill is in London. No, I'm sorry but I do not *know* how to contact him.'

Bit by bit the story came out. Bill had sold franchises for electric cars that did not exist. In fact there was only the *one* car, and Bill had borrowed that – from some people in Greece of all places – and they wanted it back!

Meanwhile, what about Ruth? How could I contact her? What could I do to save her? I rushed round to her brother who was a prominent businessman in Johannesburg. He cabled Ruth to return urgently and meanwhile began to investigate. He discovered all sorts of things. For instance there was the business of Ruth's bank statements. Like most people in Jo'burg, Ruth collected her post from a Post Office Box Number. But apparently Bill had been in the habit of collecting her post when he fetched his own. So he had intercepted her bank statements. Ruth's current account was in the red, because she had cashed two large cheques for Bill. She had given Bill her cheques in exchange for his. His had bounced, but by intercepting her mail Bill had prevented Ruth from finding out.

Meanwhile Ruth was at large with this man! Her brother made frantic long-distance calls by the dozen and eventually succeeded in contacting her. She and Bill had arrived in London! Poor Ruth was hit by a series of shocks. Shock number one was her brother's phone call. Shock number two was when the police arrived to arrest Bill – not for anything to do with electric cars in South Africa, but for a fraud he had committed in London years before! And shock number three came when Ruth examined her traveller's cheques. Bill had already forged most of them during their stay in Switzerland!

Heartbroken, Ruth returned to Johannesburg – and reached her apartment just in time to see Bill's extravagant gifts repossessed. He had never paid for them.

All told Bill took the wealthy burghers of Johannesburg, and some of the not so wealthy ones, for a reputed £250,000. But some people lost more than money. A young girl appeared at my door one day. Bill had promised to marry her, and did I know where he was? That was bad enough, but worse was to come – because another girl arrived some days later. And yet a *third* girl a week after that. Bill Livingstone had been engaged to at least three girls in Johannesburg – all at the same time and without any of them knowing about her rivals! Then there were the married ladies – people like Mrs Wolf and others. The list of broken hearts was as long as a line of creditors – Bill's creditors.

The papers were full of the story, and Stan and I slunk around town for weeks after, pretending not to know what all the fuss was about. But to no avail. Those photographs which I had taken of Bill and Stan together seemed to be everywhere. Everyone in Johannesburg had a copy in his wallet. 'Aren't you his public relations man?' they would ask Stan, and before he had a chance to answer they would add, 'But you *must* be. Bill said you were!'

That was the oddest thing – they still believed Bill, even after what happened. Stan had never been on Bill's payroll, had never arranged a meeting with the Press on his behalf, had never really done a thing for Bill. All he had done was talk about the future possibility, and pose for some photographs. And those photographs were *everywhere*.

Ruth forgave me – bless her heart. But it taught me a lesson.

Never, never, never again will I play cupid. People can do their own matchmaking without any help from me. I never told Ruth about the other girls who had been standing in line to marry her Bill – that would have added insult to injury. And just in case you think it was perfectly understandable that all those ladies were prepared to throw themselves at a man who looked like Paul Newman, let me now disillusion you. Bill was over sixty years old, with shaggy grey hair and slightly bowed legs – but boy, could he talk!

Oh, and I nearly forgot. Bill sent us a Christmas card that year.

'Having a wonderful time,' he wrote. 'Wish you were here.'

It was sent from Brixton Prison.

Stan

What with all the uproar going on in Johannesburg about Bill Livingstone, I was glad to be leaving for two weeks. Maybe some of the dust would have settled by the time we returned from Rio.

'Sir Stan's Men' tried hard to contain their excitement, but as the day of our departure drew nearer the boys didn't know what to do with themselves. Even playing football lost its excitement, compared to the prospect of flying across the world in an aeroplane.

Finally the big day arrived. Lubbe was coming with us on the trip, so he, Mila and I drove out to the airport together to meet Jack Blade and Ray Cotterill from *The Sunday Times*. We gathered in the departure lounge and waited for 'Sir Stan's Men'.

They were late, as usual, but just as I was growing anxious the mini-bus was seen – bursting along at breakneck speed with Sammy working over the steering wheel with the skill of a Grand Prix driver. He squealed to a halt in a cloud of dust, persuaded somebody to take care of the mini-bus, and – together with Gilbert – led 'Sir Stan's Men' up to the departure lounge.

They looked splendid in their blue suits. They marched across the lounge, swinging along like a squad of toy soldiers. Somehow they looked older, more mature. Every eye in the place swivelled towards them. The boys looked around, getting their bearings and not at all over-awed at being in an airport, though it was the first time for all of them. Yes, I thought, they are definitely growing up into young men of the world.

Then a monstrous wailing broke out near the departure gate. It was the mums of Soweto, who had come to say goodbye. The boys dashed over and were lost from sight in a sea of heaving bosoms and fluttering white handkerchiefs. And fried chickens. Well, it was a long flight and the mums had worried that 'Sir Stan's Men' would get hungry – so they had brought a mountain of fried chickens with them for the boys to eat on the plane.

Mila

As Lubbe was to say afterwards, Rio couldn't have given a greater welcome to the Queen of England. The reception the people of that city laid on for Stan and those boys was heart-warming, to say the least. Stan had been out of first-class football for ten years by then, but to have judged by the enthusiasm with which he was greeted he might have just played in the World Cup.

We were all bowled over by the warmth of the greeting, but the effect it had on the boys was especially amusing. Stan was met by a battery of flash-bulbs wherever he went, and he was on countless television shows, being asked his opinion about the state of football all over the world. He even lectured at the leading university, which was an ordeal for him as can be imagined, but he coped so well that I think I was the only one there to realize how nervous he was.

And after the official functions came the visits to the stadiums. I am told that visitors are absolutely prohibited from the dressing-rooms at the Maracana Stadium, but an exception was made for Stan and 'Sir Stan's Men'. In fact Stan went even a step further. He persuaded the team coach to let the boys train at the stadium the following morning, alongside a host of World Cup stars. The boys hardly slept a wink the night before, and spent most of the night after talking about it.

But the most touching moment came on the third or fourth day, when young Jimmy wanted a private word with me. Jimmy had been the spokesman when 'Sir Stan's Men' had gone on strike. For days he watched Stan face cameras and microphones, and give interview after interview. Finally Jimmy could contain himself no longer. He took me aside and whispered, 'He *is* famous after all. He is very famous, isn't he?'

I said 'Well, certainly they seem to know who he is.'

He gave me a quick look. 'He didn't need *us* at all,' he said. I knew what he was thinking. He was wondering if Stan had told me about the strike – and Jimmy's role as spokesman. I said nothing and waited.

Jimmy made up his mind to confide in me. 'I told him he needed us,' he said eventually. 'I must tell him how sorry I am.'

I shook my head, 'You apologized once already, Jimmy. Once is enough, twice would be making a fuss, and he wouldn't like that.'

Jimmy thought about that for a long moment. Then he said, 'That's why he didn't tell us he was famous, isn't it? That would be making a fuss.'

When I agreed he fell into a long silence. Then he summed up by saying, 'I shall be famous one day, and I won't make a fuss about it either.'

There was so much determination on that boy's face that I could have hugged him. But that would have embarrassed him, so I restrained myself. So all I said was, 'You do that, Jimmy, and he'll be proud of you. We'll *all* be proud of you.'

To which Jimmy nodded thoughtfully and went away. But at least he no longer felt guilty about his role in the strike that never was – or so I sincerely hope.

There was much to do and see in Rio, apart from watching football matches. We went everywhere by coach and the boys sang lustily as we travelled, so that the holiday atmosphere seemed to follow us around. It was all enormous fun and I enjoyed it immensely, but there was one thing I especially wanted to see in Brazil – and that was Mocamba.

Mocamba is the voodoo – white magic – that is practised the length and breadth of South America under a variety of names. I had heard of it, even read about it – though not much, because it attracts very little publicity in Europe. Now that I was in Rio I was determined to see it at first hand.

Not that you will find Mocamba in the guide books as a tourist attraction. Outsiders rarely get to see any Mocamba. South Americans are slow to talk about it, in fact they *avoid* talking about it if they can. The educated rich pretend to dismiss it, but they do so carefully and without sneering, just in case there is something in it. And the uneducated poor shrug and look away, reluctant to comment at all. So getting the locals to talk about Mocamba is like asking Sicilians about the Mafia. However I was determined and of course Ray Cotterill helped a lot. He used his newspaper contacts and talked of possible articles in African papers, and he eventually managed to get permission for us to visit a house on the outskirts of Rio where Mocamba is practised.

Now there are two kinds of people in this world, when it comes to the occult – the scoffers, and those who feel that any belief which has lasted centuries must have *something* worth examining. As for me, I'm a believer. Oh, I'm prepared to concede that there are charlatans and tricksters about – aren't there in all walks of life – but against them must be set the accumulated evidence in favour of the supernatural. I believe in reincarnation in the same way, and so many other things. However, I will resist the temptation to ride one of my hobby horses and instead explain about Stanley's confrontation with Mocamba.

I really didn't want him along on the visit. Well after the business with Dr Muller I knew what Stan's reaction would be – or at least I thought I did. But he insisted on accompanying us, and even persuaded some of 'Sir Stan's Men' to join us, on the basis that the trip would be educational. So eventually we were a party of ten: Ray Cotterill, Stan and I, plus seven of our boys.

The house was about twenty miles outside of Rio. It didn't look like a church or a temple – just a big house. And the reason was obvious once you were inside. Pictures of Christ and Krishna, and Buddha and Muhammad, and countless prophets of *all* religions decorated the walls. Clearly the followers of all faiths were accepted into this house – for it was a place of healing rather than worship.

The ground floor housed the Mocamba priests, each wearing a string of beads to denote his particular status. Those with the least beads were the novices, and those with the most were experienced. The diseases in which each priest specialized were denoted by different coloured beads, so it was no trouble for those in the know to find the right *doctor*. I thought the idea so much easier than searching among a dozen white-coated look-alikes in more conventional hospitals, and I was proudly explaining this example of Mocamba efficiency to Stan when something happened which quite unnerved him.

About twenty priests were tending various patients in a big room. Two of the priests were treating a pregnant woman by putting her into a trance of some kind. Suddenly she went wild. She became really violent – thrashing about her as if in a seizure, and so excitedly that it took eight priests to hold her down. I sensed Stan stiffen beside me, then he almost jumped out of his shoes when the woman started to scream. She hurled a priest across the room, but another took his place and the struggle continued. This went on for about ten minutes – shrieks and howls from the woman, grunts from the priests – and a whole series of 'Oh crikeys' from Stan. Then he grabbed my elbow and dragged me up to the first floor. If he thought it would be safer up there he was mistaken, because the first floor was occupied by the priestesses, the *real* practitioners of Mocamba. They are of a much higher order than the priests, and it is the priestesses who perform the really dramatic acts of Mocamba healing.

The atmosphere upstairs was heavy with blue-grey smoke. It hung on the air in layers, like incense in a church. A corridor ran through the centre of the house, with unglazed windows on either side, through which you looked into a series of rooms. In one people sat waiting, like the patients in any doctor's surgery. In fact a medical doctor moved among them, listening to their heart-beats with a stethoscope. He had his own small office on that floor and was on permanent call throughout the building. But it was in the next room that we saw our first Mocamba priestesses –and I realized where all the smoke was coming from. All of the priestesses puffed away on huge Havana cigars. Every priestess there had one, as if to smoke a cigar was obligatory or perhaps helped their concentration in some way. They rarely put their cigars down, even when handling a patient. Then we passed on to the next room, where I saw some real Mocamba at work.

A priestess stood with her hands on a man's shoulders. The man, who was the patient, was completely awake and quite in control of himself. He sat comfortably in a chair and appeared to be relaxed and calm. But it was the priestess who drew the eye, for she was in a very deep trance. She was in a state of trance when we arrived, so I have no idea how long it had been going on. I looked at her carefully and saw a woman in her middle years, perhaps of fifty or thereabouts. She stood as rigid as a poker. Two other priestesses stood a pace behind her, and a High Priestess looked on in what I could only suppose was a supervisory role. Then - quite suddenly - the priestess in a trance collapsed. Every bone in her body seemed to melt and she just keeled over. Her two sisters quickly stepped forward and caught her falling body to lower her gently to the floor. What happened then takes some believing, but I assure you it is true.

The priestess on the floor appeared to be completely unconscious, and yet her limbs were still active. Her hands bent backwards until the tips of her fingers touched her wrist bones, and her feet curled back on themselves until her toes touched her ankles. Then all movement subsided. Her muscles relaxed into a position of rest. Perhaps a minute passed, and then the most astonishing thing of all happened - her appearance *actually changed*. The lines which had creased her face just vanished and the years fell away from her. Even her emaciated body seemed to be fleshed out and to take on new form and strength. Watching her was like seeing one of those old Jekyll and Hyde movies where trick photography is used to change an actor's appearance. But there was no trick about this. We were standing a few yards away while it was happening. The other priestesses looked on impassively, making no move to help their sister who was lying in front of them. Next to me Stan caught his breath, but nothing would entice me to drag my gaze away from the woman on the floor. Even to describe her as a woman is wrong. For she was so very young. So young in fact that the *woman* who had looked at least fifty years old earlier, was a girl of no more than eighteen.

I stood rooted to the spot for a long time. Certainly until the girl opened her eyes and rose to her feet. Only then did I look at Stan, more for confirmation than anything, to ask if he had seen what I had seen. But I had no need to ask. He had seen it all right. His hair was not actually standing on end, but it looked as if it would be at any moment. And beyond him our boys clung together, huddled up to each other and watching with frightened eyes that were as big as saucers. Even Ray Cotterill looked shaken. Another second and every one of them would have turned and bolted downstairs. But I wasn't having that. After all, we still had the top floor to see, and the top floor was the ultimate - the home of the High Priestesses themselves. That was too good to miss, so I climbed the stairs and shamed the others into following me.

The smoke became even more dense - great billowing clouds as thick as fog. There was a chapel on the top floor, although it looked more like a simple court room, with tiers of benches rising on three sides. The same pictures of Christ and Krishna and the prophets decorated the walls, and a cross was painted on the floor. The cross was the really important part, for it was on that cross that a patient was placed when operated upon. These *operations* are performed without knives or anaesthetic and are reserved for patients whose afflictions have been diagnosed as incurable by doctors of medicine. Such patients often move their belongings into the house and live there, sometimes for months, until the High Priestesses feel the time is right for the operation. Then the patient is stretched out on the cross on the floor, while the High Priestesses - about fifteen of them - sit upon the surrounding benches to perform the *operation*.

I looked forward to seeing an operation. It was to be the high point of the visit. But Stan and the others were far from keen. In fact they were desperate to leave. None-the-less I was ready to argue the point, until I learned that no onlookers are permitted at operations. It was a great disappointment to me, but an immense relief to the others.

We were half-way back to Rio before Stan relaxed, and back in the hotel before he could talk about what we had seen. I suppose that, for people who are not into these things, the atmosphere was spooky – what with the dim light, the floating clouds of smoke, the strain and tension and occasional violence – but I had found it exhilarating. One day I will go back – but next time Stan *will* stay in the hotel.

Stan

We spent two weeks in Rio and although we watched a lot of football 'Sir Stan's Men' were not allowed to play a match because of the FIFA ruling against clubs from South Africa. I don't want to involve myself in the argument which mixes sport with politics, but it seems a poor show to me when a group of black boys from South Africa are prevented from playing another group of black boys from South America. Where is the sense in that? Anyway we were banned from playing in official matches, so I fixed up an 'unofficial' one against a local university side.

The match was to be played the day before we began the journey back to Johannesburg – so even if we were 'discovered' committing our illegal act, I felt that nothing much could happen to us. Anyway I organized the game and was looking forward to seeing how my boys would shape up against the South Americans.

Then, the day before the game was due to take place, one of the boys disappeared. He really had vanished – when I checked his room that morning his bed hadn't been slept in and his team-mates denied all knowledge of his whereabouts. Apparently the boy had gone out the previous afternoon and not returned.

'Why on earth wasn't I told?' I asked, but my questions were met with an embarrassed grin and downcast eyes.

This was really serious. The boy could be anywhere. Almost anything could have happened to him. I dashed downstairs to find Lubbe, and we rounded up Gilbert and Sammy and took them to my room for a conference.

The odd thing was that neither Gilbert nor Sammy seemed worried.

'But we *must* find him,' I insisted. 'Failing that we must contact the

police. He could be in some sort of danger....' I dried up, afraid to
express the terrible thoughts in my mind.

Gilbert shook his head: 'He ain't in no danger, Sir Stan.'

Sammy made a snorting sound and suddenly burst out laughing.

'This is no joking matter Sammy,' I told him. 'A boy has gone missing
in a strange city. He is our responsibility. If it was you – '

'Man, do I wish,' said Sammy to Gilbert, 'Do I *wish* it was me.'

'You know where he is, don't you?' I said angrily.

But the shutters had come down over Sammy's eyes. Another minute
and he would be into his routine: one hand behind his ear, eyes wide,
saying, 'What's dat, Sir Stan – what's dat you say?'

Lubbe took over: 'Where is he Gilbert? You must tell Sir Stan – '

'He ain't in no danger,' Gilbert repeated.

'So where is he?'

'With ... with a friend,' said Gilbert, staring at the carpet.

Lubbe and I battered away for another ten minutes, and got nowhere.
The most Gilbert would say was that the missing boy would be back in
the morning, and that he was staying with 'a friend'. But every time he
said 'friend' Sammy nearly died laughing.

I sent the boys away to give Lubbe and me chance to think it over.
Then Mila arrived, so of course we had to tell her all about it. A
thoughtful expression settled over her face by the time we finished, but
she made very little comment.

Then Lubbe and I went down to the lounge, where we had arranged
to meet a local reporter. It was annoying to have to give an interview
while my mind was on other things, but I had made the appointment, so
of course I had to keep it. And we were sitting there, having a cup of tea,
when I noticed two members of my squad on the far side of the room.
It was a spacious place and they hadn't seen me. So I sat there, answering
this reporter's questions, while keeping half an eye on the boys across
the room.

I ought to have explained that we were all staying at the same hotel,
so supervising the boys had been relatively easy – or at least it had until
one had gone missing. In fact Mila had remarked how well-behaved they
had all been. And so they had – except for one thing. They kept running
out of pocket money. I imagined they spent their money on food – not
that they needed to, because the meals in the hotel were excellent and
the boys consumed enormous quantities at a sitting. By now, however,
I had become accustomed to the appetites of 'Sir Stan's Men' and was
reconciled to the fact that they could eat round the clock if they chose

to. Anyway I was anxious that their trip to Rio should be one to remember, so I had scraped more money out of the kitty and kept them going.

Well the interview with the reporter was coming to an end, and I was telling him about the appetites of 'Sir Stan's Men', when a girl came into the lounge. She was quite young, in her twenties or thereabouts, but what made me notice her was that she walked directly across to my boys on the far side. And they jumped up to greet her as if she was an old friend of theirs.

The reporter followed my gaze and was grinning when he spoke to me: 'You were telling me about the appetites of your boys,' he said.

'Never stop,' I said absentmindedly, watching the girl lead the boys to the door.

'And all that pocket money?' he laughed. 'You reckon they spend that on extra *food*?'

Lubbe and I stared at him, trying to detect the innuendo. He grinned more widely than ever. 'I guess "Sir Stan's Men" are growing up,' he said, 'because that girl you saw just now is a hooker.'

'A prostitute?' Lubbe yelped. 'A *white* prostitute?'

Suddenly Sammy's laughter made a lot more sense. I remembered his words – 'Do I *wish* it was me,' he had said.

Lubbe called after me, 'Stan, where are you going?'

'To find Sammy and Gilbert. Come on.'

We dashed up to their rooms, but could find no sign of them. 'Oh Crikey,' I moaned. 'Fifteen-year-old boys consorting with prostitutes. And *I* have been financing them!'

We searched the hotel. Not one boy was to be found. The reporter was still in the lobby when we went downstairs. 'I could take you on a tour of the red light district,' he suggested helpfully.

'Are you kidding?' Lubbe demanded. 'Then Stan gets his picture in the papers too. What's he supposed to be doing – giving them a guided tour?'

We searched all the cafés in the surrounding sidestreets, but to no avail. Our lad had truly gone missing. Later, however, he turned up – in time for his tea, and looking as pleased as punch. 'This Rio is sure some place, Sir Stan,' he said happily.

We lost our match the next day – perhaps not surprisingly in the circumstances. But the boys played well enough not to disgrace themselves, and they were learning all the time, which was the important thing.

And then it was time to go home. It had been a marvellous trip, but the high spot for me came on the way to the airport. 'You know, Sir Stan,' Gilbert said, 'you were right all along. We have now seen our own skin defend. That's what we must concentrate on – when we get back.'

Mila

And so we returned to Johannesburg and the Mariston – which was fast becoming more our 'home' than 'Idle Hours' in Malta. Our life resumed the established pattern – which for me meant scuttling away into the shadows whenever the spotlight fell upon Stanley. Dozens of visiting celebrities met Stan in South Africa, and some of them met me too, but very few people ever placed Stan and I as a 'couple'. I was always part of the crowd, when I was involved *at all* that is, so that Stan and I were never obviously together. Just as friends like the Brothers and George Magri had formed a smoke screen for us in Malta, so too did people like Lubbe and Viv Grainger and others in Johannesburg. We have been lucky with our friends and we can never thank them enough.

Progress on Stan's divorce had been made, but the *progress* was painfully slow. Women's Lib really hit its stride at the end of the sixties, and by the mid-seventies you couldn't open a magazine without reading the revelations of this or that liberated lady. Maybe it suited Germaine Greer, New York actresses and the model girls in London's West End – but me, I just wanted to get married to Stan. I'd had seven years of being *liberated* and heard enough powder-room gossip about mistresses and sugar daddies to last me a lifetime. And besides, I had wanted to marry Stan from almost the moment I saw him. I wasn't being *liberated* – I was being deprived! Sadly, however, as the years passed, marriage seemed more and more of an impossible dream.

Then, one day we had a phone call from Stoke. Stan was at Soweto training 'Sir Stan's Men', and after telling the operator to call back at six, I almost forgot about it. When I remembered later, Stan said, 'It'll be Arthur or Jack.' But it wasn't. It was Mr Wilkinson, his – 'our' – solicitor. Stan took the call on the phone in the hall and I heard him say, 'Oh, can we?' and 'Why?' in a neutral sort of voice – but I knew it had to be *something* important. Stoke-on-Trent solicitors don't telephone Africa at the drop of a hat.

Then Stan came back to the sitting-room and simply said, 'We can get married.'

It would be nice to say he *ran* into the room – that he swept me into his arms and kissed me. But instead he sat down with a slightly puzzled look on his face. 'We won on a technicality,' he said. 'The other side missed one of the hearings. Robert says the decree absolute is in the post to us.'

I was unsure of the right thing to say, so I went into the bedroom and stared at myself in the mirror. Once upon a time I dreamed we would be married in Canada – high in the Rockies, overlooking a lake. But that was an amazing *seven years ago*. Then when we went to Malta I planned to marry there. But even that was *six* years ago! Suddenly the most horrible thought struck me. Perhaps Stan no longer *wanted* to marry me? I went as cold as ice. That look on his face as he sat down? Not a flicker of happiness! Not even a sigh of relief! Not really *anything*. Just sort of blank.

I arranged my hair and applied my lipstick with an unsteady hand. Be tactful, I told myself. Do what the kids say – play it cool. Let Stan make the first move. Heavens, you studied psychology – just *handle* him. Whatever you do, don't rush things. So I went back to the sitting-room and said, 'Let's get married in the morning.'

Stan fell off his chair. '*In Johannesburg*? Every paper in town will be after us. Reporters and photographers and....' He dried up with the horror of it. Then he clutched at a lifeline. 'Besides,' he said, 'I don't think we *can* – not until this decree thing arrives – '

'That's in the post.'

He nodded miserably.

Miserably! I mean he really looked *unhappy*. Depressed enough to cry! *Seven years*, I thought – hadn't I seen a film called *The Seven Year Itch*? Didn't something happen to men when they had lived with the same woman for seven years? Women get broody, men get restless. Was that it? Was that really it?

By the following morning I was the world's leading expert on how to get married in South Africa. Not that I told Stan. I never mentioned the word 'marriage'. Wild horses wouldn't drag the word past my lips. But in the hours when I wasn't on the telephone to registry offices and places like that, I was at the hairdressers and the beauty parlour. And when Stan came home I was wearing a dress he admired and I had arranged for us to have dinner with friends. Some happily *married* friends. It was a great evening, except for one thing – Stan never mentioned marriage either.

So the next day I did the same thing, except I had a steam bath as well – *and* I bought a new dress. We had dinner in the apartment, candles flickering on the table, soft music on the hi-fi. I even cooked roast beef, which is not easy for a Czech! But *nothing* – or no talk of marriage, anyway. For once I wished we both drank.... Wine, gin, whisky – something was needed.

The next day was a Friday. I prowled round the apartment all morning, reviewing strategy like Rommel in the desert, and then, quite unexpectedly, Stan came in. I was wearing an old pair of jeans and a stained pullover, my hair was a mess and I hadn't even put on a lipstick.

'It's come,' he said, waving a letter under my nose, 'the decree. We can get married!'

Then he really did take me in his arms to kiss me – and when he stopped long enough for me to get a look at him, he looked happier than I had seen him for months. But that was just the start of it.

'Nigel,' he announced triumphantly.

'Nigel who?'

'Not Nigel who – *Nigel!*'

Nigel! Of course. Nigel is a tiny place, not much more than a village really, about twenty miles from Johannesburg. A sleepy, one-horse, nice little town where nothing ever happens. Its one claim to fame is that Mr Voerster, the then Prime Minister was born there – but he left as soon as he could walk. It's the sort of place you pass through without even bothering to stop. We had – passed through it, I mean – several times on our way to Swaziland and back. Nigel seemed perfect for what we had in mind. Stan telephoned the Registrar's office who said if we spent a night there they could marry us the next morning – provided we filled in their paperwork a few days beforehand.

Stan was jubilant. 'We'll sort the forms out on Monday,' he said. 'Then we'll get married later next week.'

The only person we told was Eva Jezkova-Thonschke, a Czech girl friend of mine – and we delayed telling even her until the Sunday. She was thrilled and insisted on lending me the *something borrowed* and giving me the *something blue* to add to my regalia. I planned to wear a lemon suit with matching accessories, and Stan and I decided that the big day would be Thursday. There would be no best man, no bridesmaids, nobody to give me away and – best of all – *nobody to give us away.* The wedding would be as secret as we could possibly make it.

By the Sunday night we were like kids before Christmas and bubbling with excitement. Except that, for us, Christmas had taken seven years to come. We sat up late, played cards and talked and talked and talked – then of course we overslept in the morning! But we finally surfaced, threw on some clothes, hurried through breakfast, and left for Nigel to fill in their forms.

The Registry Office in Nigel is a single-storey, red-brick building, down a side street. Not that we really noticed the outside. Stan was full of jokes, overflowing with good humour, and once through the doors he radiated goodwill to all and sundry. The girl behind the counter was pleasantly efficient and, infected by Stan's good mood, she happily assisted us in dealing with their paperwork. Then, quite suddenly, Stan said, 'Couldn't you marry us today?' And after that I don't know what got into us. Into Stan, and me, and the girl, but within a minute we were all at it – saying that it was *preposterous* to wait until Thursday – goodness we had waited *seven years* already – and a lot more in the same vein.

It was intoxicating, and only her official responsibilities prevented the girl from being swept away by Stan's enthusiasm. But there were rules to consider, she pointed out – and besides? She threw me so many sideways looks that I tried to see us through her eyes. I was wearing an old sweater and slacks and a scuffed pair of sandals – and Stan was no smarter. We must have looked like a pair of drop outs, and middle-aged drop outs at that. But I was carried away by Stan's sense of excitement, and it's difficult to stop us when that mood takes us. I even tried bribery: 'Marry us today and I'll buy you the biggest box of chocolates you've ever seen.' And finally the miracle happened. If we returned at two o'clock, the Registrar would marry us!

When we stopped thanking her we went out for a cup of coffee – and found the most disreputable, down-at-heel café in the whole of Africa. It was full of fly-blown mirrors and peeling walls, the floor was as grubby as the counter, and our table had a leg shorter than the others, so that our coffee slopped into the saucers whenever we moved. We were on cloud nine when we arrived, but that place really brought us down to earth.

After that a sense of shock set in. A dazed look came into Stan's eyes and he looked about him as if he had just woken up. 'Well,' he said, giving me a lop-sided grin, 'that's torn it.'

I felt like pinching myself. What had we done? There wasn't even time to go back to Jo'burg to bathe and change. My something blue and all my other things were in my wardrobe with the rest of my finery. It just seemed unbelievable that after seven years of waiting I should be caught out by my own wedding day.

'At least we gave the Press the slip,' Stan said shakily.

I was too numb to answer – numb with fear. I told myself that we had to go back. Tell the girl we had changed our minds. But we couldn't do that. Not after she had bent the rules for us. She might get into trouble, and – and anyway it would seem so *juvenile*!

Stan tried again: 'I said at least we gave the Press the slip.'

Thank goodness too, I thought, that's all we needed – pictures of a tramps' wedding. The coffee tasted foul and my gloomy mood was verging on raging panic when Stan said, 'Come on – I'll buy you the best lunch in Nigel.'

But I went to buy chocolates first – and finding a *big* box wasn't easy. Maybe the citizens of Nigel hate chocolates? I went from shop to shop until, in final desperation, I bought one man's entire stock and staggered back to the car balancing twelve one-pound boxes like a juggler. Then I saw Stan coming from the opposite direction, carrying the biggest box I had ever seen. It was about five feet long and a foot or more wide, and he carried it over his shoulder like a plank.

He grinned at the expression on my face. 'It's not chocolates,' he said. 'It's your wedding gift.'

It was all wrapped up in brown paper and there was no way of seeing inside – and Stan insisted that I delay opening it until we got back to the Mariston. So finally I gave up trying to guess what it was and we went in search of some lunch. A good restaurant seemed a tall order after that coffee shop, but the one we found did us proud – once they recovered from the shock of two hippies taking over their best table. But despite the good food I was still in a panic about the situation. Being married in our old clothes, as if it was a spur of the moment thing, a casual silliness which we would live to regret. I tried to explain it to Stan.

He nodded: 'Like getting tattooed, you mean?'

That didn't help. I retreated to the Ladies to do what I could with my appearance. Why on earth did we always do these things? Poor Stan – what was he getting himself into? He was a Knight – *Sir* Stanley Matthews. Not to mention the CBE. And I would be *Lady* Matthews! How could I be a Lady? Ladies acted *sensibly*. A Lady was as serene as a Duchess, wasn't she? Not a scatterbrain like me. But it wasn't all my fault. What about him? Why should *I* feel guilty? He started it – he was the one who persuaded the girl in the first place. That's right, I told myself, nodding to the mirror. Then I puffed my cheeks into my Oliver Hardy face to say, 'Another fine mess you've got me into, Stanley', just as another customer came through the door. I left – hurriedly.

We drove at walking pace back to the Registrar's Office – but even so we arrived with fifteen minutes to spare. Our girl was delighted with the chocolates – but then we hit a snag. A best man and bridesmaids could be dispensed with, but *not* witnesses. We needed two of them. Stan and I were in such a mood by then that we would have given up, but our girl was made of sterner stuff. She and a colleague would serve as witnesses, so – having solved that problem – we were shown into the waiting-room.

I'll never forget that room. It was totally empty except for the chair. One small, hard-backed upright chair, in a room used all the time by couples coming to get married. Stan stared at it for a few moments, then said, 'It's symbolic – it's to get the bride and groom used to sharing things.' So that's what we did. He sat on half the seat and beckoned me to take the other half. We had to sit back to back, with our elbows on our knees and our chins cupped in our hands. I stared glumly at a small window set high up in the white-washed wall – a window with bars, just like a prison window. In fact by the time our girl came back to whisper, 'We're ready for you,' I felt frightened to go. The whole atmosphere was wrong. It was like leaving a prison cell to face a firing-squad. Stan looked green, and my knees trembled. Even our girl looked different. Earlier she had been cheerful and smiling, now she looked as grim as a prison wardress. Stan and I clutched each other for support and·followed her into the other room.

The Registrar had the sort of face you see in Hammer Films. I've never seen a more grim-looking man. He was tall, with a severe mouth in a stern face under a thatch of white hair. And dressed completely in black. We stood in front of his desk while he looked us over. Then he spoke in the thickest Afrikaans accent I ever heard in my life. I could barely understand him, and when he repeated something I realized there was no *barely* about it – I couldn't understand a word he said! Neither could Stan. In fact only when our girl touched my elbow did I realize that Stan and I were standing on the wrong side of each other, and that the Registrar wanted us to swap places. We did, and the marriage ceremony began.

It was a nightmare. I went limp with fear. I could have wept. This was the most important day in my entire life, and here I was – looking like a tramp – and unable to understand a word of what was going on. German I can speak, French, English, Czech, and a little Italian – but *this*?

Stanley did wonders. I was proud of him. He seemed to be lip-reading as much as listening in his effort to grasp what the man was saying, cocking his head as well, like an obedient dog trying to win a bone. Even so the Registrar had to repeat some words. Whatever Stan said, I repeated – and we got through the *I will* bit like champions. But then, just before the end, Stan hesitated. He tilted his ear to fresh angles, revolving his head like a radar scanner. I could *feel* his concentration. The Registrar repeated his double dutch to the most attentive audience he ever had in his life. Stanley fairly *strained* for comprehension. It was quite beyond me, but I willed Stan to understand. We heard the words a third time – spoken painfully slowly, one incomprehensible syllable after another. Stan was as stiff as a poker – then I felt him relax. I breathed a sigh of relief. Stan had understood!

'Long live South Africa!' he sang out triumphantly. Then he sprang to attention and his right arm shot up like a traffic cop's.

I was almost jerked off balance, but the heels of my sandals came together a split second later. 'Long live South Africa!' I cried, throwing up my arm in imitation of Stan.

The Registrar jumped backwards, bounced off the wall behind, knocked a chair over, and swung back to us, his jaw dropping and his eyes popping. Stan and I froze with our arms in the air. The man darted a look from my face to Stan. Then he burst out laughing. That serious, almost sinister-looking man laughed until tears ran down his face, and the girls behind us propped each other up in a massive fit of the giggles.

'What did we say?' Stan wanted to know. But it was a pointless question. The officials couldn't answer, and I didn't know. I was too desperate for tears. Our marriage was a fiasco before it started. But then I looked at Stan and the laughter all around got to us as well, so that we all shook with convulsions of helpless laughter.

Finally our girl recovered herself sufficiently to explain that we had been asked to say, 'So help me God.' Stan's inspired guess had let us down.

The Registrar wiped his eyes with the hem of his black gown and began again – from the very *beginning*. Oh, the concentration that went into the next fifteen minutes! Word by word we edged our way through the ceremony, delivering our responses on cue and hoping to avoid a further disaster. But then the girl behind us fairly exploded into another fit of the giggles. The Registrar was *furious*. The girl fled, shrieking with laughter, and Stan and I bit our lips to keep straight faces. I had the strong feeling that a wrong word from us then would have sent us to jail.

Somehow we managed the 'So help me God' and limped to a finish. I felt *exhausted*. Then the Registrar said something which flummoxed Stan entirely, and our girl hissed, 'You may now exchange wedding rings.'

Wedding rings! Oh *no!* Wedding rings! We had planned to buy me one tomorrow. Tomorrow! And just for me, not Stan. I went hot and cold, and then back to hot. How could we have been so stupid? Poor Stan had to explain that we didn't even have one wedding ring. The Registrar rolled his eyes up to heaven, hoping no doubt that the Good Lord was missing all this. I told myself that this was it – we would have to come back on Thursday and go through the entire performance again. But I knew I couldn't face that – not with these people.

But the Registrar obviously couldn't face it either, because he dispensed with wedding rings – and pronounced us married. Married! We were *married!* We collected our certificate from the office – and fled.

'Pretty silly if you ask me,' Stan grumbled on the way home. '"Long live South Africa" makes a lot more sense in a civil ceremony. And I can't see what was so funny anyway.'

And of course, like any other *wife*, I agreed with him.

Back at the Mariston, Stan was anxious for me to unwrap my wedding gift. I would have been keen, too, but for the fact that I felt so ill. It had started on the way home, a vague uneasiness in the pit of my stomach. But back in our apartment I felt even worse. I felt *really sick*. But Stan was so keen for me to open his parcel that I couldn't disappoint him – so I struggled with the wrapping paper, while he hopped from foot to foot, grinning like a Cheshire cat and challenging me to guess what was in the box.

I tried to concentrate, but I felt awful. And the box was enormous, as big as me.

'Guess,' Stan demanded.

'Nightdresses for evermore?'

'No.'

God, I felt *wretched*. I struggled desperately with the string and sticky tape, telling myself I felt fine – that nothing was wrong with me.

'A fur coat?' I guessed. He shook his head.

'A new dress?'

'No, not a dress.'

Finally the paper was off and I was lifting the lid from the box. It was a barbecue outfit, complete with an electric spit.

'We can take it back to Malta with us,' Stan said happily. 'It does everything – steaks, kebabs, sausages – '

Sausages did it! I reached the bathroom just in time.

'It was in a sale,' Stan shouted after me. 'Twenty per cent off.'

Then I started vomiting.

Stan dashed in: 'What's the matter?'

'Je mi zle.'

'What?'

'Potrebuji lekare.'

'Mila, speak English for heaven's sake!'

Quite suddenly *I couldn't understand a word he said.* 'Je mi zle,' I spluttered through a torrent of tears. I sponged my face with cold water and wished the room would stop spinning. 'Potrebuji lekare,' I pleaded. I tried syllable by syllable: 'Po-tre-bu-ji le-kare.'

He said something. It was worse than trying to understand the Registrar. *Why was everyone doing this to me?* Then I felt another bout of nausea churning in my stomach and I shoved him out of the bathroom.

Seven years – and now we couldn't even *understand* each other. Why did I have to go mad on my wedding day? Stan hammered on the door and I told him to go away – speaking Czech, which he couldn't understand, and getting an answer in English which suddenly I couldn't translate. Then I was being so ill that I was past caring.

Sometime later I heard voices outside. Stan was back with another man. I had stopped vomiting, so I washed my face and peeped cautiously out of the door. Stan half carried, half led me into the bedroom, and the man followed.

Stan looked as bad as I felt. 'Darling, what's the matter?'

'Je mi zle,' I told him.

The other man took over. He was a doctor, and after examining me I gathered that I was to be put to bed. Stan agreed.

'But not *here*,' the doctor protested, 'in her own place.'

'This is her own place,' Stan told him, 'she's my wife.'

The Doctor's eyes narrowed: 'That language she was speaking – what was it?'

'Czech.'

'Can *you* speak Czech?'

'No, I can't speak Czech – '

'You *can't* speak Czech! She *can't* speak English! What sort of marriage is that?' demanded the Doctor. He was very excited. 'This lady is now a patient of mine,' he snapped at Stan. 'I am responsible – '

Then my voice came back. My *English* voice, I mean. Goodness knows what would have happened if it hadn't. Even speaking in English it took me a while to convince the good doctor that we were married. *And we were!*

After that I spent the next three days in bed – being ill most of the time.

Three days and three nights! The doctors said it was the release of seven years of tension which caused it. I don't know – all I know is what my husband said: 'Crikey! That was one heck of a wedding day!'

Postscript by Don Taylor

And so, at long last, our Knight married his Lady and, as with all the best stories, they lived happily ever after. I don't say they live quietly, or uneventfully, or without a succession of adventures – but they *do* live happily.

But the tempo of life is rarely even. Sadly political pressures, ever present on the fringes of sport these days, compelled 'Sir Stan's Men' to be disbanded in 1976 – destroying Stanley's dreams of building a side strong enough to compete in the South African National League. With Stan's hopes went the dreams and aspirations of Gilbert and Sammy and Co., in what was a crushing diappointment for so many people. Stan smothered his own feelings in work and undertook another coaching tour of South Africa, going from one township to the next, sharing his love of the game with thousands of black children and spreading his talent so that they might develop their own. But without his beloved 'Sir Stan's Men' to offer the prospect of continuity the thrill was no longer the same, and at the end of that year Stan and Mila returned to the peace and tranquillity of 'Idle Hours' in Malta.

Stanley was now in his sixty-second year, and the prospect of retiring to a beautiful hillside home, overlooking the blue waters of the Mediterranean and the tiny fishing village of Marsaxlokk, would have appealed to most men of his, or indeed of any other age. It appealed to Stan – for a while.

His time was pleasantly occupied. He played football for the local post office side every week, and because he no longer needed to protect his *wife* from wagging tongues he was able to extend his circle of friends on the island. People visited and wrote to him from all over the world. He played tennis and golf, swam in his pool and helped Mila with the garden. But it was still not enough ... and he itched for the wider world.

For a while he coached The Hibernians, a local side – and to such good effect that they held the mighty Real Madrid to a draw in the European Cup. But then came the away leg. Real attacked from the whistle. The Maltese part-timers – clerks and bus-drivers and tradesmen – fought valiantly but were forever in danger of being over-run in defence. Stanley watched anxiously from the dug-out, wincing at the gaps in his mid-field. He *knew* he could close the game down if he played himself – and at the interval he decided to go on in the second half. Then he looked at the other faces in the dressing-room. Young faces, full of hope. The two reserves, biting their nails, hoping against hope that even now they would have a chance to play in that famous stadium, knowing it was the only such chance in their lifetime. Stanley changed his mind. Both boys played in the second half.

Real won, but Stan watched the game from the dug-out, content that he had made the right decision. For him a boy's dreams were more important than the result of one game.

I first met him in February 1979. I had gone out to Malta to write a novel, but writing is a lonely business ... It can take more than a year to finish a book, and during that time you live like a hermit – emerging from your study for food and drink and an occasional glimpse of the world. Suffer that for months on end, and you crave the company of people, and when you meet someone especially interesting you grab him with both hands, like a zoologist pouncing upon a rare specimen and rushing it to a microscope. So it was with me when I first met Stanley Matthews.

He is a cautious man on first encounter. He listens more than he talks. Rarely does he venture an opinion, preferring to seek your views on this and that, and paying attention to your answers – so that you are encouraged to hold forth more than you might normally. I know what Lubbe Snoyman meant when he said that initially Stan greeted him with suspicion. But it is not suspicion: it is a trick with which the shy protect themselves. They listen and watch while they make up their minds about you. And so it was when we met, as 'zoologist' and 'specimen' eyed each other with equal curiosity.

Our friendship ripened slowly. I was busy on my novel and Stan had his own life to lead, so we met once a week in Valletta for coffee – Stan often arriving in shorts, displaying legs like young trees, the muscular limbs of an athlete of no more than thirty. With typical generosity he introduced me into his circle, and I met people like Charles Pace who in turn became a good friend of mine.

But Stan was restless. Kids were growing up all over the world and he was desperate to share his knowledge of football with at least *some* of them. Then came an invitation to spend the summer coaching schoolboys and – such is the way of the world these days – schoolgirls too, in the United States. Stan was beside himself with excitement. Mila and Katie were set to work at once, packing some of the precious contents of 'Idle Hours' into the now familiar tea chests. Aer Lingus asked Stan to break his journey in Dublin, where they wanted to honour him. Then the BBC made contact – would he go to the Cup Final? It was the twenty-fifth anniversary of the 1953 Final, and his first time back at Wembley.

'How do you feel about it?' I asked him.

'Nervous,' he smiled. 'As bad as waiting in the dressing-rooms. Let's hope I'm not sick.'

I saw the 1953 Final. Alas, not at Wembley, but on television, and for me – as for millions of others – it remains the most exciting game I have ever seen – more thrilling even than England's win in the World Cup Final. The whole country seemed to have only two topics of conversation: would Gordon Richards *ever* win the Derby, and would Stanley Matthews *ever* get a Cup Winners Medal? 1953 looked like being the last chance for both of them, and when Blackpool walked out on to the turf that day it seemed that for Stan's sake the entire country was *willing* them to win. The story is now a classic, of course. Hollywood could never produce a drama to equal it. Blackpool 3–1 down with twenty minutes to go. Then winning 4–3, inspired by Matthews. As I write this I have some old newspaper clippings next to the typewriter and I see that, even in 1979 a sports writer as experienced and eminent as Frank Butler was prompted to write, 'It was the greatest one-man display I've ever seen at Wembley.' And so say all of us.

So, sitting in the sunshine outside that café in Valletta, I was prompted to ask: 'Tell me about that Cup Final.'

Shutters fell over those grey eyes. 'It was just another game,' he said, 'The Press made a lot of fuss, that's all.'

Further conversation, at least along those lines, was discouraged. After all, that happened twenty-five years ago, and Stanley wanted to talk about *now* – about what he hoped to find in the States and the exciting development of the game in that country.

April arrived, and Stan and Mila left Malta for London and Dublin, and thence on to the United States, and from there to Canada for another spell of coaching. He returned to the island in November, full of excitement about the potential of the game in North America. We had lunch together and he up-dated me on his adventures with a young man's enthusiasm.

Mila and Katie unpacked the tea chests and restored 'Idle Hours' to its proper glory. And the coffee mornings, which had lapsed in Stan's absence, started up again. Stan democratically widened the membership to include wives, so that Mila and my wife Pat joined us, and Charles brought his wife Betty.

Christmas came and went. We saw the New Year in together. Stanley tried hard to settle down, but his feet were as restless as ever.

Then, at the end of January, Mila's mother was taken ill in Prague. (Mila's long battle to win acceptance of her reasons for leaving the country in 1968 had been resolved some years earlier. The Czechs had back-dated a legal emigration visa, thus removing the threat of imprisonment if she returned. Sadly she returned almost immediately, for the funeral of her father.)

So once more Mila flew to Prague, leaving Stan alone at 'Idle Hours'.

Pat and I, and I dare say other of his friends, tried to persuade him to spend more time with us, but he preferred to stay close to 'Idle Hours'. just in case – 'Mila might phone.'

But I did persuade him to play golf on his birthday – 1 February. He was sixty-five – an old age pensioner. It seemed impossible. He strode round the course at Marsa like a young man, out-driving me down the fairways, out-putting me on the greens, out-thinking and out-playing me at every hole.

We had a drink in the club house afterwards, me sinking a gallon of beer while he sipped a fruit juice. 'You know,' he said thoughtfully, 'I've been thinking. I wonder if people would be interested in my story?'

I smiled. Two books had already been written about his career. The BBC had made two films about him: *Hall of Fame*, and *Saturday Hero*. His name had featured in a novel: *Who kidnapped Stanley Matthews?* Eamonn Andrews had spotlighted him in *This is Your Life*. Journalists the world over had written millions of words about him. Pathe and Movietone News had enough film footage on him for half a dozen feature films – and the Duke of Edinburgh had spoken for everyone when he said: 'He has become a legend in his own time, which is a distinction reserved for only the really great men.'

I wondered what of his story was left to tell? But I could have misunderstood, so I said, 'Perhaps you should do a series of articles on how you see the game today? Comparing players now with those of your day.'

He shook his head: 'No, the game is different today. Not necessarily better or worse, just different. Besides I never make comparisons.'

'What then?' I asked.

He looked around the club house. Only a few people were in the bar and, surprisingly perhaps, there was nobody who seemed to recognize him. When he turned back to me a rather shaky grin appeared on his face. 'We had a bit of trouble, you know,' he said, 'Mila and I.'

And so I heard part of their story. I had known that Mila was Stan's second wife, but no more than that. In fact very few people knew *more than that*. When Stan told me about their 'bit of trouble' I knew at once it was a story worth telling. But how to tell it? After all, it was as much Mila's story as Stan's – it was *their* story, not his or hers. Surely they should both tell it? Only then would a reader understand something of the unique relationship which exists between these two very different people.

So different, in fact, that on first examination their relationship is preposterous. Who can blame George when he said it was doomed to failure? Logic was on his side, and he was right in most of what he said. Stanley *was* an international sports star and a British institution, who was – and who still is – as English as Yorkshire pudding. Mila *was* a Slav with the widest possible interest in the arts. She had never been to a football match. He had never been to the ballet. It was an absurd relationship. And yet it worked from the moment they met.

Part of the reason lies in the complexities of Stanley's character. For behind that shy, polite exterior (he is the politest man I have ever known) hides a shrewd intelligence. Perhaps not surprisingly, in the light of his astonishing achievements. To play any sport to international standards demands a quick brain, but Stanley's intelligence goes well beyond that. His study of diet and exercise and all matters relating to physical health has been deeply analytical – it *had to be* to enable him to continue playing for so long. (The oldest player ever to score in the FA Cup. The oldest player ever to score in the League. Records which stand to this day and which look increasingly unsurpassable.) Even now – at the age of sixty-six – Stanley can play ninety minutes of football. How many men of fifty-six, or forty-six – or indeed, even thirty-six – could do as much, let alone with such skill? But while the physical achievements are obvious, the intelligence is usually masked by Stanley's disarmingly modest manner. He is deceptive. He is widely read and widely travelled, and has acquaintances in all walks of life – but he rarely talks about *his* experiences, preferring to encourage you to talk about yours. As has often been said of him, he is truly one of nature's gentlemen.

So on his birthday we talked, Stan and I, about a possible book – and decided to await Mila's return from Prague. But meanwhile Stan's restlessness was mounting. He had been back on the island for three months. Boys all over the world were playing football, and Stanley itched to coach them. Then came an invitation: would Stan go to Australia to coach the boys down there? Then another invitation – this time from Canada again: would Stan go back for a further tour? He fairly bubbled with excitement. Within hours he was closeted with his travel agent, planning dates, flights and itineraries. And his cup of joy overflowed the following day. Mila returned from Prague and John Charles telephoned from England: would Stan play in an exhibition match with his old pal Stan Mortensen in Bangor? The excitement was enormous!

It gave us a month to put their story on tape – often with both of them talking at once, so that sorting it out afterwards drove me nearly mad. But the *fun* they have! Rarely have I seen two adults get more enjoyment from each other's company. Stan says life was even more exciting before they married, so from now on he will introduce Mila as his secretary, just to liven things up. They both laugh and gloss over the more painful parts of their story, preferring to think happy thoughts rather than sad ones. And who can blame them for that? Today is what is important – today, and planning tomorrow's adventure. For one thing is certain: wherever they are, and whatever they are doing, it will be an adventure for both of them.

And then, once again, Mila and Katie were packing the tea chests and Stanley was busy with his travel agent. Have football boots, will travel – that could well be his motto. Then they were off: Singapore, Bangkok, Sydney, Adelaide, Melbourne – back to London for the Cup Final and to play in the exhibition match with Big John Charles – then on again, to Ontario and Quebec and New York ... and dizzyingly on to numerous other places. Cards and letters reached us from along the route to mark their progress. Now, as I write this, they are in Johannesburg again – next stop London – and then back to Canada ... and then ...

Much has been left out of this book. I regret it, but it is inevitable. Stan and Mila pack more into a year than most people put into a lifetime. Stanley himself is the original perpetual motion machine. Give him a ball and a group of youngsters and he will play all day. His patience and good humour is as inexhaustible as his energy. And on top of his

coaching trips come the invitation matches. Mila will say, 'Just play for twenty minutes this time.' And Stan will grin his agreement. It is a joke between them. 'Just twenty minutes.' 'Yes dear,' comes the answer. But they both know full well he will play to the end.

I remember well the time we last saw them. We had dinner together the night before they left Malta for Australia. I ought to explain that it is a tradition in Malta to see your friends off - and to be seen off - at the airport. Everyone does it. Pat and I have done it dozens of times. Everyone does it - except Stanley. He doesn't like *anyone* to see him off. So we had dinner with them the night before, and that was that. But the following day I was in my study, sorting out the tapes and wondering where to start, when my daughter came in: 'Shouldn't you be at the airport? What time is Stan's flight?'

I shook my head: 'He doesn't like people seeing him off.'

And Pat said: 'That would be making a fuss.'